The Amendment That Refused to Die

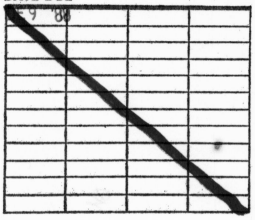

Amendment XIV

THE AMENDMENT THAT REFUSED TO DIE

Revised Edition

HOWARD N. MEYER

BEACON PRESS Boston

Copyright © 1973, 1978 by Howard N. Meyer

First published as a Beacon Paperback in 1978
by special arrangement with Howard N. Meyer

Beacon Press books are published under the auspices
of the Unitarian Universalist Association

Published simultaneously in Canada by
Fitzhenry & Whiteside Ltd., Toronto

(paperback) 9 8 7 6 5 4 3 2 1

Library of Congress Cataloging in Publication Data

Meyer, Howard N.
    The amendment that refused to die.
    Reprint of the 1973 ed. published by Chilton
Book Co., Radnor, Pa.; with new foreword.
    Bibliography: p.
    Includes index.
    1. United States.   Constitution.   14th
amendment.   I. Title.
KF4757.M46   1978   342'.73'085   77–88587
ISBN 0–8070–5419–4

Respectfully dedicated to
the Honorable William O. Douglas
who as Justice and as writer
helped bring it back to life

FOREWORD TO THE BEACON EDITION

Wounded—But Not Mortally

Eight years have passed since this book was completed. During that period the court was presided over by a new chief justice appointed by a president unsympathetic to the liberty and justice that the revived Fourteenth had, by 1969, established as integral to the law of the land.

Warren Earl Burger was sent to the court with a mission to undo decisions "seriously hamstringing the peace forces in our society," as Mr. Nixon put it, "and strengthening the criminal forces." Now the attorney general instrumental in selecting the chief justice, as well as his three junior colleagues, serves time as a convict; the man who did the appointing fled the White House to escape impeachment for high crimes, and though "pardoned" lives out his life in disgrace. But his dead hand will be effective at the nation's highest courthouse for years—in at least one instance, for decades.

This book was designed to convey to the nonprofessional reader comprehension of an aspect of American history that is not widely known or understood and that is terribly relevant to the turmoil of our times. By pure coincidence, it was completed on the eve of Chief Justice Earl Warren's departure from the court—and pretty much at the point when the Fourteenth Amendment had been reshaped to the contours envisaged by its framers.

Since this is not a treatise on law, the text need not be rewritten to incorporate the decisions emanating from the Burger courts.[1] The book, as valid history, is unaffected. But the reader is entitled to see in perspective the effect on "Big Fourteen" of eight years of a climate inhospitable to the basic rights it guaranteed.

The overall picture is a spotty one. It did not, for quite a while, justify the facile generalization that it was all bad. There were elements of holding the line, and even advance and growth, that were undoubtedly disappointing to the anti-libertarian White House of the early seventies. It could almost have been said, prior to the 1975–76 and 1976–77 Terms of Court, that where the Fourteenth Amendment was concerned some plus factors outweighed the minus.

But the setbacks of the last two years have been cause for dismay. They have inflicted on the concepts of equal protection and due process—liberty and justice—wounds so severe that their effect may not yet have been fully perceived. It may be fair to say that 1975–77 marked the emergence of the "Rehnquist court," as that sinister young activist for injustice seemed to gain intellectual dominance over a majority of his colleagues.[2]

There were early decisions after Earl Warren's departure that tended to undermine, without repudiating, the barriers that had been interposed by 1969 to protect us from lawless enforcement of the law and to insure that state and local governments would be held to the standards set for the nation by the Bill of Rights. One was the case undercutting the *Miranda* requirement that had been designed to protect accused persons against overreaching police interrogation. Over the protest of four of the justices, the court, while nominally preserving the prohibition against illegal use of improperly procured statements as direct evidence, permitted circumvention of the rule by allowing them to be read to the jury to discredit a defendant when he testified in his own behalf.[3]

In a trilogy of decisions between 1970 and 1972, the court eroded in large part its 1968 ruling on the right to trial by jury, a ruling that had helped complete the nationalization of the Bill of Rights by guaranteeing to state court defendants the Sixth Amendment's assurance of that right. The constitutionally guaranteed jury trial had always been understood to require a unanimous verdict by a jury of twelve. First came the cutback to permit a jury of six, and later the sanction to states that permitted specified majority verdicts.[4] The last aberration was produced by the vote of a single justice (Powell), who nevertheless expressed reluctance to abandon the rule of unanimity for federal trials: a schizophrenic standard that, contrary to what Congressman Bingham and Justice Black had sought, gave state court trials less fairness than federal ones.

The worst blow of all was the Rehnquist court's approval of a double-trial system, under which a defendant could not get a jury trial unless he first submitted to the ordeal of trial by a judge, or admitted that a judge would convict him—thus being forced (unless the judge acquitted him) to face a jury that would be skeptical in spite of our vaunted presumption of innocence, and less capable of delivering a fair and impartial verdict.[5]

Apart from these and some interpretive setbacks to the Bill of Rights limiting both its state and national benefit,[6] there would have been, if one wrote before the beginning of the 1975–76 Term, a number of advances beyond high water marks attained by previous courts. Sad to say, most were canceled out in whole or substantial part in what I see as the period of Rehnquist's dominance:

—A citizen could not be publicly "posted" by the authorities as an excessive drinker without notice and an opportunity to be heard as to the accusation (1971) but could be handbilled all over town as a shoplifter without an opportunity to defend himself, or even vindicate himself if the accusation were provably untrue (1976);[7]

—students were held to be entitled to the due process of notice and a chance to be heard before being suspended from school (1974 Term) but then were ruled not to have a right to clear themselves before "disciplinary" beating by teacher or principal (1977);[8]

—the imposition of the death sentence was forbidden to the states (under the Eighth Amendment as made applicable by the Fourteenth) as cruel and unusual because of the fashion in which it had been previously applied and enforced (1972), but the bar was removed when the court took at face value supposedly corrective laws passed by some states (1976);[9]

—a public school teacher with only "implied" tenure could not be terminated without due process by the state (1972), but a policeman who had been called "permanent" but without precise tenure rights could be dismissed without a hearing (1976);[10]

—a convict's parole could not be revoked without a hearing (1972), but a prisoner could be transferred, supposedly for disciplinary reasons, to a more rigorous penitentiary without notice, hearing or explanation (1976).[11]

There were advances that have not been canceled out, built on foundations laid during what I have called the Third American Revolution: the extension of the right of counsel to all,[12] and not merely felony, defendants; protection against varieties of invidious treatment to persons newly settled in a state;[13] equal rights in increasing measure to lawfully resident aliens[14] (the equal protection clause says "persons," not merely citizens) and to those whom Victorian mores had stigmatized as "illegitimates." In these last groups of cases, Rehnquist was usually dissenting.[15]

Doctrinal contributions to the concept of equality of all persons were made that the Warren court had failed to attain. The impetus of a growing, more articulate and more militant women's movement resulted in the first decision squarely treating women as "persons" entitled to equal protection; case after case followed that showed the court more and more ready to recognize that differential treatment of women and men had been based on "outdated misconceptions," "archaic and overbroad generalizations" and "old notions" of sex roles. It may be neither unfair nor inaccurate to say that the pendency of the Equal Rights Amendment helped reshape the thinking of nine (still all-male) justices.[16]

The developing commitment of previous decades to demolish past barriers to interracial justice (a principal object, after all, of the Fourteenth's framers) abated only slightly at first. It was Nixon's own chief justice who wrote (albeit in an opinion with ominous reservations), despite demagogic criticism of earlier lower court rulings and widespread white protest, that "the remedial technique of requiring bus transportation" could be ordered when necessary to dismantle dual school systems.[17] Racial discrimination in admission to private schools was outlawed, but Justice Rehnquist led a majority into a ruling condoning exclusion of blacks from private clubs licensed and regulated by Pennsylvania.[18]

Gradually, however, and with a technique shrewdly calculated to avoid public attention or popular protest, the Burger-Rehnquist leadership was drastically cutting back the purges and protections of the Fourteenth. Procedural "gimmicks" were developed and applied to bar access to the federal courthouse for enforcement of federal rights. Case after case was thrown out because of what was called lack of "standing" to sue, or unavailability of a "remedy," or to show "deference" to state courts. Numerous examples were cited in a study prepared by the Society of American Law Teachers, in an unusual public protest to the court.[19] Items: Mayor Rizzo of Philadelphia was proved to have refused to stop a demonstrated pattern of police misconduct grossly violating the rights of the people, especially black people. No power to act, said the high court. A restrictive zoning law was designed to prevent housing integration—the one simple remedy needed to make busing obsolete—but those who sued to invalidate the law were thrown out of court as lacking a clear and present "interest." [20]

The worst news of the last two terms came in decisions that, like a number mentioned above, reversed the Burger court's own earlier constructive contributions. In *Washington vs. Davis* (called by one writer the court's worst decision in eighty years) the court permitted testing for the job of police officer that had a quadruply adverse impact on black applicants, allegedly because of lack of proof of "intent" to discriminate. Legalisms aside, this was flatly contradictory to the chief justice's own (pre-Rehnquist) contribution in *Griggs vs. Duke Power Company,* which held that employment tests with a plainly disproportionate racial impact had to be thrown out unless clearly job-related, regardless of "intent." What was especially injurious in the *Washington* opinion was the gratuitously thrown-in *obiter dictum* expressing disapproval of a slew of lower federal court rulings in which, based on *Griggs* and earlier decisions, blacks and women had been granted a remedy based on wrongs proven by showing adverse impact in employment, urban renewal, public housing and allocation of municipal services.[21]

As bad in its own way—I think of it as the worst decision since the *Dred Scott* case itself—was the group of rulings reducing to a bitter memory the court's stunningly constructive 1973 decision[22] that had invalidated, as infringing on the Fourteenth's "concept of personal liberty," laws that interfered with a "woman's decision whether to terminate her pregnancy." The 1977 court decided that in the case of the poor and unemployed, who could not pay for their own medical care, the states could interfere with women's freedom of choice by forbidding funding of elective abortions while providing payment for those who "chose" to bear their children. This surrender to pressures resulting from interference with state matters by religious groups (itself a plain First Amendment violation) needs no other comment than that of Justice Marshall, dissenting: the court now permits states and cities to "brutally coerce poor women to bear children whom society will scorn for every day of their lives." [23]

What of the future? The essential principles of the Fourteenth have still not been subverted so much as they were by the *Slaughterhouse* case and its progeny. The application of these principles has been made difficult by *Washington vs. Davis* and the closing off of access to the courts in many cases. (This has been partially balanced by the independence and integrity shown by many state court judges and some federal ones, who prefer to abide by what they learned from the pre-Nixon court.) [24]

The intent of the Fourteenth to provide a foundation for affirmative action to remedy the past remains to be tested fully. The issues have been politicized and some courts bemused by the false and demagogic slogan, "reverse discrimination," in preferential admissions and hiring cases. It is to be hoped, if not confidently expected, the court will see that in the context of its first framing, the Fourteenth was a race-conscious measure, from a Congress that enacted many laws for the remedial adjustment of those formerly oppressed by slavery into a society from which they had been excluded.[25]

Notes

1. There has not, of course, been a single "Burger court." The new chief justice presided over the balance of the previous court, until and after Mr. Justice Fortas was forced off the court for an indiscretion less serious than Mr. Rehnquist's statement during his confirmation hearing (see Note 2) and then during and after two changes in composition, delayed by attempted appointments so distasteful that the full complement of Nixon appointees did not sit until January 1972; the story is well told in Louis Kohlmeier's *God Save This Honorable Court* (New York, 1972).

2. The views of the minority of the Senate Judiciary Committee, detailed in Ex Rept No 92-16, 92nd Cong 1st Sess, of Senators Bayh, Hart, Kennedy and Tunney have been fully vindicated: "Mr. Rehnquist is not sympathetic to the 'desires' for racial justice and the fundamental protection of the Bill of Rights. His nomination should be rejected." During the hearings on his nomination, Mr. Rehnquist denied under oath that a 1952 memorandum bearing his initials, written while he was law clerk to Justice Jackson, saying "that the 'separate but equal' doctrine underlying school segregation was right and should be reaffirmed" reflected his personal views (*New York Times,* 12/9/71, p. 26). In a recent and thorough examination of all facets of the 1954 desegregation decisions, *Simple Justice* (New York, 1976), Richard Kluger amassed evidence indicating pretty conclusively that Rehnquist's denial under oath was perjurious. See also, at page 222, Justice Jackson's tribute to the memory of Tourgee, as to Rehnquist's attempt to pin the views in the memorandum on the deceased justice for whom he'd worked.

3. *Harris vs. New York* (401 US 222). The *Miranda* ruling (384 US 436) was designed to prevent coercive interrogation (see text pp. 228, 232). It announced that the court would exclude any testimony about statements made by accused persons who were not warned (1) of their right to be silent, (2) that any statement could be used against them, and (3) that there was a right to the presence of an attorney when one was questioned. This continues to be undermined by the Nixon-dominated court; a notable recent example is *Michigan vs. Mosely* (423 US 96), in which Justice Brennan made the observation cited below at note 24.

4. *Williams vs. Florida* (399 US 78 [1970, 6 persons]); *Apodaca vs. Oregon* (406 US 404), and *Johnson vs. Louisiana* (406 US 404 [1972, non-unanimous]).

5. *Ludwig vs. Massachusetts* (427 US 618).

6. The full story of the undermining of the Bill of Rights *per se* (except as to the First Amendment) as applied to either the national or state governments in the early years of Nixon's court is told (and epitomized in the title of) Leonard W. Levy's *Against the Law* (New York, 1976).

7. *Wisconsin vs. Constantineau* (400 US 433) versus *Paul vs. Davis* (424 US 693).

8. *Goss vs. Lopez* (419 US 565) versus *Ingraham vs. Wright* (97 S. Ct. 1401).

9. *Furman vs. Georgia* (408 US 238) versus *Gregg vs. Georgia* (428 US 153).

10. *Perry vs. Sindermann* (408 US 593) versus *Bishop vs. Wood* (426 US 341).

11. *Morrissey vs. Brewer* (408 US 471) versus *Meachum vs. Fano* (427 US 215).

12. *Argersinger vs. Hamlin* (407 US 25).

13. *Memorial Hospital vs. Maricopa County* (415 US 250) culminated a line of such cases, including *Dunn vs. Blumstein* (405 US 330), throwing out a tradition of requiring lengthy residence for voting rights. Chief Justice Burger dissented and Justice Rehnquist did not participate in *Dunn;* Rehnquist dissented in *Maricopa County*.

14. The most recent case holding that New York could not deny state scholarships to lawfully resident aliens is *Nyquist vs. Mauclet* (97 S. Ct. 2120). And see especially *Sugarman vs. Dougall* (413 US 634), striking down denial of civil service employment. In a plaintive dissent (delivered the first day John Dean testified on the Watergate crimes before the Ervin committee) Justice Rehnquist decried the opening of the doors to persons brought up in countries where governmental corruption was condoned.

15. *Trimble vs. Gordon* (97 S. Ct. 1459) is the latest, but the court's decisions on the subject have been somewhat uneven.

16. *Craig vs. Boren* (429 US 190) is a recent case; its predecessors are discussed ably in Ruth Bader Ginsburg's "Let's Have ERA as a Signal," *American Bar Association Journal,* January 1977, p. 70.

17. *Swann vs. Charlotte–Mecklenburg Board of Education* (402 US 1).

18. *Runyon vs. McCrary* (427 US 160) forbade racial discrimination in private schools, but *Irvis vs. Moose Lodge* (407 US 163) permitted exclusion of blacks from state-licensed private clubs. (Rehnquist dissented in the school case, which was based on the 1866 Civil Right Act, but wrote for the court in the dismaying Moose Lodge case.)

19. Statement released by the Society of American Law Teachers, 500 Fifth Avenue, New York, N.Y. 10036 (October 10, 1976), 25 pp.

20. *Rizzo vs. Goode* (423 US 362) and *Warth vs. Selden* (422 US 490).

21. *Washington vs. Davis* (426 US 229), with its devastating footnote 12, versus *Griggs vs. Duke Power Company* (401 US 424). See Laughlin McDonald's "Has the Supreme Court Abandoned the Constitution?" in the *Saturday Review,* May 28, 1977.)

22. *Roe vs. Wade* (410 US 113).

23. *Maher vs. Roe* (97 S. Ct. 2376) and *Poelker vs. Doe* (id. p. 2391), as well as *Beal vs. Doe* (97 S. Ct. 2366), all decided June 20, 1977. It is to be hoped that Senator Howe's comment on the *Slaughterhouse* case (see p. 77) will be remembered.

24. In *Michigan vs. Mosely* (423 US 120), Mr. Justice Brennan noted with much satisfaction the emerging trend among high state courts of relying upon state constitutional protections of individual liberties—protections providing counterpart provisions of the United States Constitution, "but increasingly depreciated by decisions of this Court." (See Arthur S. Miller, "The Court Turns Back the Clock," *The Progressive,* October 1976, p. 22.)

25. As a prelude to *Bakke vs. California,* which may decide part of the issue, the omens are not too bad: race-conscious remedies were approved in *Hills vs. Gautreaux* (425 US 284), *Millikan vs. Bradley* (97 S. Ct. 2749), and *United Jewish Organizations vs. Carey* (430 US 144).

Sources consulted, in addition to works mentioned in the Notes:

Archibald Cox, *The Role of the Supreme Court in American Government* (New York, 1976); Stephen Gillers, *Getting Justice* (New York, 1973), a how-to as well as a scholarly and well-written book on the rights of defendants as settled by 1971; James F. Simon, *In His Own Image: The Supreme Court in Richard Nixon's America* (New York, 1973); and a memoir by Justice Powell's first law clerk, J. Harvie Wilkinson, 3rd, *Serving Justice: A Supreme Court Clerk's View* (New York, 1974 [he might not be so defensive now about Powell's role in Rehnquist's "gang of four"). *The Harvard Law Review*'s annual November studies of the court's previous term are invaluable, as are the newsletters of the Lawyers' Committee for Civil Rights Under Law, "Committee Report" (available from 733 Fifteenth Street, N.W., Washington, D.C. 20005), and the DuShane Fund Reports (available from Teacher Rights, National Education Association, 1201 Sixteenth Street, N.W., Washington, D.C. 20036).

FOREWORD

Less than forty years ago, the members of the American establishment and its supporters relied on the United States Constitution as a barrier against change and a cover for special privilege. Now they no longer do so and instead many wrap themselves in the American flag.

It will serve their purposes to do so as long as the flag is permitted to remain, as they would have it, a meaningless symbol that stands for mindless support of whatever is done in the name of the government of the United States.

But the flag cannot be divorced from the Constitution as standing for the America we should love. And, unlike the flag, the Constitution has a meaning that cannot be understood without knowing its history. Those who refuse to acknowledge the meaning of the Constitution, to know what it requires and to do what they can for its objectives, do not honor America because they do not even know what those words mean.

It is my belief that the Constitution is too important to leave to the lawyers and judges, and that too few of the professionals—let alone students and teachers, parents and sons and daughters—understand a basic structural element of our great charter. It is for the purpose of helping to create a better understanding of that element—the major overhaul that the Constitution went through from 1865 to 1870—that this book has been written.

CONTENTS

PREAMBLE:

The Twice-Made Constitution

> We the People of the United States,
> in order to form a more perfect Union,
> establish Justice,
> insure domestic Tranquillity . . .

"The most momentous chapter in American history," one chronicler of the 1787 Philadelphia Convention tells us, "is the story of the making and ratifying of the Constitution of the United States." It is true that few events in human history in the realm of the peaceful art of government have been as widely acclaimed. But those who limit its story to what happened at Philadelphia are as inaccurate as the British statesman who called the product of the 1787 meeting the most wonderful work ever struck off at a given time by the brain and purpose of man.

Look at how things stood seventy-three years later:

"A more perfect Union"? The nation had split into two hostile halves, each with its own flag, president, army and anthem. Each half held many geographic captives who were unhappy with their lot, and some talked of further secession and fragmentation.

"Establish Justice"? Things had not worked out that way at all. Absolute injustice was the treatment given one sixth of all Americans, those of African birth or descent. Even the nominally free black Americans, whose ancestors had worked for two centuries to enrich the new land, were denied citizenship by the nation, fairness by the states, and human fraternity by most of their fellow Americans. Very many white Americans were denied the freedoms of speech and association by half of the states, and by mobs and even some cities and villages in the other states.

"Insure domestic Tranquillity"? For decades the issue of slavery against freedom had disturbed the peace. In the South the slaves resisted by insurrection and flight. In the North mobs assaulted those who agitated for national freedom. There had been guerrilla warfare in bleeding Kansas and there was an armed attack on Harpers Ferry. The nation was on the verge of outright civil conflict and there would be no domestic tranquillity at all for four years during the bloodiest war fought anywhere in the world at any time.

It would hardly be an unfair judgment to have said, in 1860, that the Constitution had failed. It had contained the seeds of its own failure. It had not resolved either of the two great issues that arose in the nation during the first seventy years of its existence. Was the United States an enduring and unbreakable union? Should the states have total and permanent power to deal as they pleased with all persons within their borders?

The men who wrote the initial portion of the Constitution in 1787 had known discord, injustice and domestic disturbance before, during and after they had won the first great modern revolution. They were schooled in political science, philosophy and history. They had had the benefit of the practical difficulties encountered during twenty years of independence. It was their hope and purpose to consolidate the gains made during that revolution. What had gone wrong was not that they had failed to foresee the two great issues that brought disaster, but that they had compromised them.

To say that they had failed is not to say that they had not built well. Much of what they had done in creating a structure and system of government was admirable. The Bill of Rights which they, or most of them, added in 1789 to the original basic law cannot be overpraised: it summarized what the human race had learned in progressing from barbarism about the need to protect the individual from the tyranny of the group. The framers of the Constitution deserve to be called our "founding fathers" and to be venerated as such.

But if we mean by founding fathers only those men of 1787–89, we do ourselves and our history a grave disservice. The Constitution that failed could not merely be patched up. It had to be rebuilt. That it was done in only a relatively few words may be misleading. That those words were added without any change in the outward facade of the 1787 edifice should not be allowed—although it long has—to disguise the major contribution that they made. And that they were contained in what were called "amendments" helps to distract attention from the fact that in origin, purpose and content the thirteenth, fourteenth and fifteenth amendments—most especially the fourteenth—so changed the heart of the original American constitution as to constitute what could fairly be called a second American constitution.

Yet we do not find that the draftsmen of this second constitution are ranked with our founding fathers—we do not celebrate or examine with interested reverence the meetings that produced its components. If we were to do so we would be forced to face the fact that our second (and current) constitution had gradually been betrayed and, by the beginning of the twentieth century, made meaningless in large part—even twisted to help impose injustice.

The original constitution was the fruit of a revolution. The Civil War has been called the Second American Revolution, a phrase that has been used with some justice, although there has not been complete agreement about what was meant by it. In actuality it was a revolt against the rule of slavery at Washington (symbolized by the Dred Scott decision) and it was won when the slaves, armed and uniformed in the ranks of the United States Army, inspired by promises of freedom, equality and justice, helped to overthrow that rule. The second American constitution was an attempt to consolidate that revolution, as the first constitution consolidated the revolution of 1776.

The betrayal of the second constitution made necessary a third American revolution. It was to be a revolution unlike any other in the history of the world. It has continued for over sixty years and its purpose has been to bring about a return to the constitution. It has been unspectacular, except for the decade that began in 1960, and while it has never involved actual warfare it has never been bloodless, either. It was begun by blacks, and often the burden was carried by them alone, but it was carried on for the rights and for the benefit of Americans of all colors and of all ancestries—immigrants and native born.

It is not being won with the prospect of a third constitution but with a return to the second constitution as written. It has been wrested, bit by bit, from the changing membership of the United States Supreme Court. There have been during its course many defeats and setbacks, especially during its first thirty years. There have been so many victories that the story of all of them cannot be told in detail; suffice it to say that by 1970, just one hundred years after the ratification of the third installment of the new constitution, it had become in almost every respect the "law" of the land.

That it was not and is not everywhere enforced and honored is a problem beyond the ability of courts and congresses alone. Its failure to have achieved that which our second founding fathers had hoped for is the result of the need for affirmative action by our people and government to repair the accumulated injuries done to all Americans—injuries that have been the result of its betrayal. Squelching the new threat that the Constitution as a whole will be betrayed again is the responsibility of all Americans who love freedom and the country that was born with the revolution of 1776.

Part I

BIRTH:

The Founding Fathers of 1789 and 1866

Chapter 1

Liberty Limited

The Constitution of the United States is essentially a single document whose amendments are integral parts of it. When America entered the twentieth century, our Constitution contained a number of amendments—the first to the eighth and the thirteenth to the fifteenth—which have a special function. They do not deal with the objects of government or the division of work among its officials or the powers of subdivisions and how conflicts are to be resolved. They contain a statement of the rights of the people. They are expressed primarily in the form of rules that forbid or require certain kinds of action by men in government.

We have grown up with a feeling of regard which borders on reverence for the basic document of our national government. Its significance to the American people has been compared to the royal family's importance to the British: the single symbol that unites all sorts and classes of people around the mystique of their common heritage. Certain aspects of our constitutional history will be seen to make the analogy uncomfortably accurate. Parts of the document about which we speak with such respect have been as ineffective and as ignored by those who run the nation and the states as the members of the royal family are by Britain's government. Yet our symbol of nationhood was meant to be obeyed as well as revered.

It is hard to imagine having the reverence most of us feel for the Constitution if we were to view it without its amendments. If they were to be suddenly subtracted, what would we find? Congress could make a law limiting the printing of news about domestic disturbances or errors in foreign policy. The freedom of the press which makes such a law unthinkable was not contained in the product of the Philadelphia Convention, only in its first amendment. Without the guarantee of religious freedom which that amendment also gave us, churches whose ministers speak out on social issues might be taxed out of existence. If there were not a fourth amendment, police or federal agents could legally raid anyone's home or apartment without going to court to ask for a search warrant.

One could go on to tabulate many features of freedom, the privileges and immunities of citizens, which are absent from the original, unamended constitution. As a set of rules for dividing the powers of government between the new nation and the states that were uniting to form it, the product of the convention was a fine document. In setting ground rules for the division of authority and responsibility between the president and the congress, and in setting up the mechanics of selection of each, it was adequate and efficient. But as a charter that might be looked to for the protection of people against abuses of government it was sadly lacking.

There were only a few precautions. The right of trial by jury in criminal cases was guaranteed. The ancient right of *habeas corpus*—to have a judge pass on the legality of anyone's imprisonment anywhere—is provided. It was forbidden to pass *ex post facto* laws that make actions criminal which were lawful when they took place. A strict and narrow definition of treason was inserted, with special rules for treason trials. Each of these safeguards was really directed against royal abuses, so common in the past. Little thought was given to protecting human rights against the abuses that might occur under a popularly elected government.

There was nothing to prevent the congress, under the stimulus of a temporary popular prejudice or the pressure of a president impatient with opposition to his policies, from passing laws that would curtail the individual freedom to speak or assemble. Intolerant adherents of a particular religious sect might try to use the powers of government to aid it, or to hurt others. There are still possibilities for oppression among the standard law enforcement procedures, unless their use is controlled, and no such controls were originally provided. The rights, the privileges and the immunities of a free people which we now think of as essential to a meaningful democracy were not declared.

The omission had not been overlooked. Toward the end of the Philadelphia Convention, George Mason of Virginia arose to move that a bill of rights be included in the constitution that was being completed. "It would give great quiet to the people," he said, and such "a bill might be prepared in a few hours."

Mason was well qualified to prepare a bill of rights in "a few hours." He remembered well the experience of eleven years before when he had completed a similar assignment in a few days. Weeks before the Declaration of Independence was to be adopted by the Continental Congress, the local governmental body in Virginia decided to take the lead in the transition from resistance to the British king to revolution against his rule. The Commonwealth of Virginia was to replace the Colony of Virginia, and the first step was to replace the royal charter with a basic instrument of government. But even before the constitution was drawn, Mason had prepared the Virginia Declaration of Rights, a chapter in the history of human liberty whose words echo today in the United Nations Universal Declaration of Human Rights.

As the other colonies proceeded to adopt local constitutions, they followed Virginia's example, and in one form or another they included in their basic documents of government a list of the rights that were never to be invaded by their officials. The very fact that the individual constitutions of the former colonies each contained such a bill of rights was a factor that helped to defeat Mason's motion at the Constitutional Convention of the United States. It had been a long hot summer in Philadelphia and the delegates were impatient to leave. Why, they asked, would the people need more protection than was given by the basic laws of the separate states?

George Washington was sure that Mason's proposal had been rejected only because of the lack of an urgently felt need for a national bill of rights. "There was not a member of the convention," he wrote to his old comrade-in-arms, General Lafayette, "who had the least objection to what is contended for by advocates of a bill of rights."

Despite Washington's confidence, there may have been some delegates at Philadelphia who were embarrassed by their uncertainties about putting down on parchment a statement of national guarantees of the freedom of the individual. The source of their self-consciousness was stated by Charles Cotesworth Pinckney of South Carolina: "Such bills generally begin with declaring that all men are by nature born free. Now, we should make that declaration with a very bad grace, when a large part of our property consists in men who are actually born slaves."

What really accounted for the lateness of Mason's motion and its defeat, more than any other single factor, was the troublesome complexity of the major order of business of the Philadelphia Convention: the development of a new and unusual system of government to replace the loose alliance of individual self-governing areas that the thirteen original colonies had become after their independence had been won.

As "commonwealths" and "states," the former colonies had the right to control commerce and their relationships both with one another and with foreign nations, all of which had to be surrendered to a new nation (as Washington and most of the delegates felt) for the preservation of independence and for the sake of the future growth and security of the people inhabiting all of the states. Once this was agreed upon, the new nation would have to be able to tax, to borrow, to handle problems of citizenship and currency, to administer the post office and relations with Indians—in short, all the problems and housekeeping affairs that involved or affected more than one state.

The creation of the new constitutional structure was no easy task. Men who had fought side by side to overthrow the British rule that had encroached upon their claim to make the decisions that affected their own lives locally were now divided on whether rule from Philadelphia or New York might be just as dangerous. The form of government that was developed required a series of compromises on issues that affected small states as against large, commercial states as against agricultural, slave states as against free. The fifty-five delegates to the convention were so preoccupied with settling these differences that their inattention to written guarantees of human rights seems understandable.

When they were finished, they had produced what was basically a rough outline of an untried, dual form of government that many Americans, even today, do not wholly understand. Many details of organization and procedure remained to be worked out; the problems that could arise when each of two sets of officials—national and state—could regulate the affairs of the people could not be visualized or solved in advance. No one was fully satisfied with what had been accomplished, and a growing minority opposed it bitterly.

George Mason of Virginia, who had belatedly proposed the limitations on government to protect individual freedoms, was even more seriously concerned with the loss of state sovereignty—that is, the independence and right to have a final say in all internal and external affairs that the separate ex-colonies had had—and he complained bitterly: "The very idea of converting what was formerly a confederation to a consolidated government, is totally subversive of every principle which has hitherto governed us. This power is calculated to annihilate totally state governments. . . . These two concurrent powers cannot exist long together; the one will destroy the other. . . ."

A more judicious appraisal came from Benjamin Franklin, at eighty-two more than twenty years older than any other delegate. In an appeal for unanimity behind the final draft of the new charter, he had stood on the final day to say: "Mr. President: I confess that I do not entirely approve of this Constitution at present, but Sir, I am not sure I shall never approve it. For having lived long, I have experienced many instances of being obliged, by better information or fuller consideration, to change opinions even on important subjects. . . . Thus I consent, Sir, to this Constitution because I expect no better, and because I am not sure that it is not the best."

Chapter 2

"What No Just Government Should Refuse"

The new constitution did not go into effect merely because the men who met in Philadelphia had so voted. It did not become the basic rule book for the thirteen former colonies until it was approved by popularly elected conventions in at least nine of them. Before the conventions were scheduled to be held, the terms of the new basic law became the subject of widespread discussion and debate.

Despite the esteem in which the individual delegates who had worked in Philadelphia were held, there was dissatisfaction with their product. The grumbling became louder as it became more widely known that there were only few and scattered safeguards of the rights of individuals in the proposed constitution. It was recalled by some that when they or their parents had joined the guerrillas who were conducting revolutionary warfare against the ruler overseas, and then accepted the discipline of the Continental Army, they shared Thomas Jefferson's opinion that it was not merely independence for which they were fighting and making sacrifices.

The very nature of the government that would succeed the king, Jefferson had said, "is the whole subject of the present controversy; for should a bad government be instituted for us in future, it had been well to have accepted the bad one offered to us from beyond the water, without the risk and expense of conflict."

The increasing level of protest began to alarm the dispersed delegates, each a leader of public opinion in his home state and sensitive to popular opposition. When they first came home they did not expect too much difficulty in winning ratification for the product of their summer's work. They had expected disapproval from those who opposed the new charter because of their dislike for further surrender of "state sovereignty," the granting of greater power to the new central government; some of the dissenters, like George Mason at the convention, exploited as the basis of opposition the absence of a bill of rights and found it to be a popular issue. The founders who had labored to achieve a stronger national government had been too inconsiderate of the rights of the people, and distrust incited discontent.

Jefferson had been abroad on diplomatic business during the convention. Struck, when he returned, by the absence of sufficient evidence of attention to the ideas in his Declaration of Independence of 1776, he wrote to James Madison, who had been a convention delegate from their state. He argued for a "bill of rights providing clearly . . . for freedom of religion, freedom of the press, protection against standing armies, restriction against monopolies, the eternal and unremitting force of *habeas corpus*, laws, and trial by jury." He concluded by insisting that "a bill of rights is what the people are entitled to against every government on earth, general or particular, & what no just government should refuse. . . ."

Popular demand for the addition of a list of guarantees of the rights of individuals reached the conventions that were assembling to vote on ratification. Several of the state conventions announced officially that they would vote in favor of the Philadelphia charter only on the pledge that the very first congress would amend it by protecting the rights of the people. Sentiment was so strong for this in Virginia that a favorable vote was in doubt, A movement had even begun to insist that the missing guarantees be supplied before ratification. A new convention might have meant a fatal delay, with new battles over the compromises already agreed upon. Delegate Madison pledged unconditionally to secure the necessary amendments at the first congress, and after a severe division his pledge was accepted.

The new constitution was ratified, the first president elected and the first congress assembled. On June 8, 1789, James Madison arose in the House to fulfill his promise to introduce the amendments that had secured ratification. He was, as he told the assembly, "bound in honor to bring the amendments before you as soon as possible." To the men of short or conveniently hazy memory, who preferred to postpone action, he said: "It will be a desirable thing to extinguish from the bosom of every member of the community any apprehension that there are those among his countrymen who wish to deprive them of the liberty for which they valiantly fought and honorably bled."

The proposals that he offered were based on the human rights already guaranteed in the state constitutions, but adapted to the needs of a nation, where power and responsibility were divided among a countrywide federal government and the several state governments. After Madison's plan for a bill of rights had been unveiled, Congressman William Jackson of Georgia, among others, complained: "We are not content with two revolutions in less than fourteen years; we must enter upon a third without necessity or propriety."

The First Congress overcame that kind of opposition and redeemed Madison's pledge. His proposals underwent considerable debate and some modification in the Senate and House, both of which accepted Madison's ideas for the most part, including the new and stronger language into which he had put the additions to the nation's basic law. Previously, Virginia's pioneer declaration of human rights had said merely that "Excessive bail *ought* not be required"; the federal Eighth Amendment uses the stronger phrase "*shall* not." Virginia's language in referring to the freedom of the press did not forbid the state to interfere with newspapers, but only described it as "one of the great bulwarks of liberty." Madison's Bill of Rights for the nation is stated in absolute terms: "Congress shall make no law. . . ."

Despite the more effective wording that he used, Madison feared that the rights being declared could not be adequately protected against "that quarter where the greatest danger lies." It was not in any of the departments of the government, he said, but "in the body of the people, operating by the majority against the minority." He foresaw that prejudice, popular whim or hysteria, selfish hostility or mob action could destroy the value of the declaration of rights to be contained in our basic law.

He also had the wisdom to anticipate that Americans might be deprived of their rights by the action of state governments as well as that of the nation, and that the states might tolerate or execute such action despite a constitutional declaration that such things "ought not" to be. He therefore included in his list of proposed amendments one that by an historic coincidence was numbered the fourteenth, which provided that "no State shall violate the equal rights of conscience, freedom of the press or trial by jury in criminal cases."

The idea behind it was to protect Americans against departures from their own constitutions by state courts, which might be susceptible to local influences or to the special mood or motivation that could cause oppressive actions. The Supreme Court of the United States and the lower federal courts that were being set up by the 1789 constitution could only interfere in a case if a violation of that constitution occurred. The nature of the federal system of government as conceived gave state courts sole control over the interpretation and enforcement of state bills of rights.

Madison sensed that there might occur, within one or more states, the kind of injustice which his bill of rights was designed to forbid the new national government from perpetrating. He spoke plainly to the Congress: "If there were any reason to restrain the Government of the United States from infringing upon these essential rights," he insisted, "it was equally necessary that they should be secured against State Governments."

Although he capped his argument in favor of his Fourteenth Amendment by arguing that it was "the most valuable amendment" in the whole list, Madison lost this battle. The Senate of 1789 voted down the proposal and it was never submitted to the states for ratification. It took the first eighty years of our nation's history to teach the lesson for which words alone, in 1789, were not sufficient.

The Bill of Rights is contained in the first ten amendments. They keep the promise that had been made to induce the approval of the product of the 1787 convention. The limits placed on the power of government and the barriers erected to safeguard the rights of the individual marked a new era of civilized government.

If anything can be said to represent the heritage of the American Revolution, it is the catalogue of privileges and immunities which are set forth in the first ten amendments. Freedom of thought and expression, freedom of inquiry and association, freedom of religion: all are there. Recognition and protection of the dignity of individual personality are there too: freedom from prying and snooping and the right to fair procedures where there might be police investigations, trials and punishment. Men who had just won their freedom by revolution knew very well that these rights were required for the protection of the innocent and that to the whole nation it was worth the risk that some who were guilty might occasionally escape punishment as a result of protecting those who were innocent.

There was one great glaring omission in the Bill of Rights. That was the failure to say a word about the faith in human equality that had been expressed in the declaration of July 4, 1776. What had defeated Madison's proposed fourteenth amendment, the rejected barrier against state injustice, had also made it impossible to pledge equality for all in the new constitution: the existence of slavery in so many of the states. Human aspiration for freedom and justice would inevitably undermine the unity of the revolutionary victors.

Black men resisted oppression or sought to escape from it. Free blacks sought to help their brothers. Many whites of conscience came to recognize that the institution of slavery was not tolerable in a democratic, nineteenth-century civilization. Agitation for the abolition of a labor system which reduced human beings to "property" produced a hostile response from the owners of such property. It became impossible to speak out in a slave state, even to suggest that an African-American was as much a human being as a Scotch or German-American. Not only local laws but outright lawless mobs silenced the voices of dissent.

Such repression was in direct conflict with the constitutional rights of the people in the states that were affected. Virginia, home of the first declaration of rights, passed a law that made it a crime even to say "that owners have no property in slaves." Other states, in utter disregard for their local bills of rights, even outlawed conversations "having a tendency to promote discontent." Repression was color-blind. White men could no more speak out for freedom than blacks, native Southerners any more than visitors or new arrivals from the North.

In order to suppress the very idea that slavery was questionable or that it was immoral to treat blacks differently from whites, it became necessary to treat Americans worse than the British king had treated their parents, the colonists. The freedoms of speech, the press and assembly and the rights of petition and academic pursuit were forgotten when it came to forbidden subjects. Whites found that they had lost most of the liberties that the founding fathers had thought valuable: they had lost them because they permitted the denial of liberty to blacks.

The suppression of American freedoms came about not only or even most often from government or police action, nor did it take place only in slave states. Mobs or lawless individuals would attack those believed to be radicals on the subject of human freedom. Officials whose sworn duty it was to uphold the law and the courts established to administer justice were indifferent.

In most of the South and a good part of the North, Americans were denied the rights that their own state constitutions had provided: the rights that Madison would have secured by his pioneer Fourteenth Amendment.

The spirit of '76 which had nourished the first revolution had not been stamped out. Men and women who remembered and were dedicated to the ideas that made that revolution would not let those ideas die. A variety of groups came into being and worked to combat slavery. Others wanted to defend the rights and liberties that were denied by those who opposed agitating for freedom. They included the African-Americans, slave and free, who were united against it; some religious men and women interpreted the words in the Bible about the brotherhood of man seriously; and the sons and daughters of the revolution remembered and fought for its temporarily forgotten ideals. They wanted protection for the human rights that "no just government should refuse."

Chapter 3

A Son
of the Revolution

The lives and careers of many Americans were dedicated to the effort that caused the writing of the Fourteenth and its sister amendments and that later restored their vitality. There were so many that they cannot all be given the full recognition they deserve. Among the earliest to stand out in the story of Big Fourteen was Charles Sumner.

As a youngster, Charles did not think that he would ever want to go into politics. His grandfather left Harvard in his sophomore year to fight in the American Revolution; his father, unsuccessful at law, entered politics and was sheriff of Suffolk County, Massachusetts, when young Sumner entered Harvard Law School. There he met and worked with Supreme Court Justice Joseph Story, who doubled as a professor.

With introductions from Story, Charles Sumner went to Washington as a young tourist in 1834 and there met President Jackson, Daniel Webster and other great men of the day. He wrote to his father as his trip neared the end; "I shall probably never come here again. I have little or no desire ever to come again in any capacity. Nothing that I have seen of politics has made me look upon them with any feeling other than loathing."

A dozen years later he rejected a friend's advice that he reconsider, and said "*You* may be a senator of the United States, some day; but nothing would make me happier than to be President of Harvard College." During the following year, as the reverberations of his first great public oration were still echoing, Sumner declined an invitation to run for Congress.

Although without political ambition as a youth, Sumner had not limited his interests to the practice of law. He enjoyed working on scholarly books and had a modest interest in projects of social reform for which his contemporaries were agitating. His life was transformed in 1845 when the mayor of Boston invited him to deliver the principal address at the Fourth of July festivities—an honor annually offered to the most promising young man in the city.

Sumner accepted the assignment reluctantly—he even turned it down at first. After thinking about a subject for the oration, he began to sense what an opportunity he had, and began research and preparation that were to make his speech a major event. There had been talk of war with Britain over the Oregon border, and war with Mexico about Texas seemed imminent. He was especially concerned about the possible invasion of Mexico. To speak in opposition gave him the double opportunity of aiding the native American peace movement and defending the antislavery cause.

The audience of dignitaries, prominent private citizens and uniformed representatives of the armed forces murmured uneasily as they heard him state his theme: "In our age there can be no peace that is not honorable; there can be no war that is not dishonorable." The tall handsome youth, who carried himself with a dignified bearing that repressed the restiveness of his listeners, pressed his point.

He attacked the evils of both war and militarism. He described in great detail the public works that could have been built were it not for excessive expenditures in a standing army and navy. He insisted that all war was fratricidal, saying "God hath made of one blood all nations of men." Not only did he propose that war among the nations be outlawed: a century before the formation of the United Nations he proposed a Congress of Nations that would establish a permanent international court to resolve all disputes among them.

Even though the address offended some of the audience, the military and naval brass in particular, it created a sensation and Sumner never left the civic stage again. The injustice and the immorality of the attack on Mexico impelled him to throw himself more actively into antislavery affairs. He could no longer confine his feelings to the writing of private letters and expressions of sympathy with the movement. He had come a long way since a letter he had written ten years before to a friend who had gone to the University of South Carolina to teach: "You are in the midst of slavery. . . . What think you of it? Should it longer exist? We are becoming abolitionists at the North fast; the riots, the attempts to abridge the freedom of discussion, Governor McDuffie's message [recommending that abolition be made a capital offense in that state] and the conduct of the South generally have caused many to think favorably of immediate emancipation who never before inclined to it."

With the Mexican war, Sumner became an outspoken activist. He denounced the admission of Texas as a slave state, after Mexico had abolished slavery there. He repeatedly condemned the war while it

was being waged—even though it had been declared by Congress—
and called for the immediate and unconditional withdrawal of all of
our troops from Mexico. He made numerous antislavery addresses
and was drawn into politics with the launching of a "free soil" movement, one pledged to admit no more slave states to the Union.

In 1849 he found the opportunity, as an attorney, to attempt to
oblige his own state to obey its bill of rights. The facts of the case
that was brought to him were a forcible reminder that Massachusetts
as well as South Carolina was ignoring its state bill of rights because
of the racial prejudice that escorted slavery.

Benjamin Roberts of Boston had a five-year-old daughter whom
he wanted to send to the public school nearest where they lived. The
Boston school district at the time was divided into twenty-two attendance areas. Within each, the rules of the School Committee directed that pupils were "especially entitled to enter the school
nearest to their place of residence." But when the father took his
daughter to enroll, he found that this did not mean *all* children. A
divided school board had decided that, despite the neighborhood
school principle, young blacks were to be required to attend separate
schools.

Sarah Roberts was too young, her father decided, to have to travel
farther than his neighbors' children. He went to see Robert Morris, a
black attorney of the city. Morris was glad of the chance to mount a
fight against this kind of injustice. There was not even a state law, he
told Roberts, that required the segregation of which his daughter
was the victim.

Roberts and Morris conducted their first efforts at meetings of the
school committee. When they were turned down, they decided that
it would be useful to enlist the aid of the handsome young white
attorney who had attacked the Mexican war and slavery, and who
had become more prominent and popular during each year that had
passed after his "True Grandeur of Nations" address.

Sumner, Roberts and Morris agreed to sue the Boston school committee. To Roberts it was a chance to rectify a private injustice; to
Morris, an occasion to advance the rights of all of Boston's blacks.
Sumner saw a chance to defend and expound, as he put it, "the fundamental principles of human rights," and to test "the Christian
character of the community." *Roberts vs. Boston* was a case whose
name was to be heard again and again in the century that followed
and a ghost that still walked in 1954.

On December 4, 1849, Sumner addressed the Supreme Court of
Massachusetts. His central theme was that what Massachusetts owed
to Sarah Roberts under its state constitution was the fulfillment of its
pledge of equality. "I begin with the principle," he told the assembled judges, "that according to the spirit of American institutions,

and especially of the Constitution of Massachusetts, all men, without distinction of color or race, are equal before the law."

The revival of the spirit of the American Revolution that was to surge forward in the next twenty years was expressed by this grandson of the revolutionary soldier: "The equality declared by our fathers in 1776, and made the fundamental law of Massachusetts in 1780, was *Equality before the law.* Its object was to efface all political or civil distinctions, and to abolish all institutions founded upon *birth.* 'All men are *created* equal,' says the Declaration of Independence. 'All men are *born* free and equal,' says the Massachusetts Bill of Rights."

Some of the judges were stony faced, some were bored, few showed much interest as he continued. "These are not vain words. Within the sphere of their influence no person can be created, no person can be born, with civil or political privileges not enjoyed equally by all his fellow-citizens; nor can any institution be established recognizing any distinctions of birth. Here is the Great Charter of every human being drawing his vital breath upon this soil, whatever may be his condition, and whoever may be his parents.

"He may be poor, weak, humble, black—he may be of Caucasian, of Jewish, of Indian, or of Ethiopian race—he may be of French, of German, of English, of Irish extraction—but before the Constitution of Massachusetts all these distinctions disappear . . . He is a Man,— the equal of all his fellow men."

The opposition replied by arguing that, even though the school to which the Negroes were assigned was separate, it was "equal" and that equal facilities were all that the state need grant to the children for whom Sumner spoke. "The separate school is not an equivalent," answered Sumner. "The whites themselves are injured by the separation. Who can doubt this? With the law as their monitor, they are taught to regard a portion of the human family, children of God, created in his image, as a separate and degraded class. . . . Their characters are debased, and they become less fit for the duties of citizenship.

"Who can say that this does not injure the blacks?" he also asked. "They feel their proscription from the common schools as a peculiar brand. It adds to their discouragements. It widens their separation from the community, and postpones that great day of reconciliation which is yet to come.

"The whole system of Public Schools suffers also. . . . The law contemplates not only that all should be taught, but that all should be taught *all together.* They are not only to receive equal quantities of knowledge, but are all to receive it in the same way. . . . The school is the little world where the child is trained for the larger world of life. As the state derives strength from the unity and solidarity of its citizens without distinction of class, so the school derives strength from the unity and solidarity of all classes beneath its roof. . . . Prejudice is the child of ignorance. It is sure to prevail where people do not know each other."

For the moment it was all in vain. Sarah Roberts lost her case. But Charles Sumner was to win his battle, and having waged it he had advanced in his training for the important battles to come.

The full text of Sumner's eloquent, but unsuccessful, plea to the court was reprinted as a pamphlet and distributed by the agitators of the abolitionist movement. It helped influence public opinion in Massachusetts and was widely read in other states; its ideas took root in the minds of men who were rising in public life in the years before the Civil War. Some were to be in the Thirty-Ninth Congress.

Benjamin Roberts and the blacks—and whites of conscience—of Massachusetts pressed the fight that had been lost in court. A five-year campaign was begun with the circulation of a petition to the state legislature. By 1855 public opinion in favor of desegregated schools was strong enough to overcome segregated education. It had been aided by the growth of antislavery sentiment, nourished by events on the national scene—the Compromise of 1850, the harsh new Fugitive Slave Law, and the repeal of the Missouri Compromise, which opened new territory to slavery. The Massachusetts lawmakers used their control over local school boards to overrule the Roberts case and thus to prohibit segregation in the public schools of the state.

Sumner's plea for Sarah Roberts remained a superb statement on the evils of segregation and its inherent denial of equality. During the century that followed it was not excelled; even the advances of modern psychology and sociology did not furnish much to add to what Sumner had said on the subject when the final battle against school segregation was fought in the Supreme Court in 1952.

And Sumner's elevation of the eighteenth-century revolutionary phrases "created equal" and "born equal" to the level of constitutional right, in the concept of "equality before the law," became a significant milestone on the road to the new American freedom.

Chapter 4

Dred Scott: Four Tries for Freedom

Dred Scott tried to escape slavery by running away. He succeeded in avoiding capture for two days when he slipped off after Peter Blow sold him to Dr. John Emerson. After he was found hiding in a Missouri swamp and retaken he resigned himself to his fate—for a while. He was in personal service and better off than a plantation field hand. He dreamed of freedom and bided his time.

His new owner was an army surgeon, and when he was transferred from Missouri to a military post in Illinois he took Scott with him. After some years there, Dr. Emerson was ordered to Fort Snelling, a post in free territory at the junction of the Mississippi and the Minnesota rivers. There Scott, who had lost one wife by that cruel mode of "divorce" that was forced by a sale, married again. He and his second wife Harriet had two children, one born in free territory. The land was free soil because by the Missouri Compromise of 1820 it had been agreed that slavery should be excluded from all Louisiana Purchase territory north of a stated line, except for Missouri itself.

Dr. Emerson died in 1843. Since his widow had no need for a male household servant, she hired Dred out and permitted him to keep a small portion of what she was paid for his services. When he had saved a few hundred dollars, he made his second bid for freedom, offering to buy himself and his family from Mrs. Emerson. She refused.

Scott's third attempt to free himself and his family was begun in the Missouri state court in 1846. The word had gotten around to him that by his residence in a free state, and his family's in free territory, they had automatically become free. He used his savings to retain an attorney to win a declaration from the court that he and his family were emancipated.

The legal point was not a new one. Dr. Emerson had gone to Illinois with his property. By the law of Illinois, slavery was illegal. Since he had resided there, Dred had become Mr. Scott, a free man and a United States citizen. Why should he not remain free, even after having returned to Missouri? Had he stayed in Illinois he would have been free, having entered the state lawfully from Missouri. Why should he be worse off now than if he had slipped away while Emerson was in a free state?

In similar cases the Missouri courts had ruled in favor of the former slave. Scott was assured by the Missouri attorney that he, his wife, and children would win their freedom. The advice he gave seemed to be correct, for the lower court ruled that the Scott family were no longer slaves. But that was not to be the last word, for Mrs. Emerson's lawyers took an appeal to the supreme court of the state.

Now Dred and Harriet Scott and their little girls were made the victims of a vindictive interstate political reprisal. The high court majority admitted that under previous precedents the lower court had decided the case correctly. But it announced, over the angry protest of the Missouri chief justice, that it was changing the rules.

The judges who made up the majority of the court expressed their resentment at the growth of antislavery feeling in the parts of the United States where it was possible to discuss the issue. They conceded that they were punishing the black family whose fate was in their hands: "Times now are not what they were when the former decisions were made. Since then not only individuals but States have been possessed with a dark and fell spirit in relation to slavery . . . whose inevitable consequence must be the overthrow and destruction of our government."

While the hopes of the Scott family seemed blasted, a change in conditions had occurred while the case was in the Missouri courts which made possible a fourth bid for freedom. Mrs. Emerson had remarried in 1850 and had become ineligible to continue to act as the executrix, the person entrusted by law with the power to handle her husband's estate during the period of administration that always precedes the distribution of the property of a deceased person to his heirs. Her brother, Dr. John F. Sanford, a citizen of New York, was appointed to succeed her. If Dred Scott was legally free, said the lawyers, he was a citizen of Missouri. The chance for the fourth try was presented by the nature of the judicial system that had been created by the United States Constitution.

What the Philadelphia framers had provided for, as we have seen, was a unique federal system of government in which citizens had responsibilities to, and were governed by, their states as well as their nation. Each center of government, nation and state, had its own complete apparatus of lawmaking and law enforcement. Some areas of authority, such as foreign commerce, were exclusively national; some, such as local property relations, were exclusively state; and over some there was a dual or overlapping authority. For the national administration a federal court system was provided, with a Supreme Court of the United States at its head, and local district courts throughout the land.

But the 1787 convention did not limit the federal courts to the handling of cases presenting questions under the federal constitution and federal laws alone. It was felt that when cases arose in which a citizen of one state sued a citizen of another one or the other should have the option to sue in federal court, even if only questions of local law were presented, so that provincial jealousies or the suspicion of local prejudice could be avoided. Judges were only human, and while there was no guarantee that a federal judge would be freer from prejudice than his state court brother it was hoped that it would at least be more probable that he might, and that worried suitors from outside that state should have a choice.

Here was one more chance for Dred Scott, reasoned the lawyers, even though, ironically, he was the Missourian and Dr. Sanford was the New Yorker. The Missouri court had ruled against the local family precisely because of hostility to states like New York where antislavery agitation was permitted, so it seemed worth taking a chance on a new suit in the Missouri federal court. Freedom was a precious enough objective to be sought once more. Certainly it did not seem that Scott, and the friends who were now carrying the main burden of the cost of the lawsuit, had much to lose by another try. (One of those friends was Taylor Blow, son of the man who had sold Dred to Dr. Emerson, who now lived in Missouri and with his brother Henry had come to feel a hostility to slavery.)

The first move in the fourth bid for freedom was a failure. Federal Judge Robert Wells promptly overruled the first objection raised by Sanford's lawyers, who claimed that Scott, even if free, had no right to sue in the United States court. Their theory was one that had never been upheld by any court: it amounted to an argument that the scattered free Negroes in the several states (who had come to be victims of the meanest kinds of prejudice and discrimination, even in the "free" states) were not even "second-class" citizens—they were not entitled to become citizens at all.

After rejecting the argument that, even if free, Scott had not become a citizen because blacks could not, Judge Wells nevertheless ruled against him. He directed a verdict for Sanford since the legal issue was one of local (Missouri) property rights which he held must be governed by state law. The Missouri courts having concluded that Scott's voluntary return to the state with his master forfeited his freedom, the federal court said that it would follow that precedent.

Now the case was taken for final decision to the Supreme Court of the United States. Its decision is of course mentioned in every history book. The court helped to bring on the Civil War by reaching out to decide a question that was not even presented by the parties to the lawsuit: whether Congress had the power to forbid the introduction of slavery into United States territory that had not yet won statehood—such as the Wisconsin region where Fort Snelling had been situated.

A nationwide debate followed the court's decision, a debate that had the character of an angry majority in a ball park crying "kill the umpire" after a dubious decision against the home team. Abraham Lincoln was to emerge as a national figure during this debate over the correctness and propriety of the decision denying Congress the power to stop slavery in national territory.

Those aspects of the court's Dred Scott ruling are not of importance in connection with the story of the creation of the Civil War amendments to the Constitution. Other features of the case, not stressed as often, were to haunt the country and the court during the drafting of the amendments and again when their purpose was blunted by later Supreme Court decisions.

Apart from the explosively controversial restriction on the power of the Congress over slavery in the territories, the court also reached out to declare that no American of African ancestry, whether freed by law or born free, could even be a citizen of the United States!

This conclusion was the reverse of what federal judge Wells had ruled when the point was raised for the first time. It was not really necessary to make a decision on the point (any more than it was necessary to say anything about the power of Congress to control slavery in the territories) since, under a time-honored rule of judicial restraint, major constitutional decisions are avoided when possible. When Dred Scott's case was first presented to it, the court had decided to follow that rule. Justice Nelson was assigned the responsibility of writing an opinion saying simply that the law of Missouri, where he lived, settled Scott's status as a slave after his return. On that basis, there was no need to decide whether he had been made free by residing in territory where slavery was outlawed (and hence whether Congress had had the power to outlaw it there) or whether, if free, Scott was a citizen of the United States who was privileged to use the option of suing in the federal court for Missouri.

What the court majority did was to respond politically to the announced intention of two of its members to dissent from the decision on the point of Missouri law and to go on to explain their point of view on the questions of citizenship and slavery in the territories. Such exposition would have been logical and proper on their part, once they had concluded that the court was not bound by Missouri law. But the majority was not content to have only the two dissenters announce their views. The slavery controversy, especially the efforts of antislavery men to induce Congress to outlaw slavery in all territories that had not yet become states, had become critical in the presidential campaign of 1856. A "free soil" candidate had almost been elected. The majority of the court was composed of Southerners and sympathizers with slavery. They thought they saw an opportunity to "settle" the national dispute by pulling out the rug from under the free-soilers: a judicial decree that would forever prohibit Congress from interfering with the spread of slavery, they reasoned, would bring "peace and harmony" to the country.

Not only were they politically motivated; they also pulled political strings in their effort. One justice, John Catron, kept President elect James Buchanan informed of the state of the court's deliberations, and even urged him to influence another justice, Robert C. Grier, into joining the majority lineup. Justice Catron's letter—only disclosed in 1910, when the Buchanan papers were opened to the public—even formulated a phrase that Buchanan used in his inaugural address, one that startled many listeners when they heard the president utter it, since the inaugural was delivered at a time when no one should have known how or on what grounds the court would decide the Scott family's fate. Catron had written to Buchanan: ". . . I think you may safely say in your inaugural: 'That the question involving the constitutionality of the Missouri Compromise is presented to the appropriate tribunal to decide: to wit, the Supreme Court of the United States. It is due to its high and independent character to suppose that it will decide and settle a controversy which has so long and seriously agitated the country, and which *must* be settled by the Supreme Court.' "

Before the time came to deliver his inaugural address, Mr. Buchanan had written to Justice Grier and received a reassuring reply from him reporting that he had shown the president elect's letter to Chief Justice Roger B. Taney and Justice Noah Wayne of Georgia. "With their concurrence," wrote Grier, "I will give you in confidence the history of the case before us with the probable result." Had these events been known in 1857, many would have said: "Impeach Taney, Wayne, Catron and Grier."

Chapter 5

"There is a Mode . . . by Which It May be Amended"

A written constitution would not be of practical importance if an authority were not available to decide what each provision means and whether or not it applies to a particular case. In any government functioning under a constitution, faith in the impartiality and integrity of this referee must be maintained. He would not have any effective influence, or even remain around very long, if word got out that he made his decisions on the basis of his personal preferences.

When James Madison proposed the Bill of Rights in the House of Representatives in 1789, he optimistically expressed his faith in the impartial administration of justice. "It may be thought that all paper barriers against the power of the community are too weak to be worthy of attention," he said in introducing the first amendments. Then he stated: "If they are incorporated into the constitution, independent tribunals of justice will consider themselves in a peculiar manner the guardians of those rights; they will be an inpenetrable bulwark against every assumption of power in the legislative or executive."

He had hoped that those "independent tribunals" would vindicate his earlier wish that the Constitution "would be the great charter of human liberty to the unborn millions who shall enjoy its protection, and who should never see that such an institution as slavery was ever known in our midst." That hope was expressed at a time when enlightened white Southerners like Madison accepted the Constitution's compromises with slavery in the belief that bondage would fade away in the South as it had in the North. That was not to be. Fed by the new demands for its products and the increase in productivity made possible by the cotton gin, slavery fastened itself onto the southern states like a monster seeking vengeance. Its effect was demoralizing and it destroyed the possibilities of progress for southern whites and blacks alike.

The limited crop character of an agricultural economy based on forced labor made it expansionistic in order to survive. That expansionism became competitive with the increase of free labor and a free market economy in the states that had abolished slavery. But to that conflict there was added a new tension. The moral deficiency of slavery became more evident as enlightened ideas—themselves generated here and abroad by the prestige of the American Revolution —caused more and more men to question its right to survive. At the same time, its victims and the free Americans of African ancestry stepped up their resistance and their efforts to destroy it. Bostonian blacks like David Walker called for insurrection in 1827 and Virginians like Nat Turner tried to overthrow it by rebellion.

The result of competition, condemnation and resistance was a marked increase in intolerance of opposition in the states whose governments and political leaders were chosen from among and by the slaveowners. The insistence on holding on to their affluence and power, their "way of life" as they came to call it, caused them to try to justify its existence. The idea of the abolition of a property relationship on which the ruling class of the South depended could not be resisted by repression alone. It was also opposed by the development of excuses for the evasion of the revolutionary idea, bedrock of our independence, that "all men are created equal,"—or, as the earlier Virginia bill of rights had said, "all men are by nature free and independent."

The idea of human equality could not be erased. It was necessary, therefore, to pervert it and to prove that it did not mean what it said. That was easily done by seizing upon the obvious distinction of color between the men of African ancestry and those of European ancestry who had joined together to win the Revolution and to beat back the British in the War of 1812. By inventing a simple insertion, the slaveholders and those who depended on them, north and south, claimed to be entitled to monopolize the rights and privileges intended to be shared by all Americans. Their thinking now was that "all *white* men were created equal." An alternate way of putting it was to insist that blacks were not men, or something less than human. The tool that made it possible to develop and transmit this stratagem was readily at hand. We call it "racism" now, the belief that the lighter skinned were a race apart from the darker, superior to them, and not only entitled but also obliged to lord it over them for the survival of all.

Ralph Waldo Emerson, the great New England transcendentalist, was not a radical abolitionist or an agitator like some from his region. His words in a speech that he gave in 1845 summed up the result: "What is the defence of slavery? What is the irresistible argument by which every plea of humanity and reason has hitherto been borne down? Is it a doubt of the equity of the Negro's cause? By no means. . . . I think that there is but one single argument which has any real weight with the bulk of the Northern people, and which lies in one word—a word which I hear pronounced with triumphant emphasis in bar-rooms, in shops, in the streets, in kitchens, at musters, and at cattle shows. That word is *niggers*. . . . It is the objection of an inferiority of race."

What Emerson was describing was the insidious increase of belief in racial inferiority which tended to dominate the thinking of many. It did so in such a way as to become a part of their essential outlook, something of which they had no real doubt. It made possible the impairment of judicial integrity and honor which was reflected in the Dred Scott decision. There was not even the conscious wrongdoing that afflicts courts from time to time, ranging from frequent favoritism to the infrequent sale of justice. It was primarily the subconscious distortion of thought and the perversion of reasoning that was made possible by belief in the inferiority of the blacks and was incited by fear of the destruction or erosion of the property rights that were the foundation of society in the slave states.

The two major aspects of the Taney Court's decision in the Dred Scott case illustrate how judges can be influenced by their prejudices in deciding cases. One was quite covert. The Constitution clearly granted Congress the power to "make all needful Rules and Regulations respecting the Territory or other Property belonging to the United States." When, as part of the Missouri Compromise, the Congress forbade slavery in specified portions of the land gained in the Louisiana Purchase, that land was declared "territory . . . belonging to the United States." The court majority got around this legal truth simply by declaring that the power to regulate applied only to territory already owned by the United States in 1789, and not to territory acquired afterwards.

By this device, as even one historian sympathetic to Taney has said, the court committed a "gross abuse of trust." Its effect was not to bring the peace and harmony for which the majority members plotted with President elect Buchanan but to make the controversy over slavery even more acute. The moderates of that time had until then limited their efforts to an attempt to prevent the extension of slavery, which was thought to be quite lawful and constitutional. They had avoided espousing the objectives of the radical abolitionists, believing that Congress had no power to outlaw slavery in the states that permitted it by law and had been admitted to the Union as slave states. Now there was no more room for moderation.

The other aspect of the court's decision was not based on a play on words. It was an overt injection of the racist thinking of the day into the judicial process. The court ruled that Scott, even if free, was not a citizen because he could not possibly become one, even though native born. Justice Taney asked if one "whose ancestors were imported into this country and sold as slaves [could] become a member of the political community brought into existence by the Constitution of the United States, and as such become entitled to all the rights, and privileges, and immunities, guarantied by that instrument to the citizen? One of which rights is the privilege of suing in a court of the United States in the cases specified in the Constitution."

The response of the chief justice and the court majority to their self-created question—"Can one of African descent be an American citizen?"—was one of pure invention. There was not a word in the United States Constitution, as it stood, that defined who could or could not be a citizen of the United States. The word "citizen" had not even been in use before 1776, since all who lived here before then were "subjects" of the King of England. Many Americans of African descent were free subjects like their fellow white colonists.

When Americans became inhabitants of a free republic, the word "citizen" came into use. The initial system of government by states loosely linked by the Articles of Confederation led men to think of themselves first as citizens of the state in which they lived and second as citizens of the United States. But even in the Articles there was recognition of the beginnings of national citizenship in a provision that guaranteed "the free inhabitants of each of these states . . . all privileges and immunities of free citizens in the several states." The very use of the phrase "free inhabitants" was recognition of the fact that some, even though a tiny minority, of the Negroes in the states were not slaves, and as free men were entitled to the rights of citizens.

The new constitution did not exclude any group or class from national citizenship. It continued to protect the right of the "citizens of each state . . . to all Privileges and Immunities of Citizens of the several States." National citizenship was recognized as a fact, even though it was not defined. The presidency was restricted to a "natural born Citizen, or a Citizen of the United States, at the time of the adoption of the Constitution." This last phrase certainly meant that even before the new system of government came into being in 1789, with state control limited to local affairs, and national power granted to the federal government over national affairs, the citizens of the states were "Citizens of the United States" as well.

Not only did the Articles recognize a universality of citizenship in their reference to "free inhabitants." Northern and southern states alike—not all of them, but at least five of the thirteen—did grant the right to vote to descendants of African slaves who had the same qualifications as white voters living in those states. They were New Hampshire, New York, New Jersey, Massachusetts and even North Carolina. A North Carolina court had emphatically rejected the argument that there was any intermediate class or group of people between citizens and slaves. All of these voters had participated in the election of the delegates to the Constitutional Convention of 1787, and to the state ratifying conventions that were called to judge the new charter of government framed at Philadelphia.

In the face of this history—and without a single word in the text of the Constitution to support his conclusion—Chief Justice Roger B. Taney wrote for the court majority that Americans of African birth or ancestry were not "citizens of the several states when the Constitution was adopted." Writing with a pretense of enlightenment and sympathy, he explained, as if the period of the framing of the Constitution were a darker age than his own: "It is difficult at this day to realize the state of public opinion in relation to that unfortunate race, which prevailed in the civilized and enlightened portions of the world at the time of the Declaration of Independence, and when the Constitution of the United States was framed and adopted. But the public history of every European nation displays it in a manner too plain to be mistaken.

"They had for more than a century before been regarded as beings of an inferior order, and altogether unfit to associate with the white race, either in social or political relations; and so far inferior, that they had no rights which the white man was bound to respect. . . ."

His conclusion was that, having been considered "as a subordinate and inferior class of beings, who had been subjugated by the dominant race," they had not been intended (even though the Constitution did not say so) "to be included under the word 'citizen' in the Constitution."

Nor did the Taney Court stop at this reduction of free Negroes to a condition of statelessness, a condition which Chief Justice Earl Warren described one hundred years later, in a case denying congressional power to denationalize white military deserters, as "the total destruction of the individual's status in organized society . . . a form of punishment more primitive than torture." Also created was a completely artificial division between state and national citizenship, one wholly without warrant in the Constitution. Massachusetts or Missouri or any other state could, according to the Supreme Court, confer the right of citizenship within its own limits. But this would not serve to grant United States citizenship to African Americans. The several states were barred by the Taney decision from introducing new members from the excluded class "into the political community created by the Constitution of the United States."

This invention of a separateness of citizenship, a difference in the nature and quality of being a citizen of a state and being a citizen of the United States, was to be, from a long-range point of view, the most pernicious consequence of the Dred Scott decision. At a time when the ruling was supposed to have been erased by the Civil War and its consequences, the curious concept of separate state and United States citizenships to deprive all Americans of rights and constitutional protections provided for their benefit.

This, as we shall see, was the crowning indignity in a decision for which one sympathetic biographer of Taney has apologized by saying, "it is necessary to remember his devotion to the South, of which he was a product, and his belief that, if the trend of events continued, the South was doomed." There was a tragic irony, too, in Taney's remark that his court's opinion was not the last word. A civilized change of public opinion with respect "to this unfortunate race," he said, cannot induce the court to give "a more liberal construction in their favor than . . . when the instrument was framed and adopted. . . . If any of its provisions are deemed unjust, there is a mode prescribed in the instrument itself by which it may be amended."

Chapter 6

Moving Toward
a New Birth
of Freedom

Roger Brooke Taney naturally had his tongue in his cheek when he suggested that those who did not care for his court's reading of the Constitution need only proceed to amend it. That was the one solution which was a practical impossibility as things stood in 1857. The number of slave states had kept pace with the free, even though their population had not. The representation of the slave states in Congress was artificially inflated by the Philadelphia compromise, which increased their head count for purposes of determining representation by adding three fifths of the slaves—even though they could not vote. The provision for amending the Constitution required the concurrence of two thirds of both houses of Congress and the ratification of three fourths of the states, something that obviously could not be achieved.

This impasse was what a then obscure ex-congressman from Illinois, Abraham Lincoln, meant when he said of the decision, "now they have him [the slave] bolted in with a lock of a hundred keys." In the 1858 debates with Stephen Douglas which made him widely known throughout the nation, he said "I believe the decision was improperly made and I go for reversing it." He denounced the Supreme Court as having acted with partisan bias in a decision "based on assumed historical facts which are not really true."

Others used stronger language. The dissenting opinion of Supreme Court Justice Benjamin R. Curtis had shown how unfounded was the assumed history employed by the chief justice in justifying his pretendedly retrospective racism. A Boston paper called the court majority "great scoundrels." Three New England state legislatures passed resolutions declaring that the decision was not and could not be the law of the land. Horace Greeley's *New York Tribune* declared that the court members who had sided with Taney could be treated with the moral weight of "a majority of those congregated in any Washington bar room."

Moderate antislavery intellectuals, who had not responded to the passionate eloquence and moral appeals of the abolitionist agitators, were now thoroughly aroused. The line was beginning to blur between those who had declaimed that "Slavery is a monstrous evil: abolish it!" and those who answered, "It is wrong, but legal in some states; let us restrict it from entering new states." George William Curtis, gentle scholar, editor and educator, who had once been with the latter group, now saw "the terrible truth that slavery was a system aggressive in its very nature, and necessarily destructive of Constitutional rights and liberties." He summed up his answer to the Taney Court in an address at Plymouth Church in Brooklyn: " 'Fiddle-faddle,' says the Supreme Court of the United States, 'an African doesn't count. He is only a negro. He has no friends. Hit him again! And now that we have decided the matter, what are you going to do about it?'

"We are going to do what Patrick Henry did in Virginia, what James Otis and Samuel Adams did in Massachusetts, what the Sons of Liberty did in New York, ninety years ago. . . . We shall agitate, agitate, agitate, until the Supreme Court, obeying the popular will, proclaims that all men have original equal rights which government did not give and cannot justly take away."

But even though Lincoln could talk of "reversing" the court and Curtis of ceaseless agitation, the possibility of peaceful change by political persuasion seemed more remote than ever. The realities were discussed in a protest meeting that packed a Philadelphia church one evening. A prominent local citizen proposed resolutions denouncing the "atrocious decision" and declaring that "no allegiance is due from any man, or any class of men, to a Government founded and administered in iniquity." He told his audience that they could not take any comfort in the thought that the decision was "unconstitutional," because what the Supreme Court said "was constitutional to all *practical* intents and purposes."

A member of the audience arose. "Mr. Purvis," he asked, "is it not true that you were acknowledged to be an American citizen twenty five years ago?" The speaker, whose ancestry was as African as that of his audience, answered that he had—a fact belying the "history" recited by the chief justice. Under the administration of President Andrew Jackson (who had appointed Taney to the court), Purvis had applied for a passport, and the Secretary of State had sent an informal identity paper in return. Protests from other Philadelphians forced the granting of a full passport, giving Robert Purvis full protection as a "citizen of the United States." But the speaker added that he "was indebted for this not so much to the spirit of obeying the Constitution as to the generous impulses of General Andrew

Jackson, who still remembered his words of thanks during the War of 1812 to the many colored citizens who aided bravely in the defence of the country."

Another speaker addressed the meeting. He was Charles L. Remond, of Salem, Massachusetts, who reminded the audience that his father had come from the West Indies and yet had been formally naturalized as a citizen of the United States. Claim it no more, he told his listeners: "We owe no allegiance to a country that grinds us under its iron hoof and treats us like dogs."

Among the resolutions adopted at the meeting was one that reflected a persistent division in the ranks of the radical abolitionists. "To attempt, as some do, to prove there is no support given to Slavery in the Constitution and essential structure of the American Government, is to argue against reason and common sense," agreed the assembly; "while it may suit white men who do not feel the iron heel, to please themselves with such theories, it ill becomes the man of color whose daily experience refutes the absurdity, to indulge in any such idle phantasies."

In proposing that resolution, Purvis was expressing bitter acceptance of the viewpoint of one abolitionist leader, William Lloyd Garrison, who defiantly burned a copy of the Constitution at a public meeting on July 4, 1854. Garrison had lost patience with the elaborate arguments that had been advanced by his opponents within the movement, opponents who had sought to prove that the Constitution was potentially an antislavery instrument. "Let us be honest with the facts of history," said Garrison, "and acknowledge the compromises that were made to secure the adoption of the Constitution, and the consequent establishment of the Union." He meant such provisions as the clauses that made mandatory the return of fugitive slaves and the addition to slave state representation in Congress—and in the electoral college, which chose the president—of a population base measured by three fifths of the slave population. Garrison was outraged.

"We charge upon the present national compact, that it was formed at the expense of human liberty, by a profligate surrender of principle, and to this hour is cemented with human blood.

"It was pleaded at the time of its adoption, it is pleaded now, that, without such compromise, there could have been no union.

"To this we reply: The plea is as profligate as the act was tyrannical. It is the doctrine that the end sanctifies the means. It is a confession of sin, but the denial of any guilt in its perpetration."

The bitter frustration expressed by Purvis and his audience and Garrison's impatient defiance were understandable. The latter was the expression of a burning idealism reacting to the national political supremacy that slavery had achieved by midcentury; the former gave voice to an anger at the hopelessness of a situation in which slavery had a majority of the Supreme Court on its side, and, as it seemed, always had and always would.

They had no patience for those who had sought to use the Constitution and the original Bill of Rights as a tool of freedom. But their actions should not be permitted to obscure the contributions made by earlier abolitionist scholars, who had developed a significant body of thought that was drawn upon and helps to make understandable the language that was to be used when circumstances unexpectedly made it possible to employ the "mode prescribed in the instrument itself by which it may be amended."

In the early days of the Republic there was formed the Pennsylvania Society for the Abolition of Slavery—whose first president was eighty-year-old Benjamin Franklin—announcing as its objective the need "to extend the blessings of freedom to every part of the human race." After the 1787 Constitution was ratified, the society petitioned Congress for national action to end slavery, asserting that the power to do so could be found in the Constitution's preamble, which expressed a purpose to "establish Justice . . . and secure the Blessings of Liberty." Nine years later, the Reverend Absolom Jones, in behalf of the free Negroes of Philadelphia, invoked the preamble in an appeal to Congress in which he asserted the claims of slaves as citizens to "equal and national liberties." James Forten, who had made a fortune as a sailmaker, wrote in 1813, in agitating successfully against a proposed state law that would affect his people: "We hold this truth to be self-evident, that God created all men equal, is one of the most prominent features in the Declaration of Independence, and in that glorious fabric of collected wisdom, our noble Constitution."

As the movement for the abolition of slavery developed and broadened in the early 1830s, much of its emphasis was placed on the conversion of the sinner—a view related to the religious source of its growth. It was hoped that appeals to the Christian conscience of slaveholders and their northern allies would persuade them to repent. Some sensed the futility of relying on moral suasion, especially when the slave states imposed increasingly greater restrictions on the freedom of opinion and discussion.

These restrictions were not only prompted by fear of the force of propaganda for freedom. They were also a response to the many minor and several major slave rebellions, culminating in Nat Turner's daring effort of 1831. They were accompanied by increased vigilance against the direct action of self-emancipation through the use of patrols and other limitations on the movement of slaves. While free black leaders in the North might call for insurrection, their appeals could not reach those at whom they were directed, and only by the smoldering resistance of sabotage and sporadic acts of violence could the slaves act for their own freedom.

The other form of direct action, escape, aided by the efforts of the "underground railroad" system provided by the movement, never had a really widespread effect. It resulted in the addition of eloquent leaders to the northern free Negro population, outstanding among whom was Frederick Douglass, but this front was no threat to slavery as an institution. Some abolitionist leaders discussed the possibility of a division of the land they called "disunion," a kind of secession in reverse that they thought would cause the collapse of slavery, but there were never enough supporters to give this strategy any substantial standing. Others turned increasingly to political action.

Certain problems involving constitutional power were presented by using political action for the abolition of slavery, but they were more difficult than those faced by the groups who advocated restricting slavery to existing states. The latter felt that the express power to regulate the territories of the United States was all they needed—and they continued to hold that opinion, although with less plausibility, after the Dred Scott decision. The political activists felt a need to rummage about in the Constitution for a source of federal power, as they sensed that the early petitions to Congress based on the preamble alone were insufficient. The preamble expressed the objects of the government of the union that it had brought into being, but the Supreme Court had never ruled that the words of the preamble alone gave the federal government power to attain those aims. Federal power had to be sought since the growth of a kind of one-issue totalitarianism in the slave states made appeals to their courts and legislatures on the subject of slavery futile.

Another problem of constitutional power was created by the officially tolerated, sometimes officially incited, mob violence in the so-called free states. Advocates of abolition threatened the financial stake of northern bankers and of merchants in the cotton states, who did not hesitate to promote and exploit racial prejudice in efforts to repress the agitation. Speakers were stoned, presses were broken up, meetings were disrupted and dispersed by mass action. The freedoms of speech, of the press and of assembly were all effectually denied by the failure of local authorities to interfere, and in fact mayors were often members of mobs. The protection of the law and the enforcement of human rights were demanded by the abolitionists, and on these issues they found and recruited sympathizers. When protection and enforcement were denied them by state and local governments, abolitionists turned to the national government and sought to establish a basis for its power and duty to interfere.

The constitutional theories which they advocated and the constitutional arguments they advanced were thus prompted by the states' violation of the rights of free men as much as by their continued injustices to slaves. White men as well as blacks were being denied their rights. To restore the free Negro of the North to the status of civic equality which had existed in some states in the eighteenth century was an object sought not merely because it was morally just. The erosion of the rights that had previously existed and the increase in prejudice and discriminatory treatment were the effects of the racial antagonism promoted by slavery's sympathizers in their effort to defend their institution. To eliminate the racism that had made poor whites of the North, especially recent immigrants from peasant lands, such willing mouthpieces for establishment-inspired hostility toward abolitionism, it was felt that an important first step was to integrate, or reintegrate, social and economic life.

Chapter 7

Antislavery Origins

The early growth of the American Republic was based on the creative interpretation of the Constitution by the Supreme Court, speaking through Chief Justice John Marshall. He was able to win acceptance for the basic idea, suggested in Madison's reference to "independent tribunals of justice" (but nowhere made explicit in the document's text), that his court could enforce constitutional rights by declaring laws invalid. He launched the broad development of federal power to act on matters of national concern in a case supporting the congressional creation of a Bank of the United States, immune from state interference. The Constitution said nothing about the federal creation of banks or corporations, but there was a provision granting the power to "make all laws necessary and proper" to aid other specified powers, which Marshall made a potent, expansive weapon. In another case, he gave such a broad definition to the simply stated power "to regulate commerce" that he was given credit for having "done more to knit the American people into an indivisible Nation than any other one force in our history."

Constitutional flexibility and the capacity to adapt to the changing needs of the American people did not mean that its clear or direct commands could be disregarded. But the injection of such inventions as Taney's denial of an African American capacity for citizenship never had to be the last word—and it was not. While Taney was still alive, Lincoln's secretary of state granted a passport to the Reverend Henry Highland Garnet, defiantly describing him as a "citizen of the United States." Though born in slavery, Garnet had escaped to become an editor and community leader who had, eighteen years before, made men like Taney shudder by his eloquent defense of insurrectionists Denmark Vesey and Nat Turner and his call to American slaves—"Bretheren, arise, arise! Strike for your lives and liberties. Now is the day and the hour. . . . Let your motto be resistance! *resistance!* RESISTANCE! No oppressed people have ever secured their liberty without resistance."

In 1862, a formal ruling on citizenship came from the pen of Edward Bates, Lincoln's attorney general. A coastwise vessel had been detained by a revenue cutter on the ground that its captain was not eligible to be in command. Federal maritime law required citizenship for master's papers on an American flag vessel. Secretary of the Treasury Salmon P. Chase asked the attorney general for an official ruling. Bates replied with an opinion affirming the right of native born, free Negroes to American citizenship.

Birth in a country necessarily resulted in citizenship, declared the attorney general, and every citizen of a state is a citizen of the United States; every citizen of the United States is a citizen of the state in which he had his residence. He reasoned that citizenship by birth was a relationship that existed in all nations, and one which had to be recognized under the Constitution even though there were no words expressly so stating. All persons born in a country were equally under a duty to owe allegiance to it and were equally entitled to protection, regardless of color or race. Two years later, Chase, by then Chief Justice of the United States, would accept the application of Charles Sumner, senator from Massachusetts, to have John S. Rock, a black Bostonian, admitted to the bar of the Supreme Court, a privilege limited by court rules to citizens.

Bates' ruling was the first reward of the long and arduous struggle of the abolitionist constitutionalists to develop doctrines within the framework of the Constitution which would support their arguments. Such theories were evolved in the framework of several separate struggles. They were plausible, valid, and they enriched the thinking of the men of the Thirty-Ninth Congress who were to meet to face the problems created by the sequence of secession, rebellion, four years of war and the disastrous death of Abraham Lincoln.

They were persuasive enough to win over Frederick Douglass, who had once scoffed at the Constitution—"What is it? Who made it? For whom and for what was it made?"—and answered in Garrisonian terms that it had been "conceived in sin and shaped in iniquity." Ten years later, in the 1860 election, he identified himself with a group that proclaimed it to be the constitutional right and duty of the federal government to abolish slavery in the states.

One of the earliest campaigns during which these ideas were developed was the effort to persuade Congress to abolish slavery in the District of Columbia. Primitive and dusty though the streets were, ramshackle the houses, this was still the seat of government and the showplace of the nation. Here there was no doubt of the full power of the national legislature "To exercise exclusive Legislation in all Cases whatsoever over such District," as it is expressly stated in the Constitution. The clause eliminated the conflict of governmental authority divided between nation and state which prevailed elsewhere.

The slaveholders' legislators claimed that their rights under the Fifth Amendment—not to be deprived of property "without due process of law"—prevented congressional action. Charles Olcott responded: "The slaves (who are persons) have been deprived of liberty either with or without due process of law. If they have been thus deprived, then the law for their emancipation must also be 'due process'; one law being as much 'due process' as another. If they have not thus been deprived, there is an end to the objection of want of 'due process'; for the slaves having been deprived of liberty without due process are all free under the Constitution."

Theodore Dwight Weld, compiler of one of abolition's greatest pamphlets, "American Slavery As It Is," argued in another tract that since the slaves were "persons"—they were so referred to in the Constitution, which nowhere uses the word "slave"—in the District of Columbia they were entitled to the "protection of the laws." Such protection was warranted because of the stated purpose of the preamble—"to establish justice"—and required because of the obligation of every government to give protection to those who owed it allegiance.

One who was held in slavery in the District might be threatened or beaten and detained by his owner. Weld argued that such treatment violated local laws forbidding assault and battery and false imprisonment. A like-minded activist urged that the law declared the right of self-ownership of mind, body and soul; he insisted that "To give impartial legal protection in the District, to all its inhabitants, would annihilate slavery." This was one of the early expressions of the recurrent idea that was to be summed up in the phrase "equal protection of the laws."

The Constitution's Fugitive Slave Clause, one of the original Philadelphia compromises with the slave states, became one of the sources of productive debate. To begin with, the clause was not included in the article tabulating the powers of Congress. It was contained instead in one covering the relations of the states with one another and said simply that no person held in bondage could be granted legal freedom merely by escaping to a free state, and that the latter should return the escapee.

Without having been given power to do so, Congress nevertheless assumed the right to pass laws enforcing the clause. The federal judiciary was ordered to aid slavehunters in capturing and returning the hunted. Abolitionists argued that there was no such power in Congress and that the plain language of the clause made recapture a matter to be settled between or among the states concerned. They also argued strongly that the procedure plainly violated the Bill of Rights. There was no semblance of a trial for alleged fugitives—no right to witnesses, no right to counsel, no jury trial—all of which clearly violated the Fifth Amendment's provision that liberty could not be taken away "without due process of law." This key statement was repeatedly emphasized by freedom's advocates.

A still broader base for action was needed for the purposes of the growing abolitionist movement, whose political wing, while still a minority third party, had come to be a balance of power in some free states. The demands for due process of law and the equal protection of men under the laws in the District of Columbia as well as for due process of law as a defense against the Fugitive Slave Law were not enough to overcome the initially accepted idea that the national government could not pass laws aimed at affecting slavery in the slave states. What was needed was a plausible constitutional theory that could undermine the compromises of 1787 and make it reasonable to argue that federal power could be exerted to protect the human rights of slave and free man, white and black, which were constantly violated throughout the nation.

An important clue was found in the express recognition, in the clauses defining eligibility for election to the presidency and Congress, of the idea that there was a status called citizenship of the United States.

"We, the People of the United States . . . " began the preamble to the Constitution. These must have been, at the beginning, all who lived in the new republic, women and children as well as men, nonvoters as well as voters. These were the original citizens and to them were added as the years rolled on all who were born in the United States, or who had been naturalized under the express power granted to Congress to grant citizenship to foreigners who came here to settle. "Governments are instituted among men," according to the Declaration of Independence, in order to secure "the unalienable rights," including the rights to "Life, Liberty, and the Pursuit of Happiness," with which men were endowed by their creator.

The government of the nation that came into existence as a result of the revolution launched with the Declaration of Independence must have the power to secure the unalienable rights for the protection of which "Governments are instituted among men." These rights came to be called the "privileges or immunities of citizens of the United States." What were these "privileges or immunities" that came with national citizenship? A convenient catalogue was found in the early Bill of Rights that James Madison had prepared and offered to the first Congress as amendments for the purpose of keeping the promise that had been made to win the ratification of the yet unamended constitution.

Abolitionists looked upon the unfair treatment of free Negroes, interference with their own freedoms of speech and assembly, and slavery itself as violations of the Bill of Rights. Bondage and the discrimination and repression that attended it were deprivations of life, liberty and property without due process of law. They were denials of free speech and free press, and of the rights of the people to assemble peaceably and to petition the government concerning their grievances. They were unreasonable searches and seizures. They involved violations of every one of the ancient safeguards of the right of fair trial which were spelled out in the amendments: the privilege against self-incrimination, the right to a speedy and public trial, and the right to be tried by a jury, to be confronted with witnesses, to have the assistance of counsel and to be free from the threat of cruel and unusual punishments.

The lynching of a free black man in St. Louis, a man who was burned alive by a mob that included the aldermen of the city, was the occasion for one statement of this theme. Elizur Wright, an early agitator, argued: "When our fathers entered into Union, it was on the express condition that the rights of the citizens should be everywhere under the shield of law. The citizens of each state were to be entitled to all the privileges and immunities of citizens in the several states. No person was to be deprived of life, liberty, or property without due process of law. No person was to be punished for any crime, without a fair trial before an impartial jury, without having full information of the charge brought against him, nor without being confronted with the witnesses against him, and having compulsory process for obtaining witnesses in his favor. The people were to be secure against unreasonable searches and seizures, and against excessive, cruel, and unusual punishments. Above all, every citizen was to enjoy that noblest privilege of republicanism, freedom of speech and of the press." All of these rights were trampled underfoot by the action of the mob and by the inaction of the local government, whose obligation it was to provide the protection of the laws.

Persuasive as such statements and the constitutional arguments to which they led may seem now, there was no prospect in the 1850s that Congress would recognize the power and duty it was claimed to have. There was no hope at all that the Supreme Court would accept the ideas put forward by such men. But a growing minority was entering the Congress who were convinced of the need to recognize that "the sole legitimate end of all true government is the protection of human rights, the execution of equal and exact justice between a man and his neighbor."

This was the platform of a minor third party in 1860, a group that distrusted the moderation of Abraham Lincoln. Nevertheless there were men on Lincoln's local ticket who had absorbed and accepted the ideas of the pioneering abolitionist and constitutionalist. They included John A. Bingham, Charles Sumner and Thaddeus Stevens. But in the face of the secession crisis a thirteenth amendment was proposed (to tempt the erring sisters to return) which ironically would have guaranteed slavery freedom from national action.

Chapter 8

The Second
American Constitution

The Civil War made it clear that the objectives of the founding fathers had been frustrated. The states that seceded had destroyed the "more perfect Union." The severed portion under Lincoln continued to recognize the Constitution, but it was carrying on in circumstances never contemplated by that document; the seceders established their own provisional government, the Confederate States of America, in what Massachusetts abolitionist Edmund Quincy described as "the oddest Revolution that history has yet seen, a Revolution for the greater security of Injustice and the firmer establishment of Tyranny."

At frightful cost to the American people, that revolution failed. In its failure it was to make possible the realization of the vision of those who wanted their Constitution to be a guarantee against injustice by the separate states, as well as by the national government. The opportunity was presented—which no one could have known was so near when Taney reminded everyone that "there is a mode by which it may be amended"—to make it possible for the Constitution to stand proudly with the Declaration of Independence as a statement of the rights of all men and of the duties of their government to them.

Events moved rapidly under the pressure of war. In 1860 slavery was solidly entrenched in the United States. The guarantees of the Bill of Rights were meaningless under the laws of many states and the customs of others. When the strength and probable duration of the rebellion became clear, the response was a series of measures that the advocates of freedom never would have believed possible, however often they had called for "immediate and unconditional" emancipation.

The northern army was directed to free any slaves they found to have been used for military purposes in support of the Confederate forces. The return of fugitive slaves who crossed the Union lines was forbidden. The attorney general ruled that free Negroes were citizens of the United States. Slavery was outlawed in the District of Columbia. The Fugitive Slave Law was repealed. The Emancipation Proclamation was made, freeing legally, if not in immediate practical fact, all slaves held in Confederate territory.

Negroes had won their right to fight for the nation whose highest court called them unfit for citizenship only six years before. Their performance as fighting men began to dispel much of the racial antipathy among people in the states loyal to the Union. Many who had never been persuaded by the abolitionists' arguments began to feel that the bravery of the black soldier proved his fitness for freedom and equality. Even before the end of the war, equal rights laws and schools for all were established in the District of Columbia.

As it came to be recognized that the Confederacy was doomed and that the Union would be restored, hard questions had to be faced. The Constitution as it stood had proved to be inadequate. Half a million dead attested to its failure. The mere military victory that was in the making would not, by itself, solve the problems that had led to division, disunion and war.

An international conflict is settled by a treaty of peace that lays down the terms on which the ex-foes shall live together. The formula for terminating a civil war is a different matter—either the rebels are victors or they are crushed. But a complication presented by the American rebellion was the participation of whole states, units of the dual form of government framed at Philadelphia, led by their governors and authorized by their legislatures. Was the conflict that began for the restoration of the Union to be concluded by accepting the return of the penitent states as they were? "When a man puts a knife to my throat, and I succeed in conquering and handcuffing him," asked one minister in a sermon, "shall I be so foolish as at once to restore him to his former position, knife and all?"

At the beginning, hopeful that a short war would be the product of the offer of a generous peace, many were prepared to do just that. They argued that they were for the "union as it was," meaning with the full protection of slavery implied by the Dred Scott decision. In the summer of 1861, a majority of the Thirty-Seventh Congress resolved that the object of the war was only reunion and that no change in state control of race relations was sought. But never in history did the war aims of the victor change so much during the course of the struggle.

The war was not begun to free the slaves, but the sheer force of events made it obvious that the slaves would have to be freed if the war was to be won. As this realization spread, it came to be more widely felt that the freeing of the slaves was not merely a desirable military move but also a just and morally correct contribution to the progress of the nation. The propaganda of the abolitionists came to be confirmed by the facts of life, and this combination of persuasion and reality perceived helped make possible the first great change in the character of the Constitution.

Firsthand evidence impressed many soldiers, some of whom had resented abolitionist and Negro alike as having somehow been at the root of the difficulty which took them from their families and their civilian life. The Reverend George Cheever, whose ever popular sermons for freedom had made him an outstanding figure in New York, was invited by a group of congressmen to come to the Capitol to address the House. In the balcony was private John Geyser, whose regiment was stationed near the Potomac. Afterwards, the private wrote to the preacher: "Previous to this war, I hated the name of an abolitionist. But within the last nine months I have seen enough of the beauties of slavery to turn me right about. And I agree with you that the salvation of the country depends on the adoption by the government of a sweeping emancipation policy."

One captain in another brigade, stationed in Maryland, wrote home to tell his family "the more our officers and soldiers see of the institution of slavery the more they detest it. Five months ago, ninety of every hundred of our brigade would have been delighted to mob an abolitionist—now they want to abolish slavery, root and branch."

Lincoln's proclamation of emancipation, which came after eighteen months of war and then only as a military measure, was hailed by a resolution adopted by an entire regiment of Pennsylvania Volunteers who denounced bondage as "a curse to the land, and a great moral wrong," and told the president that they hailed "with joy the proclamation doing away with that institution in every state in which rebellion exists, and hope soon to see it forever blotted from our soil."

Petitions and public meetings in support of permanent and total abolition began to multiply. Old foemen in the abolitionist movement reunited for the last phase of their struggle. Frederick Douglass, who had broken with William Lloyd Garrison over the issue of disunion, now said, "Every man who is ready to work for the overthrow of slavery, whether a voter or a non-voter, a Garrisonian or a Gerrit Smith man, black or white, is both clansman and kinsman of ours." Even women abolitionists who at the same time were ardent leaders in their own campaign for equal rights were ready to submerge their cause for the time being. By December of 1863, a united campaign to write the death of slavery into the Constitution had been formed.

In Congress there were some, like Senator Charles Sumner, who argued that the proposed new amendment to the nation's basic charter of government was unnecessary, that Congress could sweep slavery out of existence with a single brief statute. Others, like George

W. Julian, a radical reformer from Indiana, took a contrary view. In a speech to the Congress early in the war he had said: ". . . the germ of our troubles, it must be confessed, is in the Constitution itself. . . . The Constitution received its life in the concessions which slavery *demanded* as conditions of union, and slavery, from that moment, has assumed to deal with the Constitution as its master.

"I do not say that the founders of our government are to be judged in the light of the horrible evils which have been the offspring of their mistake. . . . They thought they were simply yielding to slavery a transient sufferance, a brief hospitality, so that it might die and pass away 'decently and in order.' "

The campaign for signatures to a petition to Congress mounted. A central force in its work, a very dynamo of energy, was the Women's Loyal National League, headed by Elizabeth Cady Stanton and Susan B. Anthony. Among those urging the effort on was Frederick Douglass, who after having observed with satisfaction the change in the character of the conflict told an audience: "I hold it is an Abolition war, because slavery has proved itself stronger than the Constitution. . . . You cannot have the Union, the Constitution, and Republican institutions, until you have stricken down that damning curse and put it beyond the pale of the Republic."

That was on December 4, 1863. Nine days later, Representative James M. Ashley of Ohio introduced the resolution that was to become the Thirteenth Amendment. On February 9, 1864, two tall black men entered the Senate Chamber at the invitation of Senator Sumner. There they placed on his desk two huge bundles, petitions bearing one hundred thousand signatures. By the time Congress had adjourned in July, nearly four hundred thousand had arrived, a greater number than had ever been submitted on one petition in the history of the world.

President Lincoln and his administration were not yet ready to endorse the change in the Constitution, and the debate in Congress was sharp and bitter. One reason for the strength of the opposition was that the draftsmen of the amendment had provided two separate clauses. There was not merely a declaration stating that "Neither slavery nor involuntary servitude . . . shall exist within the United States." There was also a separate and, to its framers, an exceedingly important second section: "Congress shall have power to enforce this article by appropriate legislation." The men who wrote those added words had perceptive foresight. For one thing, they had learned the need for express congressional power from the very arguments that the abolitionists had used against the Fugitive Slave Law, namely that although the Constitution provided for the return of fugitives no express power of congressional enforcement was given.

Even more significant was their understanding that it would not be enough simply to make slavery unconstitutional, as the first section alone would have provided. It was necessary to grant freedom too, and for that the states could not be trusted. Congress must have the power to make freedom meaningful. Representative James F. Wilson of Iowa, who was Chairman of the House Judiciary Committee that reported the amendment, and its coauthor, reminded the Congress of the breadth of the need for federal action. He recalled how all persons holding political or social or economic power in the slave states used every branch of governmental power to repress opposition, and "what they could not accomplish was turned over to the mob." He concluded: "It is quite time, sir, for the people of the free states to look these facts squarely in the face and provide a remedy which will make the future safe for the rights of each and every citizen."

He did not say merely "Negroes," or "ex-slaves," but "each and every citizen." The slave states had destroyed the freedom of white men to speak and had deprived them of their right to a fair trial. That was a feature of the crusade to defend the system of race relations based on what Justice Taney had called the "subjugation" of one race by the other. Did Representative Wilson mean that Congress could enforce the abolition of slavery by making its own definition of freedom and by imposing it on the states? The opposition in Congress feared as much, and said so.

The debate over the Thirteenth Amendment did not concern itself with the virtues of slavery or whether it had a right to survive. The members of Congress who would have argued for that were AWOL, many wearing the uniform of Confederate grey. The consensus in the North, even among the many believers in white superiority who still abounded, was that slavery had to go. The controversial part of the amendment was the second clause, which was regarded as invading the federal system (the dual form of state and national government) to the extent of permitting Congress to define and enforce freedom within state boundaries.

The advocates of the amendment won the debate. Unless the Congress had the power to guarantee to the emancipated a basic minimum of rights, such as equality before the law, the protection of life and person, the freedom to live, work and move about, and the right to make contracts and buy property, the states would be free to restore slavery in all but name. It was important for this federal power to be granted so that behind the curtain of "states' rights" the black people would not be in danger of being "subjugated" once more.

The wide range of federal power was clearly conceded by the opponents and claimed by the proponents of the amendment. Many could be quoted on the point. It was not viewed, as we now see it, as one of three postwar amendments, successively granting freedom, then equality and finally suffrage. With Lincoln alive as president, it was felt that the Thirteenth was all that was needed to perfect the new American constitution. The national government, according to Congressman Ashley, who introduced the amendment, would now be able to take measures against such acts of defiance as "kidnapping, imprisoning, mobbing, and murdering white citizens of the United States guilty of no offense except protesting against [slavery's] terrible crimes." Likewise, said Ashley, there would be no more denial to "the masses of poor white children of the privilege of free schools," and free speech and free press would be restored.

The United States Senate passed the necessary resolution proposing the Thirteenth Amendment on April 8, 1864, but the storm of opposition prevented its achieving a two-thirds majority in the House during that session. Lincoln's reelection in November of that year helped to decide the issue. It is significant that the soldiers' votes helped carry Lincoln to victory over an opponent who campaigned for peace with slavery and the Constitution "as it was." After three and a half years of war, the men of the Union Army had seen enough of slavery and its works to decide that the struggle should go on, at the risk of their own lives, until victory was complete.

When Congress reconvened, the message of the polls was understood. (It was still the Thirty-Eighth Congress: under the Constitution as it was then, the new Congress would not assemble until December, unless called into special session.) The "lame ducks"—as congressmen were called who remained in office after defeat—heeded Lincoln's warning, after his reelection had emboldened him to support the amendment, and passed it.

Chapter 9

Completing
the New Constitution

James Madison had contributed to a series of essays called *The Federalist* which was intended to explain and win support for the ratification of the original constitution. In one of his papers, the Virginian had recognized the inevitability of the death of slavery. He discussed this matter while offering a defense of the clause that specified that there were to be included in the population base for representation from the Southern states "three fifths of all other Persons"—that is, black slaves. "It is admitted," Madison concluded, "that if the laws were to restore the rights which have been taken away, the negroes could no longer be refused an equal share of representation with the other inhabitants."

What had been "admitted" in 1789 by the main draftsmen of the Constitution and the Bill of Rights was no longer so obvious in 1865, even to many elected in 1864 on Lincoln's platform of freedom. Abolitionists in Congress who agreed with Charles Sumner's persistent advocacy of impartial suffrage were very few in 1865. The qualifications for voting had until then been determined by the states, and too many Northern states had come to reflect the growth of racism by excluding blacks from the vote before the war.

There was no immediate popular response to the difficult questions put forth by the National Negro Convention of 1864: "Are we good enough to use the bullets, and not good enough to use the ballots? . . . Are we citizens when the nation is in peril and aliens when the nation is in safety." Abraham Lincoln had hoped to use diplomacy to persuade the states to grant impartial suffrage, or at least not to deny the vote to "those who serve our cause as soldiers." In saying this he was trying cautiously to win acceptance, in certain quarters, of his leadership during wartime; he hoped to create new civilian governments in some southern areas, like Louisiana, from which the Confederate armies had been driven long before the end of the war. A number of congressmen differed with him on the point, and their differences were not resolved during his lifetime.

By summer, 1865, Lincoln was dead and the Thirteenth Amendment was on its way to ratification. When it became effective, the three-fifths clause would become meaningless. All would be free—but not all would be represented, despite Madison's confidence. Before the secession, a state with a million blacks and a million whites had been represented as if it had had a population of 1.6 million, and those representatives were selected solely by the million whites. Now such a state would be entitled to representation based on the entire population of two million, even if it continued to confine the privilege of voting to its whites. Its voters would outvote the voters in a free state by two to one, instead of by 1.6 to one. This reward for rebellion was so unfair that there had to be a remedy, even if legislators' prejudices—or their constituents' prejudices—would not permit them to enact prompt suffrage for the freedmen.

This was but one of the problems that arose to plague the nation after the South's surrender in the spring of 1865. Equally serious and related issues were presented as a result of the succession of Andrew Johnson to the presidency in April. Congress was not scheduled to meet until December. How and when should the states that had seceded and resisted national authority be permitted to resume full partnership in the Union? What was to be done to assist in the transition of four million Americans from slavery to freedom—if anything? When and by whom should these questions be decided: that was the thorniest question of all.

No constitution or charter of government provides rules and regulations about what steps are to be taken to restore its provisions after an unsuccessful rebellion. A number of theories were discussed concerning what should be done in and with the reoccupied portions of the United States, formerly the rebel states. Differences in opinion depended on what would most conveniently accommodate one's ideas about equal justice for all who lived there.

Those who talked about one extreme, "indestructible states," were likely to wish for little change in the way of life that had existed before, save for the nominal elimination of slavery. At the other extreme there was talk of "conquered provinces," an approach that permitted the closest possible national supervision of the physical transition from slavery to freedom. No one could claim that either approach was clearly provided by the Constitution; all that the basic law specified that was relevant was, first, that Congress had the exclusive power to decide when to readmit representatives from rebel states and, second, that Congress under the Thirteenth Amendment had the "power to enforce" the extermination of slavery "by appropriate legislation."

The thorny problems of reconstruction would have been difficult enough had Lincoln lived. Although he had had differences of opinion with congressional leaders over these questions, he had earned their respect as one committed to recognizing the rights of *all* of the loyal Americans of the South who had suffered for the Union. Congress and the president might have been able to work together in an atmosphere of mutual esteem.

Lincoln's successor was suddenly thrust into the thicket of these problems with no such advantages and with many handicaps. As a "poor white" from Tennessee, Andrew Johnson hated the aristocracy of a slave society, but he had no feeling for equal justice for blacks. He was stubbornly unwilling to listen to advice on this or any other subject that ran against his prejudices. One of his closest co-workers, ex-Confederate general Richard Taylor, deplored his friend's "obstinate, suspicious temper" and recalled afterwards that Johnson was reluctant to heed unwelcome advice or to admit error.

Unlike Lincoln in personality and lacking his political expertise, Johnson chose to ignore the slightly radical sentiment of the moderates who took part in the election of 1864. He had not been elected with the aid of votes from the self-amputated Confederacy, yet he listened to many voices there; the consensus of the people in the states that had elected him was in favor of civil rights, if not "political" or "social" rights, but this was a viewpoint he chose to ignore. He also ignored those who persistently came to him from Congress (where there was a lively sense of public opinion) with that message during the months that preceded the first, December 1865, session of the Thirty-Ninth Congress.

Instead, within five weeks after he had become president, he decided to attempt to solve the problems of reconstruction by his own one-man rule. He proclaimed amnesty for all but a few who had aided the Confederate cause. He appointed a provisional governor for North Carolina and directed that when a majority of the state's white voters had sworn future loyalty they could form a new state government and rejoin the Union. Soon afterwards a similar decree was issued for Mississippi and one by one the same provisions were ordered for the whites of each of the areas that had constituted the Confederate States of America. No condition of any kind was laid down for the protection of the whites or the blacks who had been loyal to the Union. When his Mississippi appointee used Confederate veterans as the nucleus of a new state militia, Johnson reversed Union general Henry W. Slocum's orders against that kind of "national guard."

To the defeated Confederates, sullenly and yet possibly pliably waiting to see what their conquerors had in store for them, the Johnson proclamations were like a shot in the arm. Here was the signal and a great opportunity to rebuild their society on the prewar basis of using the power of the state to force black men, as a group, to work for whites on the employers' terms, with no freedom to rise or to move or leave when they became dissatisfied with conditions. They elected to leadership in their state and county governments the members and allies of the slave-owning class that had been in the forefront of secession and rebellion.

Even as the war had ceased, widespread violence had broken out against both black and white loyalists, and especially against the returning Union soldiers, most of whom were ex-slaves. Now there was superimposed on this moral chaos a whole new legal structure designed to ensure that there would be *no* transition from slavery to freedom. Under a variety of laws called the Black Codes, a whole complex of restrictions on freedom of movement and freedom of contract was imposed whose total effect was to make the "freedmen the slaves of society," as Massachusetts' Senator Henry Wilson said, instead of, as before, the slaves of individual owners.

In every way they went too far. By the time they got to selecting added starters for the Thirty-Ninth Congress—the sole legal elections had taken place in 1864—they included nine Confederate generals and colonels, and for good measure threw in Alexander H. Stephens, their "Vice-President." Even President Johnson's confidant and friend, Secretary of the Navy Gideon Welles, was appalled. He confided to his diary: "The tone of sentiment and action of the people of the South is injudicious and indiscreet in many respects." Most moderates in the loyal states began to lose hope for Johnson, coming to agree with the viewpoint of Thomas Wentworth Higginson, former colonel of an ex-slave regiment that fought for the Union, and now a noted writer and publicist: "What most men mean to-day by the 'President's plan of reconstruction' is the pardon of every rebel for the crime of rebellion, and the utter refusal to pardon a single black loyalist for the crime of being black. . . . The truth is that we are causing quite as much suffering as a conqueror usually does. It is simply that we are forgiving our enemies and torturing only our friends."

What had happened in the former slave states during six months of Johnson's "Reconstruction—Confederate style" would not have been tolerated by President Lincoln. Although he had differed with congressional leaders over the best technique for reviving loyal state governments in the South, Lincoln had said, just before his assassination, "The restoration of the Rebel States to the Union must rest upon the principle of civil and political equality of both races." When Johnson rejected this essential ingredient of Lincoln's plan for reconstruction, the task of fulfilling the martyred president's promise of a "new birth of freedom" fell on Congress alone.

As the men of the Thirty-Ninth Congress assembled during the first week of December, they were greeted by a storm of protests against the consequences of Johnson's reconstruction policy. These pleas for national action to protect human rights did not come from abolitionists alone, nor solely from northern addresses. A new voice was being heard in the land of cotton—the voice of the articulate black man. Black soldiers paraded, black petitions came from varied places in the southland. A message from a convention in Nashville asserted that "We cannot believe that the General Government will allow us to be left without protection after knowing, as you do, what services we have rendered to the cause of the preservation of the Union and the maintenance of the laws." Richmond Negroes objected to "invidious political or legal distinctions, on account of color merely."

An ode to the Thirty-Ninth Congress came from the pen of the Quaker abolitionist John Greenleaf Whittier. He urged the men who had been elected when Lincoln was reelected to say to "the pardon seekers," the Confederates who had been trooping to the White House and bearing off dispensations to return south and rule their states once more:

Keep
Your manhood, bend no suppliant knees,
Nor palter with unworthy pleas.

: : : : : :

From you alone the guaranty
Of union, freedom, peace, we claim;
We urge no conqueror's terms of shame.
Alas! no victor's pride is ours;
We bend above our triumphs won
Like David o'er his rebel son.
Be men, not beggars. Cancel all
By one brave generous action; trust
Your better instincts and be just!
Make all men peers before the law,
Take hands from off the negro's throat,
Give black and white an equal vote.
Keep all your forfeit lives and lands,
But give the common law's redress
To labor's utter nakedness.
Revive the old heroic will;
Be in the right as brave and strong
As ye have proved yourselves in wrong.
Defeat shall then be victory. . . .

The men in Congress sensed that it was already too late to persuade the pardon seekers to be just. President Johnson's policy had helped the disloyal elements of the South to triumph over the loyal, and had made impossible a readjustment of relations between the races and between the two sections of the country on the basis of the

Thirteenth Amendment alone. The new American constitution remained to be completed. The Thirty-Ninth Congress—which included in its membership three presidents-to-be and the two towering figures of Charles Sumner in the Senate and Thaddeus Stevens in the House—was equal to the task.

Chapter 10

Justice, Equality—
and National Honor

The signers of the Declaration of Independence, which stated as its first self-evident truth that "all men are created equal," pledged in its support their lives, their fortunes and their "sacred Honor." In his Emancipation Proclamation, the document that encouraged the enlistment of 200,000 black soldiers, of whom 34,000 died defending the nation that had oppressed them, Lincoln promised to "maintain the freedom" of those he emancipated; in his Gettysburg address, he dedicated the nation to a "new birth of freedom." The lieutenant colonel in command of Thomas Wentworth Higginson's black regiment praised his men for their valor and pledged, "The nation guarantees to you full protection and justice."

The provisional governors appointed by Lincoln's successor to rule the South repeatedly proclaimed that "this is a white man's government." The president who had appointed them could not have been elected vice-president if the segment of the nation called the Union had not been propped up by the black battalions to whom such promises had been made. When the new southern governors went unrebuked by President Johnson, a member of the Thirty-Ninth Congress arose as it convened to renew the pledge of national honor: "This is not a white man's Government. . . . This is a Man's Government, the Government of all men alike. . . . Our fathers repudiated the whole doctrine of the legal superiority of families or races, and proclaimed the equality of men before the law. Upon that they created a revolution and built the Republic. . . . If this Republic is not now made to stand on their great principles, it has no honest foundation, and the Father of all men will still shake it to its center." The speaker was Thaddeus Stevens, who had assumed the practical political leadership of the House of Representatives when the war broke out, just as Charles Sumner had assumed the moral leadership of the Senate.

The virulence directed against him by slavery's spokesmen before and after secession took physical form when he was made the victim of an unusual military maneuver. On the eve of the battle of Gettysburg, in violation of Lee's orders to spare civilian property, Confederate general Jubal Early vindictively sought out and destroyed an iron foundry in which Stevens owned an interest. Saying "We must all expect to suffer by this wicked war," Stevens rejected a $100,000 fund raised by popular subscription to reimburse him for his loss, and asked that the money be turned over to the families of the men left unemployed by the action. The image of old Thad Stevens which our history books have bequeathed us is contradicted by the genuine affection for him as a public figure and the esteem for his legislative leadership that moved men to initiate and contribute to the collection.

Vermont, where Thaddeus Stevens was born, was the first state to outlaw slavery; the second was Pennsylvania, to which Stevens migrated to make his career. Afflicted at birth with a twisted or "club" foot, he did not find himself the equal of boys his age until he entered school, a fact which helps to explain his genuine dedication to the spread of free public education as well as the ideal of equality. He had the wit, the ability to think quickly on his feet, the capacity to judge people and the aggressive persistence which are required to make a success of a career as a trial lawyer. While these talents were to be of importance in his legislative career after he had entered politics, he was handicapped by a grim honesty, an irresistible impulse for sarcasm and a lack of social grace which combined with his stubborn dedication to his beliefs to keep him from rising to governor, senator or even higher. He did help to make governors and senators, and even a president, who, when elected, confirmed Stevens' distrust of humanity by breaking a firm promise that he would add the Pennsylvanian to his cabinet.

No one would have claimed that he was a hypocrite when he said that his life had been inspired by his dedication to the Declaration of Independence. He saw, as did Henry J. Raymond, founder and editor of *The New York Times* and an ultracautious, moderate congressman as well, that "Freedom of speech, freedom of opinion, freedom of political action, are more thoroughly stifled and extinguished in the South than in Austria and Russia, or the most absolute despotism on the face of the earth." But while Raymond wrote that in 1860, he was most reluctant to join in fighting, in 1865, to make the national guarantees of the Bill of Rights binding on the governments of the states and to give the national government the power and the duty to enforce those guarantees. It was Stevens who took the lead in accomplishing this monumental task, and when his work was done, after arduous months at the end (when, dying, he had to be carried to and from the floor of the House), Raymond's *Times* paid him a reluctant tribute: "He was one of the few who are not afraid to grasp first principles and lay hold of great truths, or push them to their remotest logical result."

Lacking wealth or political power, and at the age of 73 lacking the threat or promise of a political future in which he would have the capacity to reward or punish, Stevens maintained his leadership and his ability to influence more moderate men by the use of his talent at debate and maneuver. Words were his only weapons and ideas his armor, but it was not these alone that made his victory possible. The merits of the case were on his side: he could not have won without the impact of the facts that had been reported from the South during the months that followed Lincoln's death and the end of the conflict. Freedom of movement for reporters representing magazines and newspapers; visits by curious tourists and businessmen seeking investment opportunities; reports from agents for charitable and religious groups; a quantity of teachers, social workers and others who combined the functions of Peace Corps and Vista Volunteers—all of these factors produced a broad consensus.

People came to understand that the national commitment to the loyal men and women of the South was being dishonored. They felt that the need for action was urgent and told their congressmen of their concern. On December 1, 1865, Georges Clemenceau, a young French citizen, here as a political refugee from a tyrannic emperor, reported to the Paris *Temps:* "The Congress which is about to meet will settle very serious and solemn questions. It entertains no revengeful spirit, but feels its own responsibility." M. Clemenceau (half a century later to be premier of France during World War I) showed political acumen in reporting the mood of a land that was not well known to him. More than seventy proposals to amend the Constitution of the United States were to be presented to the Thirty-Ninth Congress, which assembled on December 4.

Thaddeus Stevens in the House and Charles Sumner in the Senate had chafed for many months at the inability of Congress to call itself into session. Yet in a way, time worked in their favor. Reluctantly but surely, men of practical politics were coming to join men of conscience in recognizing the wrongfulness of Johnson's course. When they saw the breach of faith and danger to the nation that would follow the granting of disproportionately greater voting strength to the overrepresented South, they reluctantly concluded that they would have to be prepared to move independently of the president. There was not yet widespread agreement about precisely what course to take; some still hoped for a compromise with the executive, who had after all been elected on the same ticket; but there was general agreement, except among the minority that had been elected in opposition to Lincoln and Johnson, that Congress would have to assert itself and act for justice and honor.

Thaddeus Stevens took the indispensable first step and launched what was to be a new constitutional convention in miniature. He presented to a caucus of the members of his party, meeting in advance of the opening session of Congress, a plan for a special Joint Committee of the Senate and the House to inquire into the condition of the area that had formed the Confederacy. The purpose of the inquiry would be primarily to determine whether or not the states involved were entitled to be represented in Washington. Meanwhile, all those claiming to represent the former rebel states would be excluded, and all questions having to do with representation from those states would be referred to the Joint Committee on Reconstruction. While this committee deferred the entire question for study, Congress would be free to decide the "serious and solemn questions" it faced, without being hampered by a prospective coalition between representatives elected in 1864 on a platform of peace with slavery and men who had worn Confederate uniforms in the previous March, when the last congress adjourned.

The Joint Committee, which was to hammer out during the next six months a constitutional amendment that would dominate the growth of American constitutional law for the next century, has never been called the "Grand Committee," as the 1787 meeting has been called the "Grand Convention," nor is its work appreciated as it should be. It met under circumstances of great difficulty, in the aftermath of the national tragedy of fratricidal conflict, a civil war more destructive than any other in the world's history. Its work was frowned upon and discouraged by the President of the United States. Its membership, reflecting that of the Congress from which it was chosen, represented a variety of points of view; while it included Stevens, leader of the House, the Senate failed to designate Charles Sumner, who had been an early proponent of the ideas pushed by old Thad. Each of the members of the committee was under mingled pressures from the prejudiced as well as from the more conscientious of his constituents. The ultimate agreement on the terms of the Fourteenth Amendment, when it was presented to the country for the ratification of the states, was rather a miracle.

The committee began by dealing separately with four types of problems, of which two seem minor now, although they caused great concern then: the war debts, national and Confederate, and the disqualification from office (for how many and for how long?) of those who had violated their oath to support the Constitution by their role in the rebellion. The more long-range issues—equitable representation and equal justice—could have been combined, in theory at least. That was an idea that Charles Sumner had advanced, long before the Thirty-Ninth Congress began, when he urged an amendment "especially providing that hereafter there shall be no denial of the electoral franchise or any exclusion of any kind on account of race or color, but all persons shall be equal before the law." Early in the work of the Joint Committee, Stevens proposed a single clause giving Congress the right to ensure equal justice and equal voting rights, but quickly saw that the mood of the membership was not ready for it.

The committee was not ready because Congress was not ready, and Congress was not ready because the country was not ready, to fulfill James Madison's promise of equal representation, the promise that had been renewed by implication, if not in words, when the black soldiers were called to the defense of the Union. Instead of a single clause, the committee began to wrestle with two: one, on representation, a search for an acceptable formula that would prevent the South from being unfairly overrepresented now that slavery was ended, and the "three-fifths of a man" idea ended with it; second, on the rights and protection of all men everywhere, with a national guarantee against injustice perpetrated or permitted by the individual states.

The solution to the problem of preventing unfairly high representation for the former slave states—in the face of the fact that the northern states were not ready to yield the right to vote to their own blacks—was made easier by the fact that more than ninety percent of all Americans of African ancestry then lived in the South. Since full equality of voting rights could not be forced, it was proposed that representation should be subtracted in proportion wherever a state denied the vote to part of its population. Apart from the fact that the impact on the North would be slight, the idea had two virtues to commend it: it prevented an unjustly high count in Congress to states that denied the vote to part of their people; at the same time it encouraged them by the temptation of restored representation to cease their discrimination.

This seemingly Solomon-like solution, practical if not wholly just, did not meet immediate acceptance. Reported as a projected separate amendment in the House, where Stevens was the acknowledged legislative leader, it passed. In the Senate it met the stubborn opposition of Charles Sumner, who was more concerned with what was morally correct than with what was practically attainable. He would not allow the Constitution to be "defiled" by a provision that countenanced continued discrimination, even though offering temptation for its termination. Abolitionists outside of Congress agreed that it was better to defeat a half measure than to accept it and risk its being the final settlement. "It proves that a Republic is ungrateful," said one, meaning ungrateful to the blacks who had helped win the Civil War. The Senate rejected the proposal when it was first submitted, but it was to return as part of a package plan that would also contain guarantees of full protection and justice in all things save for the vote itself.

These guarantees were the product of the Joint Committee during a legislative session dominated by the problems of national power and duty of the most urgent importance. They were forced upon Congress as a result of the conditions that had developed during the six-month period after the rebel states were permitted to decide for themselves how little genuine freedom to grant the emancipated. As we have already seen, the Thirteenth Amendment, which outlawed slavery, also endowed Congress with the power to maintain freedom by "appropriate legislation." Most congressmen were convinced that they could now take any action that might be needed to prevent state governments from treating the former slaves, or blacks as a class, differently from the way in which they treated whites.

Having this conviction, they passed a law—the first civil rights act in our history—drawn up by Senator Lyman Trumbull of Illinois, one of the more cautious and moderate members of his party. The senator successfully argued, first, that equality and freedom could not be thought of separately and that unequal treatment was a kind of slavery which Congress had a right to stop, and, second, that Congress also had the power to guarantee the protection of the rights of residents of a state if the state itself allowed them to become the victims of mob violence or local lawlessness.

When President Johnson vetoed this bill, Congress exercised for the first time its constitutional power to pass it over his veto. But the president's action stirred misgivings. There was a majority for freedom in Congress then—but that could always change. The rules in the Constitution were meant to protect our fundamental rights from the tyranny or breach of faith that occasional changes of majority might bring about. That was why Congress, for example, was forbidden by the First Amendment to make any law "abridging the freedom of speech": a transient, tempestuous popular majority might wish, or be provoked, to take away the freedom of speech of some particularly annoying group.

Senator Sumner had said, while the Civil War still raged two years before, that "irreversible guaranties" would be needed to secure freedom when the war was won. His vision was now seen to be realistic: the mere exercise by one congress of the national power to protect equality and to secure justice within the states was not enough. There had to be a national duty, binding on every succeeding congress, as well. That meant that a rule had to be written into the Constitution, which could not then be amended as easily as a law could be repealed.

The wish to accomplish this permanent change in the relation between the national government and the states coincided with the need to satisfy the doubts of a few congressmen as to whether the Thirteenth Amendment went as far as their colleagues thought when they passed the civil rights bill of 1866. One of the doubters was John A. Bingham of Ohio, whose misgivings were sincere and not prompted by objections to the principles of the Trumbull bill. At the outset of the Thirty-Ninth Congress he had proposed a constitutional amendment on the subject. It fell to his lot to be appointed to the Joint Committee, and in carrying on the fight there he became, under Stevens' leadership, the rightful heir of James Madison, whose own originally proposed fourteenth amendment ("No State shall infringe the right of trial by jury in criminal cases, nor the rights of conscience nor the freedom of speech, or of the press") had been turned down when the First Congress had accepted his other proposals for a bill of rights to protect the people against the national government. Now the time had come, almost eighty years later, for federal constitutional protection against abuse of power or tolerance of private tyranny by the states, protection with teeth for congressional enforcement.

Bingham was first sent to Congress in 1854. That was the year during which the conflict between slavery and freedom, particularly with respect to the power of Congress to restrict the growth of slavery, was beginning to intensify. He had paid special attention as an attorney to the legal arguments that had been developed by the abolitionist advocates of the congressional power to act. He had been impressed by the trinity of phrases they had stressed—"privileges or immunities of citizens of the United States," "due process of law" and "equal protection of the laws." His congressional career was marked by his advocacy of the ideas that those phrases represented; they were employed in speeches that became major efforts against the curtailment of freedom in the proposed constitutions for the new states of Kansas and Oregon. During one term after the war began, having failed of reelection once, he served with the army as a judge advocate from 1863 to 1865. There he learned at firsthand something more about the nature of the foes of freedom, a lesson that culminated with his service in the court-martial of President Lincoln's assassins.

Fresh from that experience, John Bingham, after his return to Congress as a member of the Joint Committee, was to learn something more about the need for a change in the Constitution that would guarantee American freedoms against interference or neglect by state governments. In its work the committee did not confine itself to study and debate on the wording of the proposals it was sifting. It conducted hearings, in one of the first of the great congressional investigations, about conditions in the various regions whose qualifications to be represented anew it had been assigned to judge.

There was not only the documented story of the state action against the freedmen that was embodied in the Black Codes that had been employed during the last half of 1865 to keep the former slaves in "their place" and to force them to work on terms and in conditions similar to slavery. There was also multiple evidence of individual and mob abuse of blacks and whites, freedmen and southern loyalists, including those who had opposed secession or had, after the war, urged their states to rebuild themselves on the principles of justice and decency.

President Johnson, the man who had made possible such abuses of the rights of white and black Americans by his one-man efforts at amnesty and his restoration of civil rule to the state leaders who tolerated them, would not interfere. When he vetoed the bills that were proposed to provide some remedy for those conditions, he set the stage for Bingham, Stevens and their colleagues to complete their work on the amendment that was to become the heart of the modern American Constitution, and to so dwarf in significance its sister Civil War amendments as to justify its being known as "Big Fourteen."

John Bingham proposed at first a simple grant of power to Congress to pass laws necessary and proper to secure equal protection for all. He and the committee found, from their inquiry into conditions in the former slave states (and from their knowledge of the effect of mob rule and interference with human rights in the prewar "free" states); that something more was needed. In their collective wisdom they drew upon the phrases so much used in thirty years of abolitionist agitation by orators who had attempted to vitalize the original Constitution to end slavery and protect human rights within the states, and they especially drew upon the concept of equality before the law that Charles Sumner had originated in Sarah Roberts' case.

Thus originated the triple-riveted (as they then thought) guarantees that are found in the second sentence of the first clause of Big Fourteen. The "privileges or immunities of citizens" were not to be abridged by state law (Bingham and his colleagues had some clear ideas about what this meant and he revealed them in debate then and later); the "due process of law" that the states were forbidden to deny to any person and the "equal protection of the laws" that they were bound to provide to all persons were not to be limited or qualified in any way by sex, color or citizenship. They were phrases that were neither vague nor general to those who knew the history of the previous thirty years.

The first sentence of the first clause, on citizenship ("All persons born or naturalized in the United States . . ."), was not the product of any thought or deliberation by the committee. It was prompted by memories of Taney's words in the Dred Scott case and was intended to make one thing quite clear: that regardless of color or place of origin, the fact of birth within our borders or naturalization made every American as much a citizen as every other one. The idea was to see to it that no later court or congress could subtract from that— an idea that within a decade was stood on its head to make possible the ripping-out of the privilege-and-immunity protection.

But no one could have known that then. Bingham's original idea, of giving Congress the power (and duty) to pass "appropriate legislation" to guarantee rights, ensure due process and see to equal protection, was also adopted, as clause five of the present Fourteenth Amendment. To complete the package was the second clause, the compromise agreed upon instead of full voting rights, which was designed to subtract representation *pro rata* whenever a state denied the vote to part of its people.

Despite this evident defect, a great change had been wrought in the character of the United States Constitution. It had been made necessary by the total abuse, before the war, of the idea of states' rights. Too many people had been deprived of rights because of the idea of states' rights; too many died because of the war that idea had caused.

The separate states were still to have the right to govern local affairs, but, at least as the framers of Big Fourteen thought, they were not to have the "right" to mistreat any part of their people any longer. They were now to be part of a single nation in a more profound sense than they had been during the first eighty years of our history. The idea of American citizenship was to stand for identical values of freedom and dignity throughout the land. The rights that Americans had won from their central government in 1789 were now not merely a limitation on the powers of the authorities in Washington. They were also a check on the rulers of every state house and city hall, and it had become Washington's special responsibility to protect all Americans in case the states should violate their rights, or fail to protect them.

That, at any rate, was the overriding idea of the new American constitution. Sumner's lofty ideas, Stevens' parliamentary skill and the dedication of Bingham and the moderates had all contributed. There were some who failed to see the dimensions of the edifice they had erected. Some were disappointed at their failure to win the vote at once for all Americans. Stevens felt this way and sadly said that the new amendment "falls far short of my wishes"; but, he added, "it fulfills my hopes. I believe it is all that can be obtained in the present state of public opinion."

He knew that his last visit to the scene of his triumphant efforts for justice and humanity was near as he closed: "I will take all I can get in the cause of humanity and leave it to be perfected by better men in better times. It may be that that time will not come while I am here to enjoy the glorious triumph; but that it will come is as certain as that there is a just God."

Chapter 11

Perfecting the Structure: Votes and Rights Laws

Just as he had foreseen, Old Thad did not live to see the "glorious triumph" of which he spoke, but it did come sooner than he had hoped. The unexpected speed of its arrival was made possible by the refusal of the regimes of the former Confederate states to ratify the Fourteenth Amendment. Congress, which had set ratification as the minimum price of the reentry of representatives from the states that had seceded, was in no mood to back down when the nearly unanimous votes of rejection rolled in during late 1866 and early 1867. Its action in proposing the Fourteenth Amendment as a peace treaty had been overwhelmingly ratified by the outcome of the 1866 midterm congressional elections. After deliberately inciting the states to reject the amendment that he had helped force into being by vetoing the civil rights bill, the president failed in his effort to build a new power base on the party that had opposed him and Lincoln in 1864 and was repudiated by the voters.

With a new mandate approving its program proposed as the basis for reconstruction of the Union, Congress was ready to act to put it into effect. The Johnson-created state governments in the South had to be put aside; there were no constitutional compunctions about this, as they had no essential validity. They were merely products of postwar presidential decrees and Congress had never authorized or approved their creation.

However, to start over, and to call for constitutional conventions in the South that would create legitimate new governments to replace regimes that had seceded and then faded away under military defeat, it was essential to remake the electorate. It would have been a waste of time to go through all the motions needed to create new governments if the end product was to be domination by the same ruling group that had come into power under Johnson's sheltering amnesty proclamations. Defeated in their attempt to sunder the Union for slavery, but not discredited among the majority of white voters, they would create the same impasse by blocking the amendment that threatened their control of labor.

The solution was fairly simple. A new popular base was there, and had been there all along, ready and waiting to be recognized. Not merely waiting: they had through their spokesmen proclaimed their readiness. "I believe that when the tall heads of this Rebellion shall have been swept down . . . there will be this rank undergrowth of treason growing up there and interfering with and thwarting the quiet operation of the Federal Government in those states," said Frederick Douglass in April, 1865. "Now, where will you find the strength to counterbalance this spirit, if you do not find it in the Negroes of the South? They are your friends and have always been your friends."

It took two years for the nation to get the message. The necessity of the situation in 1867 made palatable the introduction of impartial suffrage, an idea for which Stevens knew he could not muster a majority a year before. The freedmen whom Congress had confirmed as citizens would be made citizens in fact as well as in name. By ceasing to withhold the vote from the citizens of the United States, Congress could make it possible for new state governments to come into being, which would complete the ratification of the Fourteenth Amendment.

The necessary steps were taken early in 1867 with the passage of the Reconstruction Acts, which declared that no legal governments existed in the former Confederacy. Return to civilian government was made conditional on the adoption of new state constitutions by popularly elected conventions. No one was to be excluded from voting except those disqualified by the extent of their participation in the rebellion. When a legislature elected under the new constitution—which was required to provide impartial suffrage—ratified the Fourteenth Amendment, the state would be entitled to be restored to partnership in the Union. The Fourteenth Amendment, with its guarantee to all Americans, in every state, of national protection of equal justice, of due process of law, and of preservation of the privileges and immunities of citizens, became the supreme law of the land.

There remained the unfinished business of a federal constitutional guarantee of the equal representation that James Madison had promised ninety years before. It was only by the Reconstruction Acts that votes for all citizens were provided—and only in the former Confederate states. The inconsistency of the situation was obvious. Southern states were obliged to grant equal suffrage, but northern states were not. The instability of the situation was evident. Once a state had gained readmission, it might undo all that had been achieved if a party determined to repeal its own local provision for voting rights should gain control.

Four months after the ratification of the Fourteenth Amendment, the 1868 presidential election was won by Grant and Congress was carried by the advocates of national protection of human rights. Congress and the country were ready to eliminate the inconsistency and (as it was hoped) the instability. Said Gilbert Haven, a militant Massachusetts abolitionist: "We have no moral right to impose an obligation on one part of the land which the rest will not accept. We can have no peace till this right is made national."

The right to vote, free from discrimination, was made national and the vision of Thaddeus Stevens fulfilled as Congress completed action on a fifteenth amendment. Neither state nor nation could now legally deny any person the vote because of race or color. Once again, as in the case of the Thirteenth and Fourteenth Amendments, Congress was given the express and unconditional power to enforce the newly created constitutional pledge by appropriate legislation. In each of these three instances the intent was quite plain: it was not merely to be the function of the federal and supreme courts to void state laws or rulings that conflicted with the rights conferred; it was to be the power and duty of Congress to take its own steps, by laws governing the behavior of people in each state, to secure those rights and to prevent them from being undermined.

Congress took the first step in 1866, as we have seen, after the Thirteenth Amendment was ratified and while the various elements of the Fourteenth Amendment were being hammered out by the Joint Committee on Reconstruction. This first exercise of national power to enact "appropriate legislation" to root out slavery was called "An Act to protect all persons in the United States in their Civil Rights, and furnish the means of their vindication." Passed over President Johnson's veto, it became law April 9, 1866.

In striking back at the Black Codes by which the Johnson-created and Confederate-dominated state governments of the South sought to restore slavery in all but name, Congress began by declaring all persons born in the United States citizens. This confirmed Attorney General Bates' decision overruling the Dred Scott case and was to be reconfirmed, as were the basic principles of the act, in the Fourteenth Amendment itself. Federal protection was extended to the right of all inhabitants of any state and territory to make and enforce contracts, to buy and sell real estate, to sue and give testimony—and to have the "full and equal benefit of all laws and proceedings for the security of person and property." Federal and not state courts, prosecutors and marshals were to be entrusted with the responsibility for enforcing this law, the first in our history to use the phrase "civil rights."

John Jay, grandson of the first chief justice of the United States, was not even sure this law was necessary. He was confident that the Supreme Court would have declared the freed slaves full-fledged citizens entitled to equal rights by the sheer force of the Thirteenth Amendment itself. However, he was glad to have the law passed, to remove "misapprehensions as to the position which the American republic is henceforth to occupy before the world as regards the relationship of our people towards each other." He saw the law as fulfilling the promise of 1776 and permitting national survival in "unity, freedom, and honor."

Others, less confident in the Supreme Court, and concerned about the commitment of future congresses to "unity, freedom, and honor," had pressed for formulation of a fourteenth amendment. Their purpose was not simply to remove doubts about the constitutionality of the 1866 act, and it was not limited to preserving the principles of that act from repeal by congressional infidelity. It was expressed during congressional debate in 1871 on a further set of civil rights laws by John Bingham, the man who had fathered the first clause of the Fourteenth Amendment.

Acknowledging that he had written the clause "letter for letter, and syllable for syllable," Bingham told Congress of his concern because the Supreme Court had once ruled that the first eight amendments were not limitations on the power of the states. "Jefferson well said of the first eight articles of amendment," declared Bingham, "that they constitute the American Bill of Rights. Those Amendments secured the citizens against any deprivation of any essential rights of person by any act of Congress, and among other things thereby they were secured

>—in their persons, houses, papers, and effects against unreasonable searches and seizures;
>—in the inviolability of their homes in times of peace, by declaring that no soldier shall in time of peace be quartered in any house without the consent of the owner.
>—They secured trial by jury;
>—they secured the right to be informed of the nature and cause of accusation which might in any case be made against them;
>—they secured compulsory process for witnesses and to be heard in defense by counsel."

After this brief but incomplete catalogue of what he called "the rights dear to the American people," Bingham explained once more the deep concern he felt as a member of the Joint Committee in 1866, when he realized that these great rights, as contained in the first eight amendments to the Constitution, "defining and protecting the rights of men and citizens were only limitations on the power of Congress and not on the power of the States."

To explain his overriding purpose in the writing of the Fourteenth Amendment's first clause, Congressman Bingham then recited word for word the first eight amendments to the United States Constitution and stated flatly that it was his intent to make them limitations on the power of the states "by the fourteenth amendment. The words of that amendment, 'no state shall make or enforce any law which shall abridge the privileges and immunities of citizens of the United States,' are an express prohibition upon every state of the Union."

Bingham's detailed explanation of the larger purposes of the Fourteenth Amendment's "rights" clause came as Congress was facing a terrifying increase in lawless disorder and trying to frame a program to meet it. Several laws had already been passed by 1871, when this debate took place, to broaden the federal system of fulfillment of the promises of the three freedom amendments. Adequate though these earlier laws seemed to be in meeting particular problems, new forms of violent resistance to the law of the land continued to arise and to perplex the lawmakers. Disrespect and contempt for the law seemed to be the order of the day in every former slave state from Alabama to Texas.

In May of 1870, after the ratification of the Fourteenth and Fifteenth Amendments, a second major civil rights act was passed. This followed the passage of laws in 1866—the Slave Kidnapping Act—and 1867—the Peonage Abolition Law—which made it a federal crime to remove a person from one place to another for the purpose of forcing his labor or to enslave those without property or income by using real or pretended debts as the basis for bondage. The term "peonage" came from an old Spanish custom that prevailed in territory the United States had seized from Mexico during the 1847 war; ingenious former slave owners in other states were quick to use the idea as a substitute for the involuntary servitude that had been outlawed, and Congress was as quick to respond. There could have been little doubt that these laws were warranted under the Thirteenth Amendment.

The 1870 law established comprehensive machinery for federal protection of the newly granted nationwide right to vote. It also reenacted the 1866 Civil Rights Law; the purpose of this repassage of the four-year-old law was to make it clear that its constitutionality would rest on the federal power granted by the Fourteenth Amendment, as well as the Thirteenth, on which it had originally been based. In addition, the 1870 law took a first step against the guerrilla bands that had begun to terrorize the southern states. It was made a felony for two or more persons to band together, or to go in disguise on the highway or on the premises of any person with intent to violate the rights provisions of the act, or to injure or intimidate any citizen with intent to hinder or take reprisal for his exercise of constitutional rights.

The outlaw bands that harassed free citizens, both black and white, continued their operations. These armed and masked groups that were determined not merely to undo the work of Congress in granting citizenship rights to all but also to overthrow the governments of the states where they operated used the name Ku Klux Klan. A broader attack was mounted against them by Congress in the spring of 1871. The president was to be given the power to suppress local mob violence by military force. Conspiracies to interfere with the execution of national laws, or to deprive any person of equal protection of the laws, or to prevent the exercise of voting rights, were to be vigorously prosecuted.

It was in defense of the right of Congress to act against the Ku Klux Klan that John Bingham rose to give his explanation of the full scope and meaning of the Fourteenth Amendment's first clause. He was answering critics who claimed that there was too much "centralized power" and interference with state rights in the 1871 bill. Before his amendment went into effect, he said, "the States did deny to citizens the equal protection of the laws, they did deny the rights of citizens under the Constitution. . . . They denied trial by jury and he [the wronged citizen] had no remedy. They took property without compensation and he had no remedy. They restricted the freedom of the press and he had no remedy. . . . Who dare say, now that the Constitution has been amended, that the nation cannot by law provide against all such abuses and denials of right as these in States and by States, or combinations of persons?"

It was clear, said Bingham, that the rights provided for in the federal Bill of Rights, the first eight amendments, were now rights that could not be abridged by any state, by the intent of the Fourteenth Amendment. Moreover, he insisted, Congress had the power to protect these rights, by the appropriate legislation grant. Freedom of speech, the press and assembly, the right of trial by jury and the other aspects of a fair trial—all these were "rights of citizens of the United States defined in the Constitution and guarantied by the Fourteenth amendment, and to enforce which Congress is thereby expressly empowered."

These contributions of Bingham to the debate were evoked by opposition to the Ku Klux Enforcement Act. That opposition emanated from congressmen who stood to gain from becoming partners in a new national conservative coalition that would take over the country if the Klan succeeded in overthrowing the biracial, democratically elected state governments that were their target. They argued (contrary to the claims they advanced when the amendment was before Congress and the country for action) that it did no more than forbid discriminatory action by the state governments acting officially. Hence, they insisted, Congress could not act under the "appropriate legislation" clause against groups and individuals who mistreated others because they were black or allied with blacks in integrated governments or political bodies. This would be too much "centralized power," they said, and would destroy the dual form of state and national government they cherished. That "dual" or states' rights separation before the Civil War had left to the states the sole and unrestricted power of tolerating or legalizing the mistreatment of its people by one another. A congress that numbered many who had acted on the Fourteenth Amendment and therefore knew what they meant when they formulated it rejected such arguments for the third time when it overwhelmingly passed the 1871 Ku Klux Enforcement Act.

Understanding the meaning of these events is crucial to any real comprehension of the meaning of our entire constitutional history. For this reason, it is worth stepping beyond our story for a moment to see how it looked in retrospect to Edward S. Corwin, one of the giants among our learned commentators on the Constitution. Professor Corwin wrote in 1909, at a time when constitutional rights were at their lowest ebb in our country's history, that "there can be no kind of doubt" that the amendment's "authors designed that, at the very least, it should make the first eight amendments binding upon the States as well as the Federal Government and that it should be susceptible of enforcement both by the Federal Courts and by Congress." Continuing, he said, in words recalling the anguished protests of the racists of the 1860s and their allies: "to give such scope to the Fourteenth Amendment obviously meant to bid farewell to the old time federal balance which before the war had seemed the very essence of our constitutional system.

"It meant, in the language of contemporary protest [here he is quoting Stevens' and Bingham's opponents], 'the institution of a solid sovereignty instead of a government of limited power,' 'the transfer of municipal control of the State governments over their internal affairs into the hands of Congress,' the subordination of the 'State judiciaries to Federal supervision and control,' 'the annihilation of the independence and sovereignty of the State Courts in the administration of State laws'—in short, 'a deep and revolutionary change in the organic law and genesis of the government.' "

The passage of the Ku Klux Enforcement Act did not merely reconfirm the agreement of Congress with the original understanding of the Fourteenth Amendment that had been expressed by Bingham and was later restated by professor Corwin. It also opened the door to the supreme and culminating effort to give reality to its promise and to fulfill the pledge of national honor to the veterans of the black regiments. This was the struggle to round out the structure of guarantees of equal treatment by adding the protection of human rights to the 1866 law safeguarding legal rights. The protection of all Americans in their right to purchase property, make contracts, give testimony, sue and defend—these "legal" rights were enough to overthrow the "Black Codes" but were not enough to end the customs, practices and laws that permitted the treatment of some Americans as if they were a lower class of being. The human rights that had been trampled on, North and West as well as South, were so described by Frederick Douglass in 1870: "lucrative employments are closed to the colored race, and the highest callings open to them are of a menial character; while a colored gentleman is compelled to walk the streets of our largest cities like New York unable to obtain admission to the public hotels; while staterooms are refused in our steamboats, and berths refused in our sleeping cars on account of our color, the Negro is not abolished as a degraded caste. . . . We need today every influence that served to put the fifteenth amendment on the national statute-book to help us put the same fully into every department of the nation's life."

Charles Sumner responded by beginning what was to be his last great battle. On May 13, 1870, he introduced in the Senate a bill to prohibit discrimination by transportation companies, hotels, restaurants, theaters and other places of amusement open to the public, and so on. Initial resistance was great, and it was to require a five-year campaign to secure the passage of the capstone of the civil rights structure.

At session after session of Congress, Sumner continued his fight for this final civil rights law, until his last illness. He was not to live to see the passage of the bill for which he had fought so hard and for which he pleaded, saying that he did so "for the sake of peace, so that at last there shall be an end of slavery, and the rights of the citizen shall be everywhere under the equal safeguard of national law." As he lay dying, Sumner said to an ally from Massachusetts, "You must take care of the civil rights bill—my bill, the civil rights bill—don't let it fail." During its 1874 session the Senate passed the bill in tribute to his memory. Final approval was not won in the House until the following year, and only after provisions barring segregation in schools, churches and cemeteries were eliminated.

The full and equal enjoyment of all other public accommodations was now the requirement of the law of the land, because as Congress said: "it is essential to just government that we recognize the equality of all men before the law, and hold that it is the duty of government in its dealings with the people to mete out equal and exact justice to all, of whatever nativity, race, color . . . it being the appropriate object of legislation to enact great fundamental principles into law."

Part II
FALL:

Resistance, Struggle and Denial

Chapter 12

Two Steps Backward

While Congress was going forward step by step in expanding legal protection for the rights of all Americans, the nation had started to slip backward. In citing the laws passed to secure and protect equality and justice (the Fourteenth Amendment's pledge) and the right to vote (the Fifteenth Amendment), we mentioned only briefly the breakdown in law and order caused by the activities of armed and masked outlaw bands, some operating under the name Ku Klux Klan. Two acts of Congress were specifically directed against such lawlessness, which local authorities were unable or unwilling to check. Federal troops, thinly spread through the states of the former Confederacy, confined to garrison duty for the most part, were of little help.

It would require a broad canvas to draw the complete picture, state by state, of the disgraceful and tragic intimidation, violence and vote frauds that marked that period of our history. Those who had been defeated militarily in their war to defend a "Southern independence" based on perpetually enslaving part of their people were now fighting a guerrilla war to reestablish their dominance in local affairs. Encouraged in their initial resistance to federal law by President Johnson's opposition to and denunciation of the first Civil Rights Act and the Fourteenth Amdendment itself, they persisted in intransigent opposition to the political and civic equality that had been won by those who had previously been their slaves.

The lawless opposition was sporadic and spontaneous at first, and then became organized and effective. Its aims were economic as well as political. One objective was the outright overthrow of the biracial democratic state governments that had come into being when the Reconstruction Acts granted free and equal voting rights. Accompanying this was the purpose to curtail the free enterprise and initiative that had been exercised by the newly emancipated. The blacks were to be discouraged or prevented from rising by their own efforts in the traditional American way, or even from having the hope of doing so. Only in that way could they be forced to work for the planters on terms set by their employers and to continue to contribute to the wealth of the South (and northern cotton mills and merchants) without sharing in more than was needed to keep body and soul together.

One congressional document that has survived summarizes well the sad story of this era. It was contained in a petition to the president prepared by a convention of Alabama blacks, who met to consider how to persuade the government of the United States to fulfill its solemn commitment to them, its promise to guard them in their enjoyment of their rights of citizenship: "The investigation made in the years 1870–'71 by a committee of Congress known as the Ku-Klux committee, developed and established the fact of the organized existence, in many parts of this State, since the year 1868, of a secret, powerful, vindictive, and dangerous organization composed exclusively of white men belonging to the democratic party in this State, and whose objects were to control the labor and repress or control the votes of the colored citizens of this State. That organization, or a substitute and successor to it, under a changed name and a somewhat changed wardrobe, still exists in all its hideous and fearful proportions."

The petition pinpointed the threat to the United States Constitution. "Defeated in their scheme of secession," it said of the outlaws, "they have fallen back upon the old South Carolina plan of nullification. Being unable to defeat or nullify the constitutional amendments by their votes while the republican party is in power, or by open war, they have resolved to nullify them by secret war, violence and terror."

How could all of this have happened in the face of the laws passed by Congress in 1870 and 1871 to guard against this very evil—laws prompted by the first wave of assaults made by the Klan? It was not because of the lack, at the beginning, of a serious and sincere effort under President Grant to enforce the Constitution and the laws of the United States. Grant had appointed as attorney general, to head the newly established Department of Justice, Amos T. Akerman, a Southerner who had himself fought on the side of the Confederacy. Akerman had already proven his loyalty and was unreserved in his condemnation of the lawlessness that it became his responsibility to oppose.

"That any large portion of our people should be so ensavaged as to perpetrate or excuse such actions," he said, "is the darkest blot on Southern character in this age." He did not flinch in his task. "A spirited, yes, a desperate contest with bad men is in my judgment the most expedient course for the friends of the Government in the South."

The files of the Justice Department still contain touching samples of pleas for help in the face of the rising tide of white crime on the highways and streets of the South, as well as in the very homes of the unfortunate victims. One report tells of a lad who was flogged "for no known reason, except he was taking leave of his employer when his time expired." Another told of a man taken to a bridge at night and "shot through and through." A petition from a group in Tennessee sadly reported: "Here we are here under many dangers of our lives of the outrage Ku Kluks and other threts. What for, jest so for you," they wrote the guardians of the republic, "and now we have to call for you for help in time of need if you cannot give us sum rite to erfend ourselves."

Native white federal officers aided loyally in the execution of their oath of office. District attorney Starbuck of North Carolina assured his chief at the nation's capital that neither the wealth nor the social standing of the guilty defendant would move the prosecutor to consent to leniency: "We who were born and raised here know too well the terrible outrages committed by these bands of conspirators whose purposes were to destroy the freedom of elections and stab the Government at its vitals and who have never shown mercy to anyone," reported the North Carolinian to the Justice Department. "We do not think for one moment of asking the least mitigation of the punishment fixed by law for their crimes."

Starbuck was proud, and rightfully so, to have won forty-nine convictions in his first few months' efforts to enforce the law. But difficulties arose elsewhere. The local hostility against prosecution and prosecutors was so great that when the attorney general returned to his home state of Georgia to conduct prosecutions he was unable to secure hotel accommodations. In Alabama, too, it was difficult to proceed. The local United States attorney in Alabama reported grimly on the handicaps he faced: "Whether it is possible, under our form of government, to redress such wrongs, when a large portion of the resident population wink at them, I do not know." Shortly afterwards the federal judge at Montgomery declared that it was next to impossible to make arrests or to carry on trials without using both infantry and cavalry. In many counties along the Mississippi it was not safe for a marshal or any other United States officer to go about without military protection—eight years after Lee had surrendered at Appomattox. General Grant's compassionate generosity in allowing Lee's officers to keep their side arms was rewarded by potshots from those very weapons at President Grant's appointees.

Although many convictions were secured, the courts could not keep up with their business, so persistent and determined was the opposition to the preservation of local order by federal law. Witnesses who testified against those who had wronged them or their neighbors found it unsafe to return to their homes. The Attorney General of the United States urged them to be prepared to defend themselves: "If you take the position that the country is as much yours as it is theirs—that you have as good a right to live in it as they—and that you are determined to live in it, and enjoy all your rights; or to die in it bravely asserting your rights, when the law cannot protect you, you will teach them that you have a strength of your own; and this in the end they will respect more than the temporary exertion of the power of the U. S. Government."

Violence persisted, spread and flared up particularly at election time and during the period immediately afterward, when the ballots were counted or the winners of local offices installed. In one such eruption there were planted the seeds of a malignant obstacle that slowed down and ultimately checked the process of federal law enforcement. None of the handicaps that the beleaguered local loyalists and undermanned federal enforcement officials had faced was as difficult to overcome as the new barrier that was erected in Washington. The obstacles were created by the Supreme Court of the United States, and they proved to be insurmountable.

Two seemingly unrelated events occurred on successive April days in 1873. The first took place on Easter Sunday in the little courthouse town of Colfax, Louisiana; the second on Monday, April 14, in a courthouse in Washington, D. C. The Washington incident was the final decision in a lawsuit about the right to run a slaughterhouse; it took place in the serenity of a routine "Decision Monday" at the Supreme Court. "The decision was given to an almost empty courtroom," wrote one Washington reporter, "and has as yet attracted little attention outside of legal circles." The Louisiana story was something else, involving the killing of sixty Americans in cold blood. "Deliberate barbarous murder" was the finding of a United States Senate investigation. "It must stand, like the massacre of Glencoe or of Saint Bartholomew, a foul blot on the page of history."

The event justified the comparison. A number of the whites who lived in the parish of which Colfax was the courthouse village refused to recognize the judge and sheriff commissioned by the governor of the State of Louisiana. The threats he had heard prompted the sheriff to enlist a posse to help him defend the building used for the court and county offices. Over a hundred armed marauders attacked, using a small cannon to breach a fortification the posse had set up in front of the building. The attackers then set fire to the local symbol of law and order, and as the members of the posse emerged, shot them down.

A Justice Department investigator was able to identify ninety-six of the attackers, and a prosecution under the Civil Rights Enforcement Act of 1870 was begun. Arresting the accused was more difficult than naming and indicting them. Finally, W. J. Cruikshank and eight others were arrested and brought to trial. But the Supreme Court's decision in the case, announced on the Monday following that awful Easter Sunday, was to make it inevitable that they would go free—and the whole process of civil rights law enforcement was seen to collapse.

The court that decided the slaughterhouse cases of 1873 might not have even known of the Colfax massacre when their decision was made public. But its members knew of the very difficult battle that federal law enforcement officers had been waging to protect human rights, the rights of American citizenship, in places where state police and courts had been ineffective, or indisposed to do so. They must have known of the intention of the framers of the five-year-old Fourteenth Amendment to give Congress the power (to use the words of one member of the court) to ensure that "American citizenship should be a sure guarantee of safety" so that "every citizen of the United States might stand erect in every portion of its soil, in full enjoyment of every right and privilege belonging to a freeman, without fear of violence or molestation."

While those were the words of a member of the court in the case that was decided the day after the Colfax massacre, they were the words of a member of the dissenting minority of four. He was protesting a decision by the majority of five that seemed to him to have deliberately disregarded the intentions of the men, such as John A. Bingham, who wrote the Fourteenth Amendment.

The case of the New Orleans slaughterhouse law did not seem to present any question of human rights, of freedom from discrimination, or of fair trial. Essentially it was a struggle among white businessmen. The State of Louisiana had passed a law that required that all butchering of cattle be done in one restricted area for New Orleans and the adjoining counties by a single corporation set up for that purpose. The idea was to reduce the many sources of infection and pollution by limiting the messy business, and making it easier to inspect and control the conditions in which it was done.

There was a great uproar about this. Instead of being able, as in the past, to set up shop where he pleased with the offensive sights, smells and waste products that went with the trade, a man in the fresh meat business faced a limitation. He could import cattle from down river or over from Texas; he could sell meat to customers old and new; but he would have to take the animals to the central licensed and inspected institution for the business of killing and dressing the meat. If this resulted in a slightly increased cost of getting his meat ready for market, there was a similar effect on all of his competitors, and there seemed to be a plausible reason for the law.

Certainly this was all that the Supreme Court of the United States should have found it really necessary to decide when the case of the New Orleans butchers was presented to it for decision. But the manner in which the case was presented, the temper of the times and the personalities of the justices combined to produce a decision that went two giant steps backward toward undoing what the Thirty-Ninth Congress had tried to accomplish when it framed the Fourteenth Amendment.

What the court did in writing its decision in the slaughterhouse case was to come up with the right result for the wrong reasons. How it managed to do this takes a bit of explaining—but it is worth the effort needed to understand it. The decision of Monday, April 14, 1873, that was to make almost inevitable the freeing of the men accused of the barbarous Colfax massacre has cast a long and grim shadow over our constitutional history. It was to contribute to the making of other and equally wrong decisions for the next thirty years. It has made immensely more difficult the task of the Supreme Court in attempting, for the last thirty years, to undo the harm that came about after those first two steps backward were taken.

Chapter 13

Slaughterhouse
of Liberty

When Senator Timothy Howe finished studying the majority opinion that was handed down the day after the Easter Sunday massacre at Colfax, he exclaimed: "The American people would say, as they had said about the Dred Scott decision, that it was not law and could not be law."

Senator Howe was a fair representative of the moderates who had been in Congress when the Fourteenth was forged and who had seen for themselves its bitter necessity when President Johnson prematurely returned to the states the power to deny justice to their people. He had been a Maine man, a conservative Whig before the war, sufficiently law abiding to have displeased local antislavery men by urging obedience to the Fugitive Slave Law. He remained enough of a mainstream thinker to win an appointment as postmaster general under President Chester A. Arthur later on. But he spoke for moderates of perception and of conscience in denouncing the reasoning in the ruling on the Louisiana law. Unfortunately, he was not as good a prophet as he was a lawyer, for the American people did not react to the slaughterhouse case with the furious indignation of which they had shown themselves to be capable at the time that Taney thought he had settled the slavery question, permanently, against the slave.

Yet it was Roger Taney's ghost that emerged victorious when the contribution of the Dred Scott ruling to Supreme Court Justice Samuel Miller's written opinion is observed. Justice Miller and the court could have easily settled the quarrel among the New Orleans butchers by simply noting that the states had the power and the duty to enact local health measures; that, even if the concentration of slaughtering in one place increased the cost of doing business as a meat dealer, it was a normal and routine price to pay for a health regulation. But the attorneys for the disgruntled butchers had included in their argument against the Louisiana law the claim that it was in violation of the newly added Fourteenth Amendment to the United States Constitution. For justices who preferred the Constitution as it was before the Civil War, for men who reflected a mood of defeatism that was beginning to overcome a nation tiring of the effort to bring about law and order in the South, this created an interesting opportunity.

Mr. Justice Miller seized that opportunity with a vengeance. The lawyers for the objecting butchers had set great store, in their presentation, on the sentence in the first, or "rights," clause of the Fourteenth, which forbade the states to make laws violating "the privileges and immunities of citizens of the United States." It is part of the art of being a lawyer to take advantage of words, and it is entirely understandable that a lawyer for a butcher objecting to an interference with his business should argue that the right to slaughter his own cattle was a "privilege" that Louisiana could not take away. But it required only the briefest acquaintance with what had happened in the Thirty-Ninth Congress for one to know that it was perfectly absurd to think that the Joint Committee, the framers of the Fourteenth, were thinking of any such thing.

We know what Representative Bingham meant by the "privileges and immunities" he intended to protect. Primarily, as Senator Jacob M. Howard had also said in 1866, they were "the personal rights guaranteed and secured by the first eight amendments to the Constitution." What were these sacred rights? The "privilege" of speaking freely, and of assembling in public meetings; the "immunity" of freedom from unlawful searches and seizures; the "privilege" of being tried by a jury, and of not even being forced to defend oneself in a serious case unless enough evidence had been presented to a grand jury to satisfy it that a trial was warranted; the "immunity" of not being compelled to testify against oneself. These are only examples; they come immediately to mind as one reads the words of the first eight amendments.

The intent of the Fourteenth Amendment was not merely to forbid the states from committing such violations of personal rights. Mobs and night riders, owners of plantations and their overseers, angry and frustrated Confederate veterans, all had been violating the rights of freedmen and their sympathizers to assemble and to have a fair trial by due process of law before being punished. Congress was granted the power to enforce these rights by "appropriate legislation"—in the words of the fifth clause of the amendment. It has also been called the power "to hold over every American citizen, without regard to color, the protecting shield of law." Those were the words of Rep. James A. Garfield (later to be a martyred president) in 1866. A colleague, Rep. John M. Broomall of Pennsylvania, had said with approval that what the Joint Committee proposed was "to give power to the government of the United States to protect its own citizens within the states."

These great rights, these new national powers of protection—was all the debate and excitement over them aroused by the need to preserve men from state health and sanitary regulations, such as a restriction on the number of places in a thickly settled, swamp-infested area that might be employed for the slaughter of livestock? Of course not, and all that Justice Miller need have done was to say so.

But he and his colleagues seem to have been concerned with something much more vast and significant than that side issue. They were in revolt against the "centralizing tendency" that the congressmen opposing the Fourteenth Amendment had denounced, the alteration of the dual or "federal" form of prewar government that had left all men within a state—particularly men of African descent—to the absolutely unrestrained power of the dominant group within each state. That had been officially declared to be the nature of our Constitution by the Dred Scott decision, and Mr. Justice Miller manipulated the very sentence that had been intended to obliterate that decision and all it stood for to mangle the Fourteenth Amendment beyond recognition.

To see just how that was accomplished it is necessary to take a look at the rights clause, Section One of the amendment. It contains two sentences, the first concerning citizenship and the second setting up the triple guarantees of "privileges and immunities" for citizens, and "due process" and "equal protection of the laws" for all persons. The second sentence was the one that the Joint Committee had labored over; its first phrase forbidding the abridgment of "the privileges and immunities of citizens of the United States," expressed the sweeping purpose of draftsmen determined that no aspect or ingredient of freedom should lie at the mercy of any state government.

The full text of that first phrase becomes important in seeing just what it was that Justice Miller's majority did; it reads: "No State shall make or enforce any law which shall abridge the privileges or immunities of citizens of the United States." Those were the words that opened the first clause when it was reported to Congress by the Joint Committee. During the debate, one senator felt that, in spite of the Thirteenth Amendment, the ruling of Attorney General Bates declaring (despite the Dred Scott case) that Americans of African ancestry could be citizens, and the ruling of the Supreme Court on Sumner's motion to admit a Boston black to the bar of the court, it would be well to make it crystal clear that the infamous invention of Chief Justice Taney—the idea that no African-American could ever become an American citizen—should be obliterated forever.

In order for Justice Taney to achieve his aim in the Dred Scott case it was necessary for him to create the idea that there were two kinds of citizenship within our borders under the Constitution. Some people could be citizens of a state and not citizens of the United

States; some could be citizens of the United States and perhaps not citizens of a state. This made it possible for him to base his ruling on the proposition that even if Mr. Scott had been or become a citizen, a free citizen, of Illinois or the Northwest Territory, or of Missouri, he still had not attained United States citizenship. To put an end to this kind of idea once and for all, there was added an additional sentence to prefix the three commandments of the first clause of the proposed amendment.

The new sentence, composed and added separately from (and after) the second sentence that the Joint Committee on Reconstruction had drawn, declared that all persons "born or naturalized in the United States" were to be, henceforth and forever, "citizens of the United States *and* of the State wherein they reside." Thus they hoped to determine once and for all the concept that there was to be a single citizenship, and the belief that this was not to be considered a "white man's country" but rather a country for and of all the people born or naturalized here.

What Justice Miller did in the court's opinion in the slaughterhouse case was to stand this sentence on its head and to ignore the fact that the second sentence had been drafted separately (and previously) for the purpose of guaranteeing, against action by any of the states, "the privileges and immunities of citizens of the United States." Since the first sentence, he insisted, spoke of persons being United States citizens as well as citizens of the states and the second sentence spoke only of "privileges and immunities of citizens of the United States," there must have been a purpose to the "change in phraseology." While his argument, he admitted, was not "the most conclusive," there must have been an intention to sort out, classify and deal quite separately with two entirely separate and distinct types of "privileges and immunities."

One group he cleverly called "privileges and immunities belonging to a citizen of the United States as such," and the other "those belonging to citizens of a state as such." Only the former, said Mr. Justice Miller, almost as if pulling a rabbit out of a hat, or picking up a shell and palming a pea that had been under it, "are placed by this clause under the protection of the Federal Constitution." The privileges and immunities of the citizens of a state, "whatever they may be, are not intended to have any additional protection by this paragraph of the Amendment."

What are those rights, "whatever they may be," that were to be denied federal protection? "Nearly every civil right for the establishment and protection of which organized government is instituted . . . those rights which are fundamental." Ignoring the overwhelming circumstance that had cast its shadow over the entire decade that preceded his writing of these words, the curtailment and denial of those rights by the states and the crying need for federal protection to which the Thirty-Ninth Congress responded, Justice Miller insisted that the great rights "must rest for their security and protection where they have heretofore rested,"—with the separate states!

The supposedly defunct Dred Scott case doctrine that there were two separate kinds of citizenship and that civil rights lay within the sole power of the states to grant or deny, protect or curtail, had now been revived. The reason given for this brazen piece of judicial constitution-unmaking was the very reason that had been given in debate by the men who opposed the adoption of the Fourteenth Amendment: "To transfer the security and protection of all the civil rights we have mentioned, from the states to the Federal government . . . radically changes the whole theory of the relations of the state and Federal governments to each other and of both these governments to the people."

But that was exactly what the founding fathers of the Joint Committee and the Thirty-Ninth Congress had wanted to do, and what they thought they had done—changed the whole theory of the relations of the state and federal governments to each other and of both of these governments to the people. The theory that had been accepted from 1789 to 1861 had proved unworkable and led the nation to disaster. What the Joint Committee had confirmed by its own investigation of events during the year following President Lincoln's death was the need to end the idea that states had a "right" to abuse or to fail to protect civil rights.

The new "theory" of state, federal and citizen relations was clearly stated in the second sentence of the first section of Big Fourteen, plus the all-important power granted to Congress to enforce the pledges of that sentence "by appropriate legislation." Not even in the Dred Scott case itself had the trust placed by the American people in the Supreme Court been so abused as by the 5-4 majority that approved the revival of dual citizenship for the purpose of destroying the solemnly ratified constitutional provision protecting the privileges or immunities of citizens of the United States.

There was no congressional intention to ignore state-citizenship privileges or immunities and to concentrate on national citizenship privileges and immunities, as is evident in the deliberations of the Joint Committee. It is evident, too, from the manner in which the first sentence of Section One, the definition of citizenship, was added outside the committee after all the careful draftsmanship of the second sentence was concluded. It becomes even more evident when one asks, just what is left for national protection if we accept the idea that the really meaningful civil rights were solely state protected? What, if any, are the "privileges and immunities of citizens of the United States 'as such,' " which the court's peculiar separation leaves to national protection?

Here they are, said the justice: they are those "which owe their existence to the federal government, its national character, its Constitution, or its laws." They were such rights as the right to petition the federal government for a redress of grievances, to do business with federal officers, to use the navigable waters, to go to Washington (maybe to see the cherry blossoms) and to have protection on the high seas.

In the first place, it was perfectly evident that those were rights that hadn't the slightest relation to the widespread cruelty and violence against loyal whites and blacks being permitted in the South and in border states. No one in the Joint Committee had been the least bit upset about the inability of the people of Kentucky or Mississippi to go about on the high seas.

In the second place, there never was any need for a new amendment to the constitution to protect that limited group of rights that Justice Miller and the majority said were the kind that "owe their existence to the federal government." This narrow and limited list of rights had been protected all along by a clause in the original Constitution that made that document and federal laws passed under it "the supreme law of the land." This Supremacy Clause, as it had always been called, had been ruled sufficient to protect the Bank of the United States from federal taxation. Such rights as the right to travel to Washington, D. C., and the right to use national seaports needed no Fourteenth Amendment for their protection.

If Justice Miller and the men who sided with him to make up the narrow Supreme Court majority were right in limiting the meaning of Bingham's words ("privileges or immunities of citizens of the United States") to something that did not need further protection, then the men of the Thirty-Ninth Congress and especially the Joint Committee must have been terrible hypocrites—and Andrew Johnson and the men who fought the amendment's passage and ratification terrible fools. Is it conceivable that they were all such hypocrites and fools—and that they fooled such brilliant and passionate advocates of human rights as Charles Sumner and Thaddeus Stevens as well?

Of course not. Bingham himself had said, during congressional debates that were totally ignored (contrary to proper court practice) by the slaughterhouse Justices, that "The privileges and immunities of citizens of the United States, *as contradistinguished from citizens of a State,* are chiefly defined in the first eight amendments to the Constitution."

After Justice Miller read the majority opinion, the dissenting justices protested sharply. One of them, Justice Stephen J. Field, satirically said that if the majority was right the new amendment "was a vain and idle enactment, and most unnecessarily excited Congress and the people on its passage." As for national protection, he stressed that "no State could ever have interfered by its laws" with the narrow group of federal rights which the court majority said was all that went with United States citizenship. And Justice Noah Swayne said of the majority, in language to which people had not yet become accustomed among Supreme Court justices: "It defeats, by a limitation not anticipated, the intent of those by whom the instrument was framed and of those by whom it was adopted. To the extent of that limitation it turns, as it were, what was meant for bread into a stone."

Chapter 14

Retreat from the Constitution

Mr. Justice Miller's method of settling the butchers' battle was to undermine the rights of all Americans. The effect of his artificially created division between the rights (for that is all that "privileges or immunities" means) of United States citizens and those of state citizens was to eliminate from national protection safeguards that even the most conservative jurists summarize in the phrase "rooted in the traditions of justice and the conscience of civilized people."

It was some years before this result became entirely clear. When the full picture emerged, a lone voice spoke out from the Supreme Court. It was the voice of John Marshall Harlan, who at the turn of the century looked back at what had been happening for the three decades that followed the slaughterhouse case and then wrote in protest: "To say of any people that they do not enjoy the privileges and immunities specified in the first ten amendments is to say that they do not enjoy real freedom."

Mr. Justice Harlan was denouncing one of the last of a series of court decisions that removed from national protection the rights of the people—the very rights that the Fourteenth Amendment had been intended to guard against the actions of state and local governments. The door had been opened to these rulings by Mr. Justice Miller's revival of the Dred Scott case's idea that each American had two kinds of citizenship. The direction had been pointed by his insistence on reviving the pre-Civil War, state "right" to be free from federal interference with internal injustice.

While the door had been opened and the direction had been pointed by Mr. Justice Miller, the first major step on that pathway of retreat from the second American Constitution was taken when the case of William Cruikshank and the other accused perpetrators of the Colfax courthouse massacre came before the court. The slim majority of one in the butchers' case had after all settled only one question by their decision: that a man's "right" to slaughter his own livestock (and not have to pay a fee to a centrally inspected slaughterhouse) was not as important as the right of the state to try measures that seemed intended to protect the public health.

Something more serious was presented in the Cruikshank case. The murder of a sheriff's posse of black men, at a state courthouse, was prosecuted by the United States Department of Justice on the theory that it was a federal crime, under one of the protective Civil Rights Enforcement Laws. The murder in cold blood of any man by any other was also against Louisiana law. But the state authority had been so enfeebled by local division and lawlessness that it could not act. A state government that *could* not act because of internal weakness was no different, as a practical matter, from a state government that *would* not act because it was in sympathy with the purpose of the murderers.

It was to provide for cases in which state and local authorities failed to investigate and prosecute crimes directly involving the federal rights created by the Fourteenth and Fifteenth Amendments that the Civil Rights Enforcement Laws were passed. If a jealous husband killed his wife, or if an interrupted burglar slugged his victim, only questions of state concern were involved. But if a black man was whipped for refusing to work on slave labor terms, or a white man lynched for calling a meeting of blacks to guide them in claiming their civil rights, these were the very evils that prompted the reconstruction congressmen to amend the Constitution and to pass laws protecting the newly created federal rights.

It was under the authority of the Civil Rights Enforcement Act of 1870 and the Ku Klux Act of 1871 that attorneys general such as Akerman of Georgia had been fighting their desperate and heroic battles against lawlessness in the former slave states. A prosecution of Cruikshank and his cronies under the Enforcement Act succeeded when Justice Department investigators gathered enough evidence to convict them. An appeal was made. The decision of the Supreme Court was eagerly awaited. It was hoped that its ruling would promote obedience to the law and give heart to those fighting against such difficult odds to enforce it.

The Enforcement Act under which the Cruikshank mob was convicted made it a crime against the United States to conspire to injure or oppress persons who had exercised or sought to exercise their rights under the Constitution. There were a number of "counts," or separate charges, against the accused. They could not be charged with murder as such, since that was not a federal crime. They were charged with interfering with the murdered blacks' right to assemble; also, in separate counts, with plotting to deprive them of their lives "without due process of law" and of banding together to interfere with the victims' rights to the "equal protection of the laws."

For an entire year the nation waited to learn if its government would be permitted to redeem the pledge of national honor. Was there some hope that law and order would be restored in the South, in the face of all the heartbreaking handicaps that federal law enforcement officers faced? The answer that came from the 1876 Supreme Court was a loud and obstinate "No." Instead of the 5-4 split about the property rights of white butchers, there was now a unanimous rejection of federal protection of the human rights of blacks who volunteered to aid a sheriff.

The First Amendment protects the right of the people to assemble peaceably. If the Fourteenth Amendment had made this right to assemble a "privilege or immunity" of citizens of the United States with which the states were forbidden to interfere, then the federal government would have had the power to protect that civil right. But it did not, said the new chief justice, Morrison Waite. We have, he recalled from the butchers' case opinion of Justice Miller, two kinds of government, federal and state, and the rights of citizens under each of these governments are different. It had always been solely the obligation of the states to protect the right of free assembly—and the Fourteenth Amendment had changed nothing. So said the court in 1876.

The slave states had always forbidden blacks to assemble in groups of three or more, off plantations, and tightened control after Nat Turner's revolt in 1831. By the Black Codes, which the states passed to limit the freedom of movement of the newly emancipated after the Civil War, these very limits placed on the right of assembly were repeated. It was against such actions that the Thirty-Ninth Congress tried to act in framing the Fourteenth Amendment. But the butchers' case decision of April 14, 1873, which frustrated the "privileges and immunities" clause of the Fourteenth Amendment by a limitation that practically eliminated it, was applied to set free the murderers of April 13, 1873, on this count. The privilege of peaceful assembly granted by the First Amendment was not one of the "privileges and immunities" federally protected, and the tentative steps backward indicated by Mr. Justice Miller were reaffirmed.

A new and equally devastating step backward was taken in dealing with the charges accusing the Cruikshank mob of plotting to deprive men of their lives without due process—in their cold-blooded murders—and of denying equal protection of the law. Such is not the business of the United States government, wrote the new chief justice. The first clause of the amendment forbids only the *states* from denying "equal protection" or from violating "due process." Even though the amendment forbids violations of these fundamental guarantees, the judge insisted that it "adds nothing to the rights of one citizen against another."

By these few words, without explanation or justification, the court nullified the fifth paragraph, the "national power" clause, of the Fourteenth Amendment. This was the section specifically giving Congress the power to enforce the provisions of the amendment "by appropriate legislation." The states had repeatedly failed to protect "the rights of one citizen against another," before and during the Thirty-Ninth Congress; and it had been thoroughly understood by all of its members that Congress could fulfill the promise of "equal protection of the laws," if it judged state authorities to be incapable of doing so.

The strongest possible evidence of that understanding lay in the passage of the Enforcement Acts by a congress that included most of the men who wrote and passed the Fourteenth Amendment. Those who had said that Congress should have the power to enforce civil rights by "appropriate legislation" certainly knew what they meant and it was their judgment that the Enforcement Act that was before the court in the Cruikshank case *was* appropriate legislation. But the court said no. By saying so they licensed mobs to do, without national interference, the very things against which the amendment was supposed to protect their victims.

As long as there was no "state action," the federal government was forbidden to interfere with the taking of lives or the destruction of property without due process of law. But it had been "private action" and not state action that had caused so much of the bloodshed and grief in the South during the early reconstruction period. On the mind of every congressman who had debated the pros and cons of the "centralizing tendency" of the Fourteenth Amendment had been the question of federal protection against private action.

When news of the court's decision got around, it was not only U. S. Attorney James R. Beckwith of Louisiana who was astounded. The other federal attorneys who had been trying, in good faith, to stem the rising tide of civil rights crimes were similarly dismayed. Their discouragement was increased by a decision on the same day in March, 1876, placing drastic restrictions on the federal power to protect the right to vote. From that day on, while a few attempts were made to restore law and order, they were the exception.

Just as the U. S. attorneys and the friends of law and order were thunderstruck, the lawless ones who had by force been regaining power in the former slave states were exuberant. One leader of the Louisiana bar described the reaction vividly, when news spread that the Colfax courthouse assassins had gotten away with murder: "When the decision was reached and the prisoners released, there was the utmost joy in Louisiana, and with it a return of confidence which gave best hopes for the future."

The "joy" of which this respectable citizen spoke and which he shared was limited to members of the race to which he and the freed murderers belonged. It took some time for southern whites to learn that they were being shortsighted and self-deceiving in cheering the subversion of the congressional attempt to protect the rights of all Americans.

With the completion of the two major steps backwards—the undoing of the guarantee of privileges or immunities and the subtraction of the promise of national protection—there began a seepage of the rights of both blacks and whites. The first case to prove this point was to do so with an ironic twist.

Joseph Walker ran a coffeehouse in New Orleans. Charles Sauvinet was tired and thirsty. He wanted a place to sit and sip the brew so popular among Louisianans. Walker looked at his prospective customer and shook his head. Sauvinet's skin was too dark to suit him.

Charles Sauvinet knew his rights. Louisiana's lawmakers had been elected while that state still obeyed the commandment of the Fifteenth Amendment. Its biracial legislature complied with the requirement of the Fourteenth Amendment that it furnish to all persons within its jurisdiction the "equal protection of the laws." The owner of a public place, such as a cafe, was obliged by act of the state assembly to be open to the "patronage of all persons, without distinction or discrimination on account of race or color." Violators could be sued for damages—and Sauvinet sued.

Anticipating the possibility that biracial juries might disagree in such cases, the General Assembly had devised an ingenious limitation on the right of trial by jury. Instead of the customary provision for a new trial when the jury was unable to agree upon a verdict, it was made the duty of the judge presiding at the trial to decide the case on the evidence as he saw it. Walker, the white cafe owner, protested bitterly when the judge discharged the jury that disagreed on the merits of Sauvinet's suit and announced his intention to award the verdict to the disappointed coffee-sipper.

Walker's claim was that he had been denied his constitutional right to a trial by jury. The Louisiana courts disagreed, setting the stage for a vivid lesson on the damage done by the slaughterhouse decision to the rights of all Americans. The disgruntled, racist coffeehouse host, who had been billed $1000 for his lack of hospitality, appealed to the Supreme Court of the United States.

Before the Civil War, before the Fourteenth Amendment had become part of the United States Constitution, state courts were not obliged by federal law to grant jury trials. The Bill of Rights did provide, in the Seventh Amendment, that in private civil law suits, "where the value in controversy shall exceed twenty dollars, the right of trial by jury shall be preserved." Under the prewar ruling that had so stirred Congressman Bingham, the privileges and immunities in the Bill of Rights were protected only against action by the national government. Judges in federal court cases were obliged to grant jury trials; state court judges were free to follow whatever the local state law and constitution provided.

Suddenly the shoe was on the other foot. It became very important to the racist, "states' rights," side of the case to persuade the court to honor Bingham's intention to protect individuals against state intrusions on their privileges and immunities. If the Fourteenth Amendment made the Bill of Rights a limitation on the states, Walker was quite correct in his claim that his right to have a trial by jury had been violated. That right had been defined in the Seventh Amendment and Bingham had said that the privileges and immunities of American citizens "are chiefly those defined in the first eight amendments to the Constitution."

Not at all, said Chief Justice Morrison R. Waite, in a decision issued just a month after the Colfax murderers were freed. Trial by jury in state civil suits was deemed *not* "a privilege or immunity of national citizenship." It cost Mr. Walker $1000 to learn that when the great purpose of the Fourteenth Amendment was frustrated the court (as Louis B. Boudin was to write, half a century later) "had to put some others beyond the protection of that Amendment along with the Negroes."

Chapter 15

Election Returns and an Unexpected Dissenter

A great deal of debate took place during the 1900 presidential election and afterwards over whether or not inhabitants of lands conquered and annexed by the United States had any rights. The question popularly put was "Does the Constitution follow the flag?" After President McKinley, who had launched our first armed interference with the affairs of the people of Southeast Asia, was reelected, the Supreme Court upheld the denial of a jury trial to a Philippine man prosecuted by presidential authority.

"No matter whether the Constitution follows the flag or not," said Mr. Dooley, a character invented by the most popular newspaper columnist of the day, "th' Supreme Court follows th' illiction returns."

Justices sworn to uphold and enforce the Constitution as it was written would hardly form the independent tribunals that James Madison expected if they were to allow their decisions to be influenced by political events. It goes without saying that judges should not be influenced by their feelings about wealth or property, race or color. An extreme example of judicial decision unfairly influenced by extraneous factors was the Dred Scott case. When in 1873, the court revived Taney's "two citizenship" idea with such a devastating effect on the future of the Fourteenth Amendment, its members cannot be said to have "followed" the election returns, as did Mr. Dooley's court of a later day. What the court did was to anticipate and influence the outcome of the election of 1876.

The opposing candidates had been Rutherford B. Hayes, whose platform and campaign during 1876 called for enforcement of the Constitution, and Samuel B. Tilden, whose followers confidently expected him to govern as if the Fourteenth and Fifteenth Amendments had never been made part of the nation's basic law. The enthusiasm of many of the voters for fulfillment of the promises embodied in those amendments had worn thin as the guerrilla insurgents of the South, the Ku Klux Klan and similar bodies, had proved to be difficult to prosecute. That sense of national honor had slipped back still further when the court read "privileges" and "immunities" out of the Fourteenth and made national protection almost mythical.

Even so, Hayes might have been elected with ease. If the laws that protected freedom and the right to vote had been enforced, the result would not have been close—and Hayes might have tried to live up to his platform's promises. But when the returns came in from states where the votes were counted by the type of man placed in power by actions such as those of the Cruikshank mob, Tilden had taken most of the southern states. The results in others were so doubtful, with more than one electoral body claiming to be authorized to certify the returns, that a National Electoral Commission was appointed to determine the outcome.

The decisions of that commission were made not as the result of an honest inquiry, but as the fruit of a secret and sordid deal. Hayes was to be allowed to become president, but he and his party were to accept Tilden's program of allowing race relations and "justice" to be controlled by the individual states. The power to rule which had been gained illegitimately in the southern states was to be recognized. The men who wielded that power were to be left free to take the vote away from part of their people, or to count it dishonestly.

No promises needed to be made concerning the role that the Supreme Court would play. Long in advance of the 1876 election a majority of the justices had committed themselves in the slaughterhouse case to the proposition—contrary to the ideas of both the framers and their opponents—that it was not the purpose of the Fourteenth Amendment "to transfer the security and protection of civil rights" from the states to the nation.

The court had shown its intention more clearly when the freeing of Cruikshank and his mob invited the widespread intimidation of voters in the 1876 presidential election. In the years to come the court was to continue doggedly on the course of eroding the amendment. So much did its decisions frustrate the plain purpose of the draftsmen that a member of the bar of the court, chosen years later to deliver a memorial eulogy of Chief Justice Waite, declared that when the court announced the narrow scope of the first clause of Big Fourteen "many of the framers of these Amendments received information regarding their intentions which was new" to them.

There was no national outcry, little public resistance to the path of nullification on which the justices had chosen to embark. The inauguration of President Hayes in 1877 was accompanied by the development of a public consensus that placed the "national unity" of white Americans on a higher footing than the national honor that had been pledged to fulfill the promise of the new amendments. The first response by the new president, and a symbol of the bargain that he had made as well as a gesture of appeasement toward that unity sentiment, was the appointment of a Confederate ex-officer to be postmaster general.

When a Supreme Court justice resigned the day after his inaugural, Hayes reached out to make another appointment in the same spirit. This time a Kentuckian, the son of a slaveowner, was chosen. But John Marshall Harlan was to surprise his supporters and amaze the surviving radical senators who opposed and delayed his confirmation.

Born in 1833, the son of a Kentucky politician and officeholder who had named him for the great chief justice, Harlan had been for slavery before the Civil War and against its abolition afterwards. To launch his own political career, as a young lawyer he had joined and actively supported the local version of the bigoted, native American "Know-Nothings," a group that played upon prejudices against Catholics and the foreign born. He had supported the candidacy of ex-General George McClellan, who ran against Lincoln in 1864 on a platform of peace with slavery, and he had opposed the passage of the Fourteenth and Fifteenth Amendments.

With all of that against him, he was nevertheless able to cite, in support of his confirmation by the Senate, such evidence of a change in heart as a speech he had made in 1871 as unsuccessful candidate for Governor of Kentucky: "The most perfect despotism that ever existed on this earth was the institution of African slavery," he told his listeners, and perhaps that was why he was not elected. "It was an enemy to free speech; it was an enemy to good government; it was an enemy to free press. . . . I rejoice that these human beings are now in possession of freedom, and that that freedom is secured to them in the fundamental law of the land, beyond the control of the state. . . . Let it be said that I am right rather than consistent."

The change in his outlook and his dedication to freedom and to its protection against "the control of the state" had come about over a period of ten years. Despite his family's ownership of slaves and his own opposition to emancipation, his patriotism had prompted him to help resist the sentiment for secession in Kentucky. He helped to raise a volunteer regiment and accepted a commission in the Union Army. His unit served in Kentucky, Mississippi and Tennessee.

It falls to some men, dictatorial though the command structure of an army may be, to learn something more of the common humanity and worth of man in their military life than they had ever been able to understand before. In Harlan's case, the association with men of every rank and station and the comradeship with Catholics and foreign born was not merely an education; it was also an experience that caused him to repent and wish to make amends for the bigotry that he had shared and helped to popularize in the 1850s.

His firsthand experiences with slavery and with the slaves helped to bring about the beginning of an end to his support for that institution. Political life in postwar Kentucky completed the transformation and made him a genuine believer in the new constitutional amendments that he had opposed and in the laws that had been passed to fulfill their promise. His personal sense of morality and commitment to law and order were offended by what he saw between 1868 and 1871, as Kentucky underwent a repeated pattern of raids and intimidation by lawless groups of men determined to maintain their "skin-color supremacy."

By 1871, when he first ran for governor (he was to run again, also unsuccessfully, in 1875) he had become convinced of the incorrectness of his earlier views. He acknowledged that the new amendments were necessary "to place it beyond the power of any State to interfere with the results of the war." He learned at first hand that the blacks who sought to participate in political life were as worthy as those with whom they competed. He felt strongly that those who loved the South and had belonged to its "better" classes before the war owed it to their section to try to bring about a cessation of racial hostility and to begin rebuilding their economy on the basis of a just and equal relationship among the people.

When Hayes, the candidate, was still speaking out for the enforcement of justice and equality under the Constitution, Harlan as head of the Kentucky delegation to the national convention was able to clinch his nomination by swinging his delegates away from their "favorite son" candidate—his own law partner—at the crucial moment. During the disputed election fight, while serving as a visiting electoral commissioner in Louisiana, he was believed to have helped certify those votes for Hayes. His services were sufficiently valuable for him to have been offered the ambassadorship to Great Britain. He was not interested in that post. Then, unexpectedly, came an opening on the Supreme Court. For the next thirty-three years there was to be one justice, at least, who never yielded his stubborn belief in obedience to the Constitution or his devotion to the task of carrying out the intentions of the men who wrote it.

Mr. Justice John Marshall Harlan (the first, for a namesake grandson sat until recently on the court) was more stubborn than he was successful. He revived the tradition of writing "dissenting" opinions, as they are officially called—argumentative explanations of their views by justices whose conscience will not permit them to join silently in majority opinions that they believe are wrong. The man for whom he had been named had been able to discourage the practice for many years, during his own leadership and afterwards. His ambitions to build the prestige of the court and to win acceptance of the major constitutional ideas which he fathered explains his desire for unanimity.

John Marshall Harlan came to the court at a different time and saw his obligation differently. When great questions of human rights were presented, he would not accept the idea that the vote of a majority would have to be the last word. He had seen the nation suffer too much agony in a bloody conflict that had been made inevitable by one improper Supreme Court decision. The basic idea of the Dred Scott case, that the several states were separate islands free to inflict as much injustice as the ruling class within each saw fit, had been written out of the Constitution and five hundred thousand lives had been paid for that change. The refusal to obey that undoing of injustice was too important to be left unrecorded; more than that, Harlan saw it as his duty to express his dissent as a document for a democratic debate. Although he knew that the debate might not be won in a year or a decade, he felt sure that right would triumph and he continued to speak out.

Others have been given the title, and more glamor has surrounded their names; but John Marshall Harlan was *the* great dissenter in the history of the Supreme Court: a Kentuckian from Olympus. He looked the part, too. Over six feet tall, with a massive body and deep-set eyes, he commanded attention whenever he entered a room. Though his bearing was regal and his voice boomed out in startling contrast to those of his brethren of the bench, he never ceased to want to mix with and talk to the common man. He rode a trolley car to the court building each working day, and until late in life conducted a bible class at his church's Sunday school. He was a popular and well-loved figure in Washington—though some have called him an "eccentric" because of his view of the Constitution. There were few who were around in 1908 who were able to forget the sight of the baseball game he played at the age of seventy-five: the Supreme Court nine against the junior Washington bar. The old dissenter cleared the bases with a triple to center field, and heroically ran every step of the way to third base.

Chapter 16

A Banker, a Burglar and a Bootlegger

Albert Twining was a banker and John O'Neil a businessman. Charles Maxwell was accused of robbery, Joseph Hurtado convicted of murder. Each lost his battle with the law. A plain and direct command of one of the first eight amendments was disobeyed in each case and the liberties of all Americans were diminished.

From the time that Hurtado's appeal came before the court in 1884 until Twining's in 1908—three years before his death—Justice John Harlan persisted in appealing to a future day from the kind of justice that was dispensed in his. His appeal was essentially for a return to the Constitution, from which he felt the court had departed when it reduced the "privileges or immunities" protection to a mere garland of words. It is one of the strange quirks of history that Justice David Davis, whom Harlan replaced on the court, had voted with the Miller majority in the slaughter of liberties.

The commandments of the Bill of Rights were not created overnight. They were the fruit of the experience of many generations spent resisting the abuse of power. Men had learned enough about the weaknesses of their fellow men in positions of power to know what to guard against. Everything, from the First Amendment's "Congress shall make no law respecting an establishment of religion" to the Eighth's "nor cruel and unusual punishments inflicted," is there to safeguard against interference with freedom of thought and conscience or against unfair or inhuman methods of law enforcement, or both. Such forbidden methods of law enforcement as the illegal search of a man's home or the denial of counsel had been used to suppress dissent.

One of those specific prohibitions of the Bill of Rights was the Fifth Amendment's opening, "No person shall be held to answer for a capital, or otherwise infamous crime, unless on presentment or indictment of a Grand Jury. . . ." The institution of the "Grand Jury" that is mentioned is an ancient one, not to be confused with the trial jury that is convened and selected in the prosecution of a case. The grand jury specified by amendment is a group of twenty-three citizens, usually selected by the month for each county, which must pass on the evidence gathered by the prosecutor at a closed hearing. Only if twelve of the grand jurors vote that the evidence provides "probable cause"—that is, sufficient evidence to justify forcing a man to face a trial—will an "indictment," an accusation, be voted for.

The need for such a method of procedure in the interest of simple fairness becomes evident if one thinks for a moment about what a man faces when he is forced to defend himself in court against a serious accusation. The publicity and expense alone may well ruin him, or do serious damage. To be found "not guilty" is small consolation after a trial that may take weeks and cost job and savings.

Joseph Hurtado was accused of having killed José Stuardo in Sacramento in 1882. California's constitution of 1879 had dropped the requirement of indictment by a grand jury and provided as an alternate method an "information," a sworn charge by a district attorney. The attorneys for Hurtado objected. Since the slaughterhouse case had determined that the privileges and immunities of the first eight amendments were not protected against state action by the Fourteenth Amendment, they tried another approach. They claimed that when Hurtado was forced to trial without having been indicted he was denied "due process of law."

Now this appeal relied upon the precise words of the Fourteenth Amendment, the second prohibiting clause in the first paragraph. Even if such rights of fair procedure were not "privileges" or "immunities" under the first prohibiting clause, they could well be within the second. There seemed little doubt that the framers of the Fourteenth Amendment intended a generous overlapping or double protection by the three phrases "due process," "equal protection" and "privileges or immunities." What could "due process" mean, in plain English, except "fair procedure"?

Hurtado's lawyers presented the court with a Massachusetts precedent that seemed difficult to answer. That state's constitution had contained no direct pledge of grand jury procedure. It did provide that no one could be denied life or liberty save by "law of the land." These words, in Latin *(Per Legem Terrae),* go back to the first bill of liberties wrested from an English ruler, the Magna Carta of 1215. The phrase "due process of law" was but an alternate way of stating "law of the land," developed during the course of English history.

The Massachusetts high court had held that the protection of grand jury inquiry before trial was required in that state by the use of the words "law of the land." Its chief justice had written in so deciding that the right of citizens to be free "from the trouble, expense, and anxiety of a public trial before a probable cause is established by the presentment and indictment of a grand jury, in case of high offenses, is justly regarded as one of the securities to the innocent against hasty, malicious and oppressive public prosecutions, and as one of the ancient immunities and privileges of English liberty." Here was a direct and persuasive precedent that "due process of law" required that a grand jury must indict a man before he could be forced to face a criminal court, and that Hurtado had been deprived of his rights even though the explicit requirement of the Fifth Amendment for such protection was not since slaughterhouse a "privilege" or an "immunity" of a citizen of the United States.

Not at all, said the court majority. It was for them, the justices, to decide what rights are so fundamental that to take them away would be a deprivation of "due process." The grand jury is merely a form of procedure which the states can abolish at will. Moreover, the Fifth Amendment (unlike the Fourteenth) contains the words "due process of law" in addition to the specific direction that "no person shall be held to answer" without a grand jury indictment. We must assume that the words "due process" mean the same in both the Fifth and the Fourteenth Amendments, and that those words as used in the Fifth cannot be understood to include the grand jury requirement, since that is spelled out by other words in the same amendment. (There is more than one answer to that argument, the simplest and most direct being that the court itself did not apply the same test to the phrase "nor shall private property be taken for public use, without just compensation"; instead it held that the words "due process of law" in the Fourteenth Amendment did require just compensation when a state took private property for public use.)

"My sense of duty compels me to dissent," announced Mr. Justice Harlan. He anticipated the court's later ruling on "just compensation" and its application of a different standard to property rights from that which it was applying to human rights. He placed his finger on the important feature of the grand jury system as a guardian of liberty—that it is based on a "body of private persons, *who do not hold office at the will of the government or at the will of the voters.*" (The justice himself underlined those words to indicate the importance of setting people free from popular passion and prejudiced acts in such cases.)

"In the secrecy of the investigations by grand juries, the weak and helpless (proscribed, perhaps, because of their race, or pursued by an unreasoning public clamor) have found and will continue to find security against official oppression, the cruelty of mobs, the machinations of falsehood and the malevolence of private persons who would use the machinery of the law to bring ruin upon their personal enemies."

It was not too often in that period of our history that justices were concerned with the problems of the "weak and helpless," or of those who were "proscribed, perhaps, because of their race." John Marshall Harlan, long in advance of his time, saw the importance of enforcing the full protection of all of the rights of all Americans, and did not give up easily. Having become convinced of the purpose of the Fourteenth Amendment—to extend the protection of national constitutional rights to black and white, rich and poor—he continued to speak out even though he knew that he would not win during his lifetime.

John O'Neil was not poor, helpless or black. He was a successful merchant and dealer in wines and liquors. The products he sold were perfectly lawful in New York State, where he had his business; neighboring Vermont, however, had responded to the temperance movement by outlawing the sale of intoxicating liquors. O'Neil's place of business was in Whitehall, in upstate New York, and for a number of years thirsty Vermonters mailed orders to him, which he filled by railway express. One unhappy day Mr. O'Neil (who believed that his shipments in interstate commerce were immune from punishment by Vermont law) was picked up in Rutland, jailed and held for trial.

The charge against him was that he sold intoxicating liquors without the authority of the law. The Vermont court found that he had made four hundred fifty-seven such sales and he was sentenced to serve 19,914 days in jail—or almost fifty-five years. He appealed this harsh sentence, claiming that such lengthy imprisonment was cruel and unusual punishment. By such action he was asking the United States Supreme Court to apply the protective language of the Eighth Amendment to the United States Constitution in judging the action of the state of Vermont. His lawyers argued plausibly that half a century in jail for selling intoxicating liquor was out of all proportion to the offense—just as the whipping post might be considered extreme nowadays for stealing a loaf of bread—and therefore "cruel and unusual."

This commandment of the Bill of Rights was a direct inheritance from the English revolution of 1689 that drove the Stuarts from the country. In revulsion against the savage cruelty with which previous popular movements and expressions of dissent had been punished, the successful rebels secured from the new king a pledge against excessively disproportionate retribution. The promise was repeated in the pioneer Virginia and Massachusetts bill of rights and carried into the national catalogue of freedom by Madison in 1789. The outlawing of "cruel and unusual punishment" was meant to ensure a standard of human decency, both for its own sake as a mark of civilization and as a safeguard against tyranny by men in power.

If a state government resorted to such methods before the Civil War, the nation could not interfere: the Eighth Amendment, like the rest of the Bill of Rights, was treated as a barrier only against the wrongs that federal officials and judges might do. It is easy to see why this was so in a nation that was composed of slave states as well as free: not only for the repression of discontented or rebellious slaves but also to curb those who spoke out or acted against the barbarism of slavery, the slave states would tolerate no limits on the methods used.

Here was a perfect example of the need felt by the Thirty-Ninth Congress to frame a constitutional amendment, in the root-and-branch elimination of slavery, that would protect all Americans, white and black. John A. Bingham saw this and said so, during the debate on his paragraph of the Fourteenth. "Cruel and unusual punishments," he told his listeners in Congress in 1866, "have been inflicted under State laws within this Union upon citizens, not only for crimes committed, but for sacred duty done." He paused, and looked around the rows of congressional chairs and desks—including the empty ones that waited to be filled by representatives from the states that had been excluded by Stevens' resolution.

"It was an opprobrium to the Republic that for fidelity to the United States they could not by national law be protected against the degrading punishment inflicted on slaves and felons by State law." He paused, and then said with emphasis: "That great want is supplied by the first section of this amendment."

The court had spoken differently in the butchers' case and divided five to four. It had reaffirmed its rejection of national protection in freeing the Cruikshank mob. Hurtado had hanged, with Harlan alone dissenting. Now in the case of the businessman from New York, bootlegger in Vermont's eyes, two other justices joined Harlan in a belated attempt to give effect to the intentions of Bingham and the Thirty-Ninth Congress. Justice Field, who had been in the minority in the slaughterhouse case, and who then acquiesced in the backward steps of the court majority in the case of the Louisiana massacre of blacks—and the California denial of grand jury protection to an Hispano-American—joined a recent arrival, Justice David J. Brewer, in espousing Harlan's determined fight. Having abstained from the fight in those two key cases, Justice Field spoke out with clarity and vigor in a belated attempt to right the wrong done by the slaughterhouse decision.

Of the first ten amendments, Mr. Justice Field said: ". . . so far as they declare or recognize the rights of persons, they are rights belonging to them as citizens of the United States under the Constitution; and the Fourteenth Amendment, as to all such rights, places a limit on state power by ordaining that no State shall make or enforce any law which shall abridge them. . . . The State cannot apply to him, any more than the United States, the torture, the rack, the thumbscrew, or any cruel and unusual punishment, any more than it can deny to him security in his house, papers, and effects against unreasonable searches and seizures, or compel him to be a witness against himself in a criminal prosecution."

"I fully concur," said Justice Harlan, adding that being sentenced to more than fifty-four years in jail "inflicts punishment, which, in view of the character of the offenses committed, must be deemed cruel and unusual." What he meant was that the Eighth Amendment barred not only fiendish or barbaric methods of hurting prisoners but also jail sentences that were out of all proportion to the crime. The majority of the court, though, adamant and consistent with its recent history, decided the case as if the Fourteenth Amendment did not exist.

That was in 1892. Field was soon to retire, and Brewer to switch sides. Oliver Wendell Holmes, Jr., joined the court and silently sided with the majority. Harlan continued to fight on alone for the application of the Bill of Rights to the states. His last great utterance on the subject—delivered shortly after the base-clearing triple that he hit at the age of seventy-five—was in the case of an unfortunate banker, Albert Twining of New Jersey. In Twining's case, the court was to declare the states to be free from the limitations of the Fifth Amendment's barrier against compelling individuals, in criminal cases, to bear witness against themselves. This was the violation which Justice Field had compared with "the torture, the rack, [or] the thumbscrew" (all of which were barbaric methods of extracting evidence from people as well as primitive ways of "punishing" them) and with the unreasonable searches and seizures that were the hallmarks of English royal oppression.

Twining's case marked John Harlan's last great stand for the right of all Americans to be protected by their nation against the state governments that were supposed to have been curbed by the Fourteenth Amendment. How badly the rights of white Americans had been whittled down was shown in 1900, eight years before Twining's case came before the court. Charles Maxwell had been charged with robbery in Utah; for reasons of its own, that state had chosen to limit the jury in criminal cases to eight members. The Sixth Amendment's guarantee of a jury trial in federal cases had in an earlier case been carefully considered in the light of its history and declared to require a jury of twelve.

Maxwell's lawyers based their argument on two branches of the Fourteenth Amendment. It was a violation of his privileges and immunities to deny him a proper jury trial, they contended, and a denial of due process of law as well. Reaffirming the slaughterhouse case on "privileges" and "immunities" and the Hurtado case on due process, the court turned down Maxwell's appeal and stated that since the right of jury trial could be abolished altogether by the states it could be cut down to a jury of eight.

Justice Harlan's dissent was an eloquent reminder of the origins of trial by jury as the safeguard of a free people, "vital to the protection of liberty against arbitrary power." He spoke with measured emphasis as he quoted from a work by an earlier justice, Joseph Story: "The great object of a trial by jury in criminal cases is to guard against a spirit of oppression and tyranny on the part of rulers, and against a spirit of violence and vindictiveness on the part of the people. Indeed, it is often more important to guard against the latter than the former." Tartly, he reminded his brethren that they had recently held that "due process" in the Fourteenth Amendment required "just compensation" for property taken by the state, even though the Fifth Amendment contains an explicit pledge of just compensation quite apart from the due process guarantee. "It would seem that the protection of private property is of more consequence than the protection of the life and liberty of the citizen," Harlan wrote.

His dissent had shaken the court, and the writer of the majority opinion in Twining's case showed it. Admitting, as the majority now did, that the slaughterhouse case gave much less effect to the Fourteenth Amendment than some of the public men framing it intended and that the "criticism of this case has never entirely ceased" are large concessions. Despite the stubbornness shown by the majority, and the number of times he had already spoken out on the point, the great old dissenter was not content to remain silent!

"As I read the opinion of the court, it will follow from the general principles underlying it"—age had not tempered the great voice or stilled his wrathful indignation—"the Fourteenth Amendment would be no obstacle whatever in the way of a state law or practise under which, for instance, cruel or unusual punishments (such as the thumbscrew or the rack or burning at the stake) might be inflicted."

For all that the justices who had refused to overrule the slaughterhouse decision seemed to care, the states' right to burn the guilty at the stake was not threatened by the Fourteenth Amendment. And when the time came that the court was obliged to take action to protect free speech, or to prevent unreasonable searches by state officials, or double jeopardy—all of which Justice Harlan foresaw in his dissenting opinion—the court awkwardly, and to some to this day unconvincingly, gave protection to these privileges and immunities under another, less accurate label.

Chapter 17

Law and Order
in Chicago

Those decades during which the heart was being whittled out of the Fourteenth Amendment are known as our "Gilded Age." Profits that had been piled up during the Civil War years were on hand for investment. Virgin lands teeming with timber and mineral resources were ripe for the taking. Immigrants, the poor and hungry of other continents, were pouring into the ports to guarantee a labor supply at low cost for the owners and managers of the mushrooming industries.

That first Gilded Age was marked by the growth of great personal fortunes, unprecedented in number and size. The affluence of the rulers of new empires of railroads and steel, coal and oil, was acquired by methods that earned them the title of robber barons. They were hard working and hardheaded, unconcerned with the welfare of their workers, and they often used ruthless and unscrupulous means to destroy their competitors. To guarantee the peaceful enjoyment of their booty they were insistent upon "law and order."

Their idea of law and order was entirely one sided. It was of a law that protected property no matter how it was acquired. It meant an order that required of laboring men that they stand in line, hat in hand, to learn the wages, hours and working conditions under which they would be employed. "Labor agitators" who sought to organize workers to improve their lot were enemies of the society that the robber barons dominated, the government that they controlled and especially the press that they owned. Even worse than the agitators were those who had a vision of a social order in which wealth and poverty alike were abolished. One of their leaders answered the question "What is Property?" by saying "Property is theft." This idea was much too accurate a description of the robber barons who founded some of America's great fortunes. Those who spread it were targets of greater vilification than the labor agitators.

"Anarchos" is a Greek word that means, simply, "without a ruler." Some of the advocates of social change in the 1880s were proud to bear the name "anarchists," believing as they did that it was the kind of rule that men had that caused them to hate one another and exploit their fellows; they believed in a liberty that consisted primarily in the removal of all forcible control over the individual by the community. Since all forms of government rested on violence, they argued, all were wrong and harmful. They saw the police as perpetrators and the press as advocates of violence against workingmen and their leaders and many concluded that only by violence in self-defense could their cause be advanced.

In Chicago particularly the police were seen, over and over again, to employ violence as a means of terrorizing workers who sought to organize to improve working conditions. In that city, too, there gathered a number of followers of the anarchist creed who at the same time offered their services in the cause of labor organization. Their dream of a better society was not forgotten, but they were willing to ally themselves with those they saw as the victims of the factory owners, merchants and bankers for the sake of helping them to improve the awful conditions under which they lived and labored. Preachers, politicians and the press, all under the influence or the control of the men whose purses were threatened by the prospect of labor organization, combined to convert much of the nation to the belief that radical labor agitators must be exterminated in order to save America.

The fear and hatred that had been aroused as a result of industrial conflict and radical social theory converged in a criminal trial in Chicago in 1886. The outcome was a jury verdict that found guilty of conspiracy to murder eight men who had been proved not to have worked with the murderer in question, nor to have aided him, nor to have instructed or urged him to do his awful deed, nor even to have known him. They could not have, for no one knew or ever found out who the murderer was.

Recollections of the jury that had found men guilty without evidence might still have stirred Justice Harlan's memory as he wrote his dissent in Maxwell's case, the Utah decision in which he stood alone in arguing that the Fourteenth Amendment guaranteed a fair trial by an impartial jury. His remark about the relative importance of the protection of personal rights as against property rights, and his reference to the need to protect against a spirit of violence and vindictiveness, evoked memories of Chicago's Haymarket hangings of 1886, when the Supreme Court of the United States, with Harlan himself concurring, refused to interfere. He may have regretted in later years his failure to dissent, especially when he read the review of the case by an Illinois governor that came too late to save the lives of five innocent men.

Militant labor's May Day, the first of the month celebration that seems to be honored more abroad than here, was born on American soil. The first May Day was marked in Chicago as part of a Great nationwide general strike in support of the reduction of working hours to eight a day. While the organized labor movement was not very strong, and workingmen and their unions were not favored by law, the spirit of the American worker was fresh and responsive. The idea of a nationwide demonstration for a shorter work day caught on like wildfire, and hundreds of thousands joined the movement. In Chicago there was a flurry of strikes for independent grievances that had already begun earlier that year, including one that lasted many weeks at the McCormack farm equipment factory. Public tension was higher in the midwest city. Owners of the media that molded public opinion were particularly hostile to two of the leaders of the local eight-hour movement, Albert R. Parsons and August Spies.

These men were American radicals, editors who at the same time would speak whenever and wherever they could for industrial and social democracy. Parsons was a son of the American Revolution, one of his ancestors having been a major general in Washington's army. He had been a freelance labor agitator for a dozen years, and though based in Chicago had been known far and wide as one willing to live on little and to go wherever he might be called for the cause. Spies had come to America as a young man and learned whatever he knew of socialism and anarchism in the American labor struggles of 1877 and the years that followed.

Parsons and Spies were marked men. The police had watched them for months, hoping to find occasion to arrest and imprison them. On the eve of the first May Day, one major Chicago newspaper had singled them out for denunciation: "There are two dangerous ruffians at large in this city; two sneaking cowards who are trying to create trouble. One of them is named Parsons; the other is named Spies . . .

"Mark them for today. Keep them in view. Hold them personally responsible for any trouble that does occur. Make an example of them if trouble does occur."

These almost seem the words of one privately aware of some coming trouble, one who had perhaps arranged it for the very purpose of discrediting men like Parsons and Spies and the movement. In the light of what was about to happen, it is not unjust to conclude that there was a "frame-up" in preparation.

Before the French Revolution, men who held obnoxious or dangerous opinions were placed in the Bastille without trial by sealed letters under the king's hand. Wherever there has been a despotic regime, dissenters have been disposed of by command. For the crime of being the king's enemy, no witness, judge or jury was needed save for the king himself. The resistance movement that produced the Magna Carta began a long struggle whose fruit is found in the Bill of Rights to our own constitution. But men whose opposition was obnoxious also aroused hatred in a republic, and mob violence or rigged trials choked their opinions and discouraged others. The Fourteenth Amendment was supposed to end all that.

The phrase "frame-up" is an American contribution to a more picturesque English language. It means, of course, an action employing the forms of law for the purpose of jailing or executing a person who is innocent of the crime he is charged with and who is being put away for his opinions or political activity. A frame-up is not too different from a lynching; the latter merely lacks the mock or imitation trial used to cover up the act of vengeance and intimidation. The purpose of the Fourteenth Amendment's guarantee of "due process of law," and the idea behind the attempt to give federal protection to all of the Bill of Rights' privileges and immunities, was to terminate both lynchings and frame-ups. The Supreme Court in Cruikshank's case vetoed the action that Congress had taken against lynchings. In the Haymarket case, it was to disclaim the power to interfere with brazen frame-ups. This was during the period when it was stripping itself of the power to interfere with any state's bypassing of the procedures that were intended to make certain that only the guilty were punished for crimes.

The "trouble" that the *Chicago Daily Mail* had so confidently predicted arrived soon after the successful demonstrations and one-day strikes that Parsons and Spies had led on the First of May. On the third, Spies addressed a meeting composed mainly of lumber workers in an open area near the McCormack plant, whose striking employees also attended. He urged the workers to stick together and to keep up their united fight for the eight-hour day, for in that lay their only strength. All was peaceful until a factory bell rang near the end of his talk and strikebreakers began to emerge from the McCormack plant.

The sight of the men who had replaced them at their jobs after passing through their picket lines enraged the McCormack strikers, who surged away from the meeting to voice their feelings to the "scabs." There was some pushing and shoving, and additional police were called. Suddenly a massive number of Chicago police reserves arrived on the scene, with pistols drawn. Firing freely, they charged the ranks of strikers, wounding many and killing at least one. Spies, who personally witnessed the brutal actions of the police, joined a group of radical labor leaders in calling a protest meeting to be held in Chicago's Haymarket Square.

Parsons, who had been out of town on organizing work, returned to speak at the Haymarket meeting. It was a cold and dreary night, and the attendance was disappointing. Although one circular announcing the meeting and inviting attendance began "Revenge! Workingmen, To Arms," the meeting was entirely peaceable. Carter

Harrison, the Mayor of Chicago, came personally and mingled with the crowd. He wanted to see for himself what went on, but heard nothing in the speeches to give him concern. While Parsons was speaking a drizzle began to become uncomfortably like rain and the crowd dwindled. After hearing enough of Parsons' speech to satisfy himself that the speaker meant what he said when he declared "I am not here for the purpose of inciting anybody . . ." the mayor decided to leave. Before departing, he told the police officers in charge of the detail on duty at the square that reinforcements would not be needed.

Nevertheless, while the next (and last) speaker was droning on to his conclusion, and the crowd kept thinning out, there was a sudden interruption. As soon as police captain Bonfield learned that the mayor had gone, he marched upon the meeting at the head of a large detachment of uniformed men and shouted a command to the crowd to disperse. Before the speaker, Fielden, could fairly finish his protest that "We are peaceable . . ." a dynamite bomb sputtered through the air from somewhere in the dark. It exploded with deadly effect somewhere near the ranks of the police. Between the explosion and the shooting that followed, about ten people were killed.

The aftermath was grim, and if one can judge an event by its consequences the throwing of the Haymarket bomb could well have been the act of a deadly enemy of the radical labor movement, for the leaders of that wing of the movement suffered the most as a result. Not since the firing on Fort Sumter had the nation been so shaken. The middle and upper classes were frantic with fear and forebodings. The careless and merely romantic talk of the anarchists about the necessity of force to meet the force of police attacks on workers suddenly assumed a sinister aspect. All their wild words were played up by press, pulpit and politicians to make them appear to be enemies of the people. A ceaseless, daily chatter described them as threatening the safety of every home and the sanctity of all property. The wealthy and their spokesmen and allies, who had persistently pressed to destroy the prospect of real social revolution, saw their chance—if, indeed, they did not manufacture it.

Despite the many police on the scene and the feverish days of investigation that followed the explosion, no one was ever identified and arrested as the thrower of the bomb. The arrests were those of men who had been the leaders and spokesmen of the movement for radical social change. The charge was murder, despite the fact that no one could prove that the thrower of the bomb was not a police agent or a demented "loner." The conviction of the eight defendants could not have been obtained unless the jury was ready to convict them regardless of what the evidence might show. Such a jury was provided by a court bailiff who summoned for jury duty only "such men as would be sure to convict," a bailiff who boasted about the result of his efforts "that he had gotten ten or twelve men that would be sure to hang those fellows."

The admission that he had used such methods for this purpose did not come out until after the trial, but the stenographic record of the examination of the jurors as to their qualifications clearly showed that a hanging jury had been selected. After the Haymarket defendants—including Parsons and Spies—had been convicted and sentenced to hang for a murder perpetrated by an unknown person, a petition for review was brought to the Supreme Court of the United States. It was presented to Justice Harlan with a request for a stay of execution during the court's review of the case, and he deemed it sufficiently troublesome to refer it to the full membership of the court.

Since, prior to the ratification of the Fourteenth Amendment, the states were not bound to observe the safeguards of the Bill of Rights, local criminal convictions had not previously been examined by the United States Supreme Court. Despite the intentions of the Fourteenth's framers, the court in the slaughterhouse case had said that "privileges" and "immunities"—such as the right to a jury trial— were still not protected against state action. In Hurtado's case, the court had denied that the federal requirement for a grand jury accusation before forcing a person to defend himself against a serious criminal charge was binding on the states. Now it wavered, as it was faced for the first time with the question of whether a "frame-up," cast in the form of a trial, could be set aside by a federal court under the new addition to the federal constitution. The lawyers for the Haymarket Eight brought before the court such examples of jury selection as one who admitted frankly what his bias was but was ruled qualified to render an impartial verdict:

Q. You heard of this Haymarket meeting, I suppose?
A. Yes.
Q. Have you formed an opinion upon the question of the defendants' guilt or innocence upon the charge of murder?
A. I have.
Q. Have you expressed that opinion?
A. Yes.
Q. You still entertain it?
A. Yes.
Q. You believe what you read and what you heard?
A. I believe it, yes.
Q. Is that opinion such as to prevent you from rendering an impartial verdict in the case, sitting as a juror, under the testimony and the law?
A. I think it is.

Unwilling to go so far as to say that the denial of a fair trial was beyond its power of examination under the Fourteenth Amendment, the court chose another route for permitting the convictions and death sentences to stand. A court of law is more conscious that its role is played as part of the process of history than the other institutions that have power and exercise it in society. The Supreme Court was only too willing to yield to the mass clamor that called for death to the anarchists, but felt that it must justify itself not only to its audience of the day but also to the perhaps soberer and sterner judgment of those of a time to come. To shut the door on the Fourteenth Amendment by saying that no matter how gross the fraud on justice federal courts could not interfere with state convictions—that was the logic and direction of the course it had taken since the time of the rejection of the butchers' appeal. But to do so in the Haymarket case would have left the implication that injustice had been done. The court, therefore, would not deny its own power; instead it tortuously examined the cases of some of the jurors who had been wheedled and cajoled by judge and prosecutor into saying that, despite their preconceptions, they would render an impartial verdict. It was for the trial judge to say whether or not they were telling the truth when they denied the hold that their own prejudices had on them—and he was not "manifestly" in error.

And so the State of Illinois was permitted to hang four men, not because of their guilt in any crime, but "for their opinions," as William Dean Howells, respected writer of the day, noted. They were "judicially murdered," said Eugene Victor Debs a decade after their hanging. "They were called anarchists, but at their trial it was not proven that they had committed any crime or violated any law." When the time came for the name of Albert Parsons to be placed in the *Dictionary of American Biography,* it was to be said of him: "He was brave, upright, truthful, and passionately devoted to the cause of freedom and justice." When he and his comrades were about to be hanged, John Brown, Jr., son of the man executed for the raid on Harpers Ferry, sent them a gift of fruit from his farm "as a token of sympathy for them and their cause."

Within a few years after their death a governor of Illinois took office, John Peter Altgeld, who had been troubled by the trial and execution and was determined to study the record. One of the opinions that had moved him was that of Lyman Trumbull, distinguished framer of the Fourteenth Amendment from Illinois, who had said that the trial took place "at a time of great public excitement, when it was about impossible that they should have a fair and impartial trial." Although he must have known or suspected that to do his duty would cost him reelection and bring his career to an end, Altgeld freed the three remaining Haymarket prisoners. He did so after writing a careful analysis of all the evidence, weighing it and concluding that the trial had been unfair, the judge stubbornly determined to see the defendants convicted, and the prisoners innocent of the crime.

Most people who attacked and condemned Altgeld for doing his duty as he saw it were obsessed with an idea as erroneous and irrelevant to real "law and order" as the contention of an editor named Browne, who rose after a meeting at which a young lawyer named Clarence Darrow had read a paper concluding that the Haymarket Eight were innocent.

"Don't you think it was necessary," he asked Darrow, "in order that society be protected, that these men be hanged as an example, even if they were innocent?"

"Why, Mr. Browne," answered Darrow, "that would be anarchy."

Chapter 18

A Carpetbagger's Lost Cause

John Marshall Harlan labored long and lovingly over the writing of his dissenting opinions. Before he finished his many years of service on the court he had dissented from its decisions more than three hundred times, a record that still stands. He tried to be as clear and as persuasive as he possibly could, when he wrote in dissent, for he knew that he was asking a court and a public of some future day for vindication.

It was inevitable, in view of the damage done to the Fourteenth Amendment by the slaughterhouse and Cruikshank cases, that the time would come when the court would strike down Charles Sumner's Civil Rights Law of 1875. That law depended on the intent of the framers that all the privileges and immunities of citizenship should be given national protection, and that Congress should have power to act on its own to protect all Americans in being treated equally as citizens. These cases had knocked out those props before Harlan had even been appointed to the court.

A story has been passed down that Justice Harlan spent a sleepless night trying to get started on his dissenting opinion. When she saw how he struggled, his wife brought down from a hiding place a treasured souvenir that they had acquired from a collector when they arrived in Washington to live. It was said to be the inkstand that Chief Justice Taney had used, the very one, perhaps, in which his pen had been dipped when he wrote the fateful words that fastened the shackles more firmly on Americans of African ancestry. Harlan's thoughts were unblocked. "His pen fairly flew," his wife recalled, once he had the benefit of the inkwell haunted with such memories.

David J. Brewer was a fellow justice who ascended the bench after the decision in the civil rights cases. He was called on to speak at a dinner given for the Kentuckian to celebrate his twenty-fifth anniversary on the court. He began by saying, "My talk will not be long, no longer than one of Harlan's dissents, and perhaps no better." He made his intentions quite clear by going on to say, "All men are said to have their hobbies, and Justices of the Supreme Court are no exception. Mr. Justice Harlan has a hobby—a judicial hobby—and that is the Constitution of the United States."

Returning to the bantering manner that marks such talks, Justice Brewer continued: "Some mistakes a man may never regret. Brother Harlan made a mistake in holding the Civil Rights Bill constitutional. The Court said so; and in our governmental system the Supreme Court, on constitutional questions, is infallible."

Becoming serious again, Brewer continued: "But it was a mistake on the side of equal rights, and no act done or word said in behalf of liberty and equality ever fails to touch humanity with inspiring, prophetic thrill."

Justice Brewer did not have quite the sense of prophecy to join Justice Harlan in another dissent that was filed a dozen years after the civil rights case, but he was troubled enough about it to abstain from joining the majority. This was *Plessy vs. Ferguson,* the case with which Harlan's name is most frequently associated. In that 1896 dissent, John Marshall Harlan correctly prophesied the evil consequences of the majority's ruling and forecast correctly that it would one day be erased from the tablets of the law. In writing it he had the assistance of an attorney, the advocate who represented Homer Plessy, whose contribution to our constitutional history is not given as much credit as it deserves.

Albion W. Tourgee was uniquely fitted to help Justice Harlan spell out the answer to the seemingly knotty question that was to be presented by Plessy's case. His qualifications did not come from years of experience as a constitutional lawyer, or in appearing to argue cases in the Supreme Court of the United States. He had attended law school, but for the decade and a half before the Plessy case came to court he had hardly touched a brief or advised a client. His ability was the product of life itself.

Tourgee had been a real live "carpetbagger," a northern resident who had migrated to the South following the Civil War. His life gives the lie to the propagandists of the period whose version of events after the war was concocted to justify and excuse the Cruikshank mobs and their subversion of the states that had established biracial governments during reconstruction. That version was that the former slaves had been unready for self-government, that they had been misled and imposed upon by two types of white scoundrels: the "carpetbaggers," scheming adventurers who went south with all their possessions in a suitcase ("carpetbag"), and "scalawags," renegade white Southerners who sold out their own people to combine with the carpetbaggers in misleading the Negroes.

Tourgee had his family name from a French Huguenot ancestor who had come to the colony of Rhode Island to escape persecution in the late seventeenth century. Albion divided his youth between Massachusetts and Ohio, and managed to acquire a good deal of New England idealism that blended in him with a tendency toward gallantry and romanticism. His greatest interest as a student at the University of Rochester was in literature, but his desire to become a writer had to be deferred. His childhood sweetheart's interest in abolitionism and the national crisis of 1861 combined to draw him not only into the army but also into the cause for which the war came to be fought.

A serious back injury sustained in the line of duty forced Captain Tourgee to leave the army by the end of 1863. This prevented the fulfillment of an ambition to obtain the command of a company in one of the multiplying black regiments. He had requested the transfer as the fame of these new outfits had begun to spread.

He returned home to complete his legal education. An industrious young man, he did his law clerking during the period that preceded the close of the war and also worked as a newspaperman and later as a teacher at a prep school. As the nation's civil conflict came to a close, a secret ambition to return to the South revived. He had been fascinated with its landscape and its people, and he had the added impetus of medical advice that a warmer climate the year round would be easier on his aching back.

After making inquiries and receiving encouragement from North Carolina's postwar governor, Tourgee took his family to settle at the pleasant piedmont town of Greensboro. His purpose in going south was not to enter politics, nor did he expect that the law practice that he opened as an adjunct to a business in which he invested his savings would take more than a fraction of his time. But he was to find a larger group of pro-union local residents than he expected; the independent whites who owned no slaves were naturally attracted by his ability and his outspoken opinions. His resentment at what he saw in the local treatment of the newly freed Americans, the Southerners who had been loyal to the nation for which he had fought, aroused in Tourgee an indignation which made it difficult for him to resist allying himself with them.

Much of what he experienced on a local scale, at the grass roots, resembled what the Joint Committee on Reconstruction had heard described as the condition of life in the former rebel and border states. Tourgee decided, on the basis of his own experience, that the Fourteenth Amendment—splendid though its ideals might be—was but a "makeshift" that was doomed to fail. He warned his antislavery friends in the North that "No law, no constitution, no matter how cunningly framed, can shield the poor men of the South from the domination of that very aristocracy from which rebellion sprung, when once the States are established here."

The future would prove correct his prophecy that once the re-bellious states were readmitted, even with the protections of the Fourteenth Amendment, the masses of poor, uneducated and inexperienced white and black loyalists would not long hold power against the wealth, experience and ruthlessness that would be orga-nized against them. Meanwhile, he continued to fight the good fight.

He accepted nomination to the constitutional convention that was held under the Reconstruction Act. His platform included political and civil equality for all, elimination of property qualifications for jurors; free schools and prison reform. Elected to North Carolina's Constitutional Convention of 1868, his skill as a debater and his ag-gressiveness made him a leading figure. He was able to put over all but one of his platform pledges, and he helped to introduce lasting reforms in the state's legal procedure. It was but natural and proper that he was elected a judge of the state superior court, a position he was to hold through the next eight years with credit and distinction.

The esteem that was to be privately expressed for Tourgee as a judge was some small compensation for the barrage of abuse pub-licly directed against Tourgee the carpetbagger. Even while the con-vention was still in session his dedication to progressive principle won for him the false accusation of a criminal past. Journalists re-ferred to the meeting as consisting of "Baboons, Monkeys, Mules, Tourgee and other Jackasses." The campaign for judicial office was marked by such vignettes as this—a brief excerpt from a diatribe that greeted the readers of one morning paper: "This Tourgee is the meanest looking man it has ever been our misfortune to meet. The pirate; the cutthroat; the despicable, mean, crawling, sneaking vil-lain have been portrayed by nature, with a master hand, in every lineament of his countenance. The mark of infamy is stamped indel-ibly on his brow. . . ."

Such language did not discourage him, nor was he frightened by the threats to his physical safety. His judicial assignment covered a group of eight counties and he traveled from one courthouse to an-other, frequently alone, driving his own horse and buggy. From the roadside and from the bench he learned at first hand what the prob-lems and prospects of a democratic biracial society were. Dominat-ing the scene, wherever he went, was a breakdown of law and order that was caused by underground opposition to the reconstruction of life and race relations on the basis of the new amendments to the Constitution.

Tourgee saw the courage and simple dignity with which the newly freed American citizens sought to establish themselves in little farm-steads or workshops. Others asked no more than to work on the farms and fields where they had labored before, but they asked fair treatment and the right to live as free men. There were some who were interested in playing a part in political life: they had fought for the country and its flag, and its Constitution had been amended to invite their participation. Among all there was a thirst for education, and courageous teachers came from the North to help satisfy this need.

Tourgee and his wife befriended the teachers and offered them the warmth of home surroundings to make up for the cold and hostile reception they were given by the "better people" in the community. But the judge's courage and stubbornness could not prevent widespread interference by the Klan that was aimed at the modest hopes and ambitions of the freedmen. His pessimistic prediction of 1867 was to be fulfilled: integrated democracy was a delicate plant that could not merely be sown and left alone to grow. It was uprooted and destroyed because of neglect by the nation.

The time was inevitably to come when Tourgee could no longer remain in North Carolina. He had ignored threats against his life and escaped attempts at assassination. He saw political allies—both black and white—murdered in cold blood. One case he was to describe a few years later, the death of a friend to whom he gave the name of Jerry, which took place near the courthouse and in sight of a village church early on a Sunday morning: "Upon the limb of a low-branching oak not more than forty steps from the Temple of Justice, hung the lifeless body of old Jerry. The wind turned it slowly to and fro. The snowy hair and beard contrasted strangely with the dusky pallor of the peaceful face, which seemed even in death to proffer a benison to the people of God who passed to and fro from the house of prayer. . . . Over all pulsed the sacred echo of the Sabbath bells. The sun shone brightly. The wind rustled the autumn leaves. A few idlers sat upon the steps of the court-house, and gazed carelessly on the ghastly burden on the oak. The brightly dressed church-goers enlivened the streets. Not a colored man was to be seen."

This passage was written for a novel that Tourgee was to have published, after he left the South, under the title *A Fool's Errand.* The fool was the judge himself, the foolishness the mission on which he had spent ten years of his life, trying to make a reality of the Constitution of the United States in his adopted state. Yet it was a noble foolishness, a heroic foolishness, and he did not depict it as anything else.

With the publication of *A Fool's Errand,* Albion W. Tourgee, ex-judge and refugee carpetbagger who bore the title proudly and defiantly, began a new career. The impulse to self-expression and the love for literature that had marked his student days had never left him, and now they came full flower. His first books, especially *A Fool's Errand* and its immediate sequel, *Bricks Without Straw,* portrayed in fiction the essential truths about reconstruction and the people who had played a part in it. They may be usefully consulted to this day to remedy the picture given in most histories written since then in which, in the name of truth, fiction is offered for what had happened in the South after the Civil War.

That fictional treatment of history was already in process when Tourgee began his novels, and in more than one passage he referred to it. He saw contemporary newspapers permeated with falsehoods— the papers that later would be cited as evidence by historians. "The most amazing thing connected with this matter, however, was the fact that the press of the North, almost without exception, echoed the clamor and invective of the Southern journals." Especially was this true of the treatment of the radical whites, whose ideas were transformed from the abolitionist movement into the Fourteenth and Fifteenth Amendments, and whose actions consisted of efforts to make those amendments a reality. "In nothing has the South shown its vast moral superiority over the North than in this," Tourgee wrote in *A Fool's Errand*. " 'I pray thee curse me this people,' it said to the North, first of the 'abolitionists,' and then of the 'carpet-baggers;' and the North cursed, not knowing whom it denounced, and not pausing to inquire whether they were worthy of stripes or not. Perhaps there is no other instance in history in which the conquering power has discredited its own agents, . . . espoused the prejudices of its conquered foes, and poured . . . contempt upon the only class in the conquered territory who defended its acts, supported its policy, promoted its aim, or desired its preservation and continuance."

Tourgee's first books were immensely popular. *A Fool's Errand* sold over two hundred thousand copies and was described, in various publications, as being "as serviceable in enlightening the North about the startling events of the reconstruction period as 'Uncle Tom's Cabin' was in illustrating the phases of an earlier epoch." The effect of the books was almost sufficient to bring about a reversal of the trend in the rest of the nation to turn its back on the South, where most of the blacks of the United States still lived. But it was only an 'almost' because of an assassin's bullet.

The election of James A. Garfield in 1880—partly as a result of the sentiment created by Tourgee's best sellers—might have marked a new effort at a national reconstruction. The president elect had been influenced in his views by Tourgee's writings and meetings with him, and there were phrases in his inaugural address that had the earmarks of Tourgee's thinking and writing: "The elevation of the Negro race from slavery to the full rights of citizenship is the most important political change we have known since the adoption of the Constitution of 1787 . . . there was no middle ground for the Negro race between slavery and equal citizenship. There can be no permanent disfranchised peasantry in the United States. . . . So far as my authority can lawfully extend, they [the blacks] shall enjoy the full and equal protection of the Constitution and the laws. . . . To violate the freedom and the sanctities of the suffrage is more than an evil. It is a crime which, if persisted in, will destroy the Government itself."

Soon afterwards, an assassin's bullet brought an end to the hopes that were inspired in Tourgee and others by that inaugural. The so-called "Lost Cause," the cause of the Confederacy, to establish in each state the "right" to regulate race relations and to deprive its inhabitants of the freedoms of the Bill of Rights had prevailed.

Even then, Tourgee would not give up. Like Don Quixote, dreaming the impossible dream, he persisted in his own cause, which a dozen years later would bring him before the Supreme Court of the United States to offer the arguments in Homer Plessy's case. Meanwhile he continued a career of writing and lecturing in which he sought to create, in behalf of the Fourteenth and Fifteenth Amendments, "a public sentiment that would not only permit, but demand their enforcement, in letter and spirit, in every nook and hamlet in the land."

Chapter 19

Color Caste
or Color-blind?

The publication of *A Fool's Errand* naturally led to heated controversy. Any book that presents a partisan picture, even if its one-sidedness is justified, will arouse discussion and attacks that seek to discredit its author and its message. Often the attack will be welcome, for it will help to draw attention that the book might not otherwise receive.

So it was with the carpetbagger's novel. There were not merely attacks. Whole books were written in an attempt to diminish the damage done to the Ku Klux cause. At least four were published whose names survive today; one was so extreme as to begin with a full-fledged defense of slavery itself.

The most popular attack on Tourgee's version of the events of reconstruction was entitled *A Reply to a Fool's Errand By One of the Fools*. It was written by William C. Royall, a Confederate veteran from Virginia who had come as a reverse carpetbagger himself (like so many of his fellow Southerners) to settle and prosper in New York City, where he had become a well-known and successful attorney.

Royall denounced Tourgee's book as "a willful and malicious libel upon a noble and generous people." Although the ex-judge had already compiled a supplement to his book, based on a full Senate investigation of the Klan, documenting his charges and called *The Invisible Empire*, Royall ignored the evidence and produced nothing in support of his version. He was, as the *New York Tribune* put it, "satisfied with pronouncing the statements of Judge Tourgee as 'false as hell'—a mode of reasoning which can hardly be called conclusive."

Stubborn and prejudiced though he was in defending his version of the facts of reconstruction, attorney Royall spoke differently about the constitutional amendments—particularly the Fourteenth—that had been drawn to curtail invasion of human rights by the states. It was almost as if his loyalty to people of his class in the

South had blinded him to the truth of what Tourgee had written, while his integrity as an attorney compelled him to tell the truth about the purpose and meaning of the new birth of liberty launched by the Thirty-Ninth Congress.

In a rambling postscript to his criticism of the carpetbagger's defense of his role in the South, Royall reached out to reprove the Supreme Court for certain recent decisions concerning the exclusion of Negroes from jury service. Pouncing on what he called the court's 'inconsistency,' he condemned it for having, in the slaughterhouse case, declined to grant the protection of the Fourteenth Amendment to "all the ordinary matters of personal right—those fundamental matters of citizenship without which human liberty cannot exist." The slaughterhouse decisions, wrote Royall, were an "emasculation of the Amendment." The states, he insisted, should have been prevented from interfering with "those privileges and immunities of a citizen which are fundamental, and without which true liberty cannot exist."

In his criticism of the drastic limitations placed by the court on the Fourteenth Amendment, Royall had been even more outspoken in an essay he had written for a professional journal, *The Southern Law Review.* He was bitter about the separation the court had created between the rights of citizens of the United States "as such"—like the right to go to seaports and come to Washington in cherry blossom time—and the rights of citizens as state citizens, which included the really important rights of free assembly, fair trial and the like. Those, the court had ruled in 1873 in the case of the butchers' quarrel, "must rest for their security and protection where they have heretofore rested," with the separate states. The decision was pure nonsense, said Royall: "Ninety nine out of every hundred educated men, upon reading this section over, would at first say that it forbade a state to make or enforce a law which abridged any privilege or immunity whatever of one who was a citizen of the United States; and it is only by an effort of ingenuity that any other sense can be discovered that it can be forced to bear."

And, after doing the perfectly lawyerlike job, which Justice Miller and his majority had failed to do, of examining what Thaddeus Stevens and Congress had said were their intentions in framing the Fourteenth, he noted: "There was perfect unanimity of opinion between senators and representatives, Democrats and Republicans, upon one point, to wit, that the purpose of the first section was, and its effect would be, to incorporate the Civil Rights Bill bodily into the Constitution. The Republicans contended for its adoption because that was its purpose and that would be its effect. The Democrats opposed its adoption because that was its purpose and that would be its effect."

When the court majority slashed away nine tenths of the ground that was intended to be covered by the "privileges and immunities" guarantee of the first clause of the Fourteenth Amendment, it was doing so for a good motive, from Royall's point of view. The purpose—to curb the progress of federal power—was patriotic, he agreed. "But was it wise? Can it ever be wise for the court to force a meaning upon the language of the Constitution to avert a fancied or threatened danger?" Of course not, said Royall.

Tourgee resented Royall's attack on his book. But he must have had great respect for the honesty with which the ex-Confederate had exposed the betrayal of the Fourteenth Amendment by the 1873 court. The death of President Garfield had put an end to the hope of immediate renewal of national leadership for interracial justice. The resentment with which the slaughterhouse decision and its result, the freeing of the Cruikshank group, had been greeted had quickly subsided. Sectional lines were beginning to blur for business reasons as Northerners came to accept the idea that the separate states should "solve" their race relations problems on their own. To make this possible, most men quietly assented to the misreading of the Constitution by the court. That was what made the perception of a maverick Southerner like Royall especially striking.

Another ex-Confederate soldier, wounded twice in battle for his "bonnie blue flag," described the state of mind that made possible the court decisions stripping national protection from civil rights. "The popular mind in the old free states," said writer George Washington Cable of New Orleans in a commencement address at the University of Alabama in 1884, "weary of strife at arm's length, bewildered by its complications, vexed by many a blunder, eager to turn to the cure of other evils, and even tinctured by that race feeling whose grosser excesses it would so gladly see suppressed, has retreated from its uncomfortable dictational attitude and thrown the whole matter over to the states of the South."

And so Sumner's civil rights bill went down. While the court majority was declaring that Congress was as powerless to protect American citizens from the humiliation of being turned away from the door of public places as it was to protect them from mob violence, Justice Harlan's pen, dipped in Taney's inkstand, angrily answered: "Constitutional provisions, adopted in the interest of liberty, and for the purpose of securing . . . rights inhering in a state of freedom, and belonging to American citizenship, have been so construed as to defeat the ends the people desired to accomplish, and which they supposed they had accomplished by changes in their fundamental law."

During the rest of that difficult decade Tourgee and Cable were outstanding among the few whites who continued to fight and work for the restoration of justice. Cable's idea was to arouse a "silent

South," the whites of conscience who spoke his drawl and shared his background, to insist that their own state governments return to decency and law and order. Tourgee felt that only national action would be effective. Undiscouraged by the seeming hopelessness of his effort, he was militant, vocal and persistent.

His purpose was to persuade blacks and whites to unite in order to reverse the tragic trend in the land. He argued, as did Cable, that the existence of a dominant race that treated another as inferior was as injurious to the ruler as to the ruled. He called for "protest, remonstrance, denunciation—continuous, passionate, determined." While he had many friendly correspondents who supported his efforts, which were carried on not only through public lecturing but also through the pioneer example of the regular newspaper column commentary on public affairs, he was also the target of many venomous attacks.

He was a man agitating for an idea whose time had not come. The trend was to go from bad to worse. Assured of immunity from federal interference, the dominant whites in the South now wanted to place legal dress on their relationship with the Americans of African ancestry who lived among them. The tyranny of the mob had kept the black man in his place: away from the polls, fearing to assert his rights as a citizen. There began the passage of laws designed to make mob action less necessary: to write on tablets of stone that one race was, as a group, inferior to the other.

What was desired was a kind of "final solution," something that would put the stamp of law and order on that which had been achieved by lawlessness and disorder. Ideally it was to make every black American conscious of a supposed inferiority, to admit it, to accept it. At the same time, whites had to be made to understand that no spark of conscience was to disturb them, that moral or religious ideas about the "brotherhood of man" were irrelevant to the mistreatment of a different kind of man. They were not to think that it was for economic advantage, for the material convenience of a ruling group, that the former slaves, or free blacks and their descendants, were to be forbidden to rise, or to think themselves citizens, or even to employ skills as workmen that they had acquired before the Civil War. They were to be persuaded that this was not injustice, but the way things ought to be.

It came to be felt that the solution had been found in the imposition of the force of state law behind the idea of a caste system. The word "caste" may not have been in their minds, but it represented exactly what they were trying to achieve by a whole new thicket of laws that came to be called "Jim Crow" laws. The word caste came from the Portuguese word for "race" but its modern meaning referred to a class system with rigid separation between each race. It originated with the application of the word by Portuguese explorers to the social system found in India. There, with the support of the power of religion and of the state, the population was divided into severely separated classes, with the members of each taught from the cradle to believe that the officially described superior classes were as God decreed and the state rightly required.

It is usually difficult to do evil in a democracy unless it is disguised. Sometimes the deception is achieved by an explanation that makes the evil course seem fair or proper. That was what happened when the introduction of the caste system into America was accompanied by laws to keep colored Americans from voting. The force and threats that had kept blacks from the polls, or the fraud that had kept their ballots from being counted, were replaced by a pretext. The pretense of the laws was that it was not the Negro who was disfranchised but the ignorant. "Literacy" tests became the great barrier to obedience to the Fifteenth Amendment. Yet ways were found to permit ignorant whites to vote.

The disguise with which the evil of segregation was introduced was the use of the word "equal" in the first laws requiring the separation of American citizens regardless of their wishes. Accommodations, schools, all sorts of facilities were required to be equal by the new breed of Jim Crow laws. This fooled no one. If clues were needed to the real intent, they were found in the common provision that separation was not forced when the contact came about with the black man or woman in the role of servant.

From his earliest days as a carpetbagger, Tourgee had thrilled to see the resistance to oppression that repeatedly arose among black Americans. Only when their cause was hopeless, when it became clear that the United States government would not honor its commitment, did self-defense subside. As the new aggression of the Jim Crow laws began to spread, Tourgee was delighted to learn from afar of a new upsurge of resistance. He was pleased and flattered that he was called upon to guide and lead it, from a distance of a thousand miles.

In a letter from an admirer, a militant black who was passing through New Orleans, he had learned of the plans of a group there to fight a new state law. Louisiana, locale of the butchers' battle that had cost the heart of the Fourteenth Amendment, Cruikshank's murderous conspiracy, and Charles Sauvinet's fight for the right to sip coffee, was to be the battleground again. When the law was passed compelling railways "to provide equal but separate accommodations" Louis Martinet, a black attorney and physician who was a fighting editor as well, called for a boycott of the railroads and a test case.

"Submission to such outrage," Tourgee wrote Martinet when he heard of the impending fight, "tends only to their multiplication. It is by constant resistance to oppression that the race must ultimately win equality of right." The organizer of the New Orleans fight was glad to have Tourgee's encouragement. The former carpetbagging judge, novelist and crusading columnist was to become lawyer again, chief counsel to the "Citizens' Committee to Test the Constitutionality of the Separate Car Law," with "control from beginning to end."

The fateful case began in June of 1892 with a deliberate violation of the Jim Crow law by Homer Plessy, who had volunteered to take the step. When he refused to leave the "white" car, Plessy was arrested and brought before Judge John Ferguson. An appeal under Louisiana procedure was brought with the names of the contending parties as *Plessy vs. Ferguson,* a name that was destined to live in infamy.

Tourgee was almost bound to be defeated. It was 1896 now, the Civil War and the contribution of the black regiments to the saving of the nation thirty years past and forgotten. The interests of men of wealth and the prejudices of the poor whites coincided. The militant leader Frederick Douglass had died, and by 1896 the most quoted Negro figure was Booker T. Washington, who seemed to be willing to have his people forgo their rights for an indefinite period, so difficult appeared the task of recapturing them. Harlan, the white Southerner, alone of the justices on the nation's highest bench seemed attentive to Tourgee's words.

The reward of the appearance of the carpetbagger in the Supreme Court chamber was the most striking collaboration between advocate and judge in constitutional history. Examples abound, of which the best known is found in Justice Harlan's words: "Our Constitution is color-blind, and neither knows nor tolerates classes among citizens." The source of that phrase was Tourgee's pungent "Justice is pictured blind and her daughter, the Law, ought at least to be color-blind." Even more important than this colorful figure of speech was the underlying point that Tourgee was trying to make: the Thirteenth and Fourteenth Amendments were intended to eliminate the special kind of "caste" system that slavery stood for; it was this that was being reintroduced behind the mask of "equal but separate."

"A law assorting the citizens of a State," argued Tourgee, "on the basis of race, is obnoxious to the spirit of Republican institutions, because it is a legalization of *caste.*" He underlined the word himself in his brief, the written argument that is often more important than what is said in the courtroom. Said Harlan in response: "There is no caste here. In my opinion, the judgment this day rendered will, in time, prove to be quite as pernicious as the decision made by this tribunal in the *Dred Scott* case." Such regulations upon the basis of race, he went on, are "cunningly devised to defeat legitimate results of the war . . . [and they] can have no other result than to render permanent peace impossible, and to keep alive a conflict of races." Tourgee had asked, in his brief, whether it was believed possible that the people in granting citizenship to all Americans "meant to restore that very sovereignty which was the excuse for the resistance to national authority and which the bloody tide of war had only just overthrown?"

If such laws could be passed, Tourgee asked, to emphasize how far they would go, "Why not require all colored people to walk on one side of the street and the whites on the other? Why may it not require every white man's house to be painted white and every colored man's black?" In responding to Tourgee's logic, Harlan went further and forecast the sorry path the nation would take in its abandonment of the Constitution: "Why may a State not so regulate the use of the streets of its cities and towns as to compel white citizens to keep on one side of a street and black citizens to keep on the other? . . . Why may it not require sheriffs to assign whites to one side of a court room and blacks to the other? . . . The present decision, it may well be apprehended, will not only stimulate aggressions, more or less brutal and irritating, upon the admitted rights of colored citizens, but will encourage the belief that it is possible by means of state enactments to defeat the beneficent purposes which the people of the United States had in view when they adopted the recent amendments to the Constitution."

Many attorneys have had the supreme legal thrill of knowing that they contributed, by their skill and talent, to a victory for constitutional rights. Albion Tourgee did not have that satisfaction. He did see, as the fruit of his efforts, Justice Harlan's powerful dissenting opinion. And the ultimate victory was to be Tourgee's, half a century after his death. His statement of the meaning of equality, as reflected in Harlan's dissent, had remained as a spur and a target for Americans fighting together to restore their constitution.

Chapter 20

This is Due Process?

The distant future was of little importance in 1896, and the immediate effect of Tourgee's defeat was disaster. The trend that had been moving from poor to bad in human relations now went from bad to worse. All across the South (and in some parts of what we might think of as the North as well) there was a stepping up of the drive to put the caste system into effect. The rules that were meant to ensure that whites would remember their "superiority," and that blacks would stay put in their place, were spreading like a contagious disease.

Separate cars on railroad trains naturally led to separate waiting rooms and even separate ticket windows. Finally, there was separation in streetcars and taxis in cities and towns, at drinking fountains in the street and at bars and soda fountains off the street, in restaurants, hotels, hospitals and jails. In many places, a "colored" Bible and a "white" Bible were kept for swearing in witnesses at court trials.

The separation that was being introduced was never "equality." In the trains, the coaches for colored were dirty and filled with cinders from the burning coal of the locomotives. The drinking fountains for blacks were less sanitary, the seats in theaters less comfortable. All the forces of state power were put into gear to show black Americans that their place was a second place, an inferior place.

Worst of all were the schools. Within a few years most states were spending from ten to fifteen times as much on the education of white children as they were on the education of blacks. This was taking place at a time when perhaps ninety percent of the Americans of African ancestry lived in the states that practiced this evil. Our nation still suffers from the consequences of this savage injustice.

One of the lowest depths to which the court sank was in its decision in the case of Berea College. This little private institution had been established in Kentucky before the Civil War, with a charter that proclaimed the brotherhood of all men under one God. Attendance at Berea was voluntary and no state aid was requested or received. Students were accepted regardless of race or color. But all that was to be stopped by brute state force in 1904, when Kentucky's state legislature forbade even the voluntary, private association of persons of different colors in educational buildings. The justices of the Supreme Court of the United States ruled, when the case reached them in 1908, that the forced separation of the Berea College students—seven hundred young white Southerners who *wanted* to learn side by side with their black brothers—was not in violation of the Fourteenth Amendment. Even Oliver Wendell Holmes, now a member of the high bench, silently joined in the court's action.

But not John Marshall Harlan. At seventy-two years of age, in one of the last of his great dissents, his voice boomed out again. The decision reflected how much Americans had become "inoculated with prejudice of race." He chose as the ground for his decision one which he hoped would shake up his brethren on the bench. It would not be enough, he decided, to remind them of the "equal protection of the laws" to which they had for so long turned their backs. The right to give instruction, he insisted, was a right of "liberty and property." That liberty and property could not be impaired by the State of Kentucky without violating the Fourteenth Amendment.

Liberty and property! These words, in the Fourteenth Amendment, were straight out of the due process clause: "nor shall any State deprive any person of life, liberty, or property, without due process of law." As originally written, the phrase meant that no one suspected of having committed a crime could be jailed without fair and legal treatment before and during the trial. It had been included in the amendment as a guarantee of fair procedure. Too many blacks and whites, loyal to the nation, had been unjustly punished by the states, or harassed by mobs with state connivance.

Due process of law—and its denial—had had a long and seamy history since those words were first written into the Fifth Amendment as an intended check on the potential tyranny of the national government. We have seen how the "process" by which the alleged fugitive slave had been deprived of liberty was not "due"—it was totally unfair. No right of counsel, no right to call witnesses, no jury trial— these and other injustices combined to make up the process for recapturing human property, a process that disregarded the commandments of the Fifth Amendment.

The framers of the Fourteenth Amendment had intended and sought to revive the rights protected by the Fifth, and to extend them to the protection of people in the states against acts of their local governments. This intent had been defeated in a variety of cases, as we have seen, involving bankers and anarchists, burglars and bootleggers. The privileges and immunities clause of the Fourteenth

Amendment, and its due process clause as well, had been nullified as far as the protection of human rights went. Chicago could prosecute and hang anarchists without evidence of guilt by the verdict of an admittedly biased jury.

Meanwhile, on another front, "due process" had been turned topsy-turvy. The words that had been put together to protect the underdog and the poor, to preserve the rights of all Americans, were being twisted to serve as a tool to prevent their protection. At the very same time that the court was permitting state interference with liberty of association at Berea College, and condoning the manipulation of state courts as instruments of possible injustice, it was forbidding state action to protect laborers and farmers from those who preyed on them.

The plain and ordinary meaning of words can sometimes be twisted by lawyers, and judges are only lawyers who have been able to achieve an ambition. The outcome of trials that embody charges against people can involve a possible threat to their lives, in cases in which the death sentence is a penalty, their liberty, when they may be imprisoned, or their property, when they may be fined or subjected to forfeiture as a penalty. The process that leads to the imposition of such penalties must be fair: that was all that was intended by the first statesmen who provided for processes that were "due" in written constitutions. But the pressure of the growth of a capital-based system of economic relations, and the persuasiveness of the advocates retained by the owners of capital, resulted in the transformation of these words and the reading of an entirely new meaning into them.

The judges did not work their transformation immediately after the Fourteenth Amendment was written into the Constitution. Nor, it must be remembered, did the change that they wrought outlast the 1930s by long. But for a period of about four decades they did succeed in using the Constitution as a barrier against industrial and social democracy at the very same time that they denied it any value for the protection of civil rights and liberties.

The story of the use of the Fourteenth Amendment to interfere with state action taken in the interests of workers and small farmers begins, in a way, with the same slaughterhouse case that settled the butchers' battle of New Orleans. In rejecting the plea of the ousted slaughterers, the court did more than take the protection of "privileges or immunities" out of the amendment. The lawyers for the butchers deprived of the right to do their own slaughtering—as all lawyers will, in such a case—beset the court with every kind of argument they could conceive of. One fairly novel claim that they made, one that the framers of the Fourteenth Amendment would hardly have recognized, was that their clients were being deprived of property without "due process of law" by being forced to pay others to kill their cattle. The court made short work of this pioneer attempt to use words intended to guarantee fair procedures for the peculiar purpose of interfering with business regulation. "It is sufficient to say," answered Justice Miller, "that under no construction of that provision that we have ever seen, or any that we deem admissible," could the Louisiana law "be held to be a deprivation of property."

While the court continued to hold tenaciously to the idea that the personal rights, the privileges and immunities, of citizens were all but completely at the tender mercy of the states, it soon began to tiptoe away from the perfectly sound treatment that Justice Miller had given to the businessmen's claim to "due process" protection. In the cases of Hurtado, the Chicago anarchists, O'Neill and so on, it repeatedly rejected the argument that the protection of the specific commandments of the Bill of Rights had been intended by the Fourteenth to shield individual citizens against unfair procedures by the states. But as it did so it took a series of tiny steps away from the ruling that Justice Miller had made in 1873. The total effect, after twenty years or so, was to discard what was correct in the slaughter-house decision while preserving what had been totally wrong.

To understand how the court began to shift its ground, and to torture and reshape the words of the Constitution into an instrument of injustice in economic relations, just as it had made it a barrier to interracial justice and human rights, it is necessary to recall how life in the United States had been changing after and as a result of the great industrial upsurge that came with the Civil War years. The centralization of farming and manufacturing gave way to concentrations of power and private control of economic relations. Wealth and influence were increasingly drawn into the hands of a few, who owned or controlled the railroads, the textile and other clothing factories, the steel mills and the banks. Laborers lost their independence and the power to make any decision affecting their lives, unless they could organize themselves for the advancement of their mutual interests. Few could do so in the reaction that came after the Haymarket prosecutions. Farmers could lose the value of much of their crops to railroads, grain elevators and middlemen unless they could unite for their common good. As one leader said: "You farmers need to raise less corn and more hell."

There was a valuable political power that working men, and especially in the first postwar years the farmers, could bring into play. The time had not yet come when it was felt that the power of concentrated wealth could be controlled somewhat in the common interest by national political action. On a local scale, efforts were made to pass laws that would protect the farmers and their communities against the power of the railroads and the banks. Later on, movements were to become effective that sought to remedy the inequality of power that made it possible for owners of factories, mills and mines to treat workers as "wage slaves"—men, women and even children obliged to work under abominable conditions.

From the beginning of the popular movement to limit their power, the wealthy and the greedy turned to the courts for protection. When some states passed laws trimming rail freight charges and storage rates for grain, the great corporation lawyers moved into action. Each time that their influence over the press and their corruption of some legislators failed to stop the passage of laws chopping profits down, they turned to the courts to cry foul. By 1878 Justice Miller was moved to remark that "the docket of this Court is crowded with cases in which we are asked to hold" that states had violated "due process of law. There is here abundant evidence that there exists some strange misconception of the scope of this provision as found in the fourteenth amendment."

As the years rolled on, the capitalists continued their fight. Judges died and new ones were appointed, many who had themselves been successful railroad lawyers. New decisions were made in which the court decided that it did have the power to veto laws regulating business. It began with a decision that held that the control of railroad rates interfered with the use of property and therefore was a taking of property. The "taking" would then be reviewed by the court to decide if it was "reasonable."

There was one influential private organization that helped to bring about the court's shift to a position in which it had the impudence to judge the reasonableness of what "reasonable" men—elected legislators and governors—had decided was in the public interest. The American Bar Association, a nationwide league of lawyers, was formed principally as a pressure group to get the court to adopt the curious new due process creed. Addresses at annual meetings and agitation at community groups promoted the idea that it was necessary for courts to limit state action in regulating the old-fashioned crimes; holdups by railroads, slow murder by near starvation and bloodshed by industrial accident were privileged liberties of the corporate clients of the leaders of the American bar.

The great growth of wealth and the concentration of economic power in the control of those clients came as the court was persuaded to interfere not only with rate-making but actually with any and every kind of regulation of private business activity. A totally new kind of legal idea was concocted for the purpose. It was too farfetched to call state interference with working conditions in a factory a "deprivation of property." Throughout English history, laws had always in some way affected the use to which owners could put their property, and no one had ever called that "depriving" one of property rights. The lawyers saw that they would have to persuade the court that laws limiting profits affected "liberty."

A new "liberty" was invented to meet the needs of the times, one that could not conceivably have entered into the thinking of anyone who played a part in the fight for the Fourteenth. The key phrase was to become "liberty of contract": any law that imposed limits on the extent to which an employer could exploit a workingman was said to be interference with the freedom of free men to agree with each other. Realistically this was pure poppycock. Conditions in those times were such that few workmen could refuse to accept the terms laid down by the owners of factories or railroads, or the banks that controlled them.

It was in 1896—the year that the idea of "freedom of contract" as a "liberty" protected by the due process language of the Fourteenth Amendment made its triumphant entry into the opinions of the court majority—that Plessy's prosecution was approved by the court. Harlan's dissent acknowledged and protested the invention of the new shield that the framers of the Fourteenth Amendment would never have recognized; at the same time, he denounced the violation of the right of all Americans to free association and the condemnation of blacks to inequality. "There is a dangerous tendency in these latter days," wrote Justice Harlan in his Plessy dissent, "to enlarge the functions of the courts, by means of judicial interference with the will of the people as expressed by the legislature."

Less than a year later, the legislature of New York State—responding to a movement for social justice that grew as the dawn of the twentieth century approached—decided that sixty hours of work in a week, or ten hours in any one day, was the limit that human beings should be expected to give in a bakery or confectionery establishment. The particles of flour and other ingredients in the air, on the floor, on the walls, which were inevitable at that period, and the intense heat from the ovens and other equipment—these were the factors that made it possible for popular agitation to succeed in getting a law passed that would put a mild limit on human exploitation in this industry.

But baker-boss Louis Lochner did not choose to obey the law. Arrested when caught, he was fined twenty dollars. This was no doubt a loss that he felt he could afford, considering the number of times he had gotten away with his offense and the profits to be made by violating the law. For another year and a half, law and order did not catch up with him again. Then he was nabbed a second time, and this time fined fifty dollars, the legal minimum for a second offender. Now he decided to fight rather than pay the fine, and before he was through he had paid many times fifty dollars in a four-stage appeal that served the interest of all bakery employers—and all employers who feared that the conditions in their industry might justify maximum hour or minimum wage laws.

Lochner lost the fight all the way to the United States Supreme Court, but there he and whatever industrialists helped finance his fight, got their money's worth. Symbolic of a Supreme Court that distorted due process hundreds of times over a forty-year period in striking down state legislation to reduce profits, the majority overruled the conviction of Lochner and threw out the sixty-hour law. "The general right to make a contract in relation to his business," wrote Justice Rufus W. Peckham, "is part of the liberty of the individual protected by the Fourteenth Amendment. [Laws] limiting the hours in which grown and intelligent men may labor to earn their living, are mere meddlesome interferences with the rights of the individual." One of the best answers to this perverse idea of freedom came thirty years later from Mr. Justice Harlan F. Stone, as the court, its ways still unchanged, was in the process of overthrowing many of Franklin Delano Roosevelt's New Deal laws: "There is grim irony in speaking of the freedom of contract of those who, because of their economic necessities, give their services for less than is needful to keep body and soul together."

The Supreme Court's verdict for the baker-boss did not go unchallenged by Justice Harlan, who dissented, as did Justice Holmes, the latter being more sensitive in these matters than he was in cases of interracial injustice. Anticipating Justice Stone's eloquence, he said that employers and employees are not on an equal footing, and that it is therefore unjust to say that the actions of workers in submitting to orders to work longer than sixty hours are an exercise of their freedom. "We are not to presume that the State of New York has acted in bad faith" and hence denied the employers "due process." The majority decision, he correctly predicted, would be "far-reaching and mischievous," and would "seriously cripple the inherent power of the States to care for the lives, health and well-being of their citizens."

Harlan's forecast was correct. In the name of freedom of contract, the pre-1937 court outlawed attempts by the states not only to regulate hours of labor but also to set minimum wages based on what was needed for mere subsistence. The protection of workers from forced "yellow dog" contracts, binding them not to join unions, was forbidden, as were attempts to curtail the abuse by the courts of their injunction procedures for the purpose of repressing agitation. Other states' rights were taken away in the name of due process: the right to protect the people of a state against excessive employment agency fees, and even unconscionable ticket brokerage charges for hit plays.

Only one great states' right survived the turn of the century unscathed, the "right" to oppress a portion of a state's people and to deny fair and humane procedure when liberty or life is really at stake. A "constitutional revolution" was still needed to breathe life into the practically dead Fourteenth Amendment and to take away the most peculiar face placed on it by the profit-protecting freedom of contract idea. No constitutional revolution, however, has ever been possible without a people's revolution to make it obtainable and to lay its foundation. One came, soon after the new century began.

Chapter 21

This is Democracy?

The President of the United States went to the Congress during Holy Week of 1917 to perform a constitutional duty. From the moment of our nation's birth it has been part of our fundamental law that only Congress can declare war. President Woodrow Wilson had concluded that it was necessary for the United States to intervene and take part in an unprecedentedly bloody and devastating European war. He asked for a declaration of war on the German Empire, saying: "We shall fight for the things which we have always carried nearest our hearts—for democracy, for the right of those who submit to authority to have a voice in their own governments."

The words were cheered and the proposition carried. The Americans who were to be drafted were black and white, but the five hundred congressmen and senators voting did not include a single American of African ancestry.

The fact that the Congress that voted to declare war did not include any black Americans meant something more than that it did not represent any. It is also fair to say that that Congress—and many before it, as well as many since—did not represent the American republic. America was not the land that James Madison and the founding fathers had envisioned: "We may define a Republic," Madison had written in the *Federalist Papers*, "to be a government which derives all its powers directly or indirectly from the great body of the people." Moreover, he added, "it is *essential* [Madison himself underlined that word] to such a government that it be derived from the great body of society, not from an inconsiderable portion or favored class of it."

By Madison's definition, the United States had never been a republic. It was not until 1920 that the exclusion of women from participation in government was ended. Apart from that, the greatest move in the direction of democracy was the passage of the reconstruction laws of 1867, when for a brief period the control of a favored class over the rest of the people was halted. But the nation started to slip back into its state of rule by only a part of the people after the Supreme Court's decision in the Cruikshank case.

The Fifteenth Amendment had been intended to declare and to guarantee the "right of those who submit to authority to have a voice in their own governments"—the right, using those very words, for which Wilson had sent out a quarter of a million Americans to foreign lands to die. But that right had not existed here; it had been destroyed by the end of the nineteenth century, seventeen years before the war that was advertised as the one to make the world safe for democracy.

In the United States, the reconstruction-created right of those who submit to authority to have a voice in their governments had been whittled away until it no longer existed. Its disappearance began the moment the Supreme Court made it plain that it would not aid congressional enforcement of the Fifteenth Amendment. The sordid story of state-by-state destruction of democracy in so large a part of the United States as to devitalize it for the nation as a whole is too long to tell in all its details. It began with the violence of the 1870s with which the Supreme Court refused to interfere. It ended with the legal trickery of the 1890s, the passage of laws designed to make permanent the illegal rule by a portion of the people of a dozen states over the rest.

The purpose of those laws of the 1890s was loudly avowed by men brazen enough to believe that they could openly defy the United States less than thirty years after their rebellion had been put down. In addressing one state constitutional convention, a local judge admitted: "Sir, it is no secret that there has not been a full vote and a fair count in Mississippi since 1875 . . . we have been stuffing ballot boxes, committing perjury, and here and there in the state carrying the elections by fraud and violence." Explaining that the convention had been called to find a way to maintain undemocratic rule without such methods, one journalist put it very well: "The old men of the present generation can't afford to die and leave their children with shotguns in their hands, a lie in their mouths and perjury on their souls, in order to defeat the negroes. *The constitution can be made so that this will not be necessary.*"

They were correct in their confidence that there would be no interference from the Supreme Court, which had struck down the Sumner Civil Rights Act and which was to reject Tourgee's fight for Plessy and against state-structured segregation. When the major test came, it was Oliver Wendell Holmes who spoke for the court majority. This may surprise some who have been led to revere Holmes as a "Yankee from Olympus." We tend too often to overlook or gloss over the serious imperfections in our great men.

In detached and hostile language, Holmes refused to interfere with the statewide fraudulent registration scheme. "How," he asked cooly, "can we make the Court a party to the unlawful scheme by accepting it and adding another voter to the fraudulent list?" Two other justices, Brewer and Brown, joined Harlan in his dissent from the majority opinion of the man who—at least in matters of racial injustice—had not yet earned his later title as the "Great Dissenter."

For the time being the Fifteenth Amendment was a dead letter. The consequences were not merely the creation of state governments that were no better than separate little fascist dictatorships. The effect was not limited to the poisoning of all congressional action by the presence of unconstitutionally selected senators and representatives. In an important turn-of-the-century appraisal, an almost forgotten black academician pointed out the other evil effects on his fellow Americans.

"The law which deprives him of the badge of citizenship, changes at once his legal status and cuts him off from respect. His disqualification as an elector shuts him out of the jury box in courts where what few rights he has left are adjudicated and his grievances redressed. His disqualification as an elector and as a juror discredits him as a witness."

Pointing out the admissions of Southerners that the purpose of all this was economic—the control of the Negro as a laborer—the writer, John Love, foresaw the planting of the seeds of our current national crisis: "These disfranchising enactments, in that they lower the legal and economic status of the black man, tend also to lower his educational and social status. The political and economic supremacy of the southern oligarchy is dependent upon the ignorance and social degradation of the Negro . . . and that consequently there must be a decrease in the amount of money expended for his education. . . . The nation cannot put up with many more of these instruments of disfranchisement."

Too few Americans understood as clearly as John Love the injury to their nation that was inflicted by the nullification of the Fifteenth Amendment. There were some, in 1901, who did remember that even before the Fifteenth was ratified the Joint Committee on Reconstruction had provided clear and explicit directions, in the Fourteenth, for responding to the mass denial of the right to vote in any state. Thaddeus Stevens had led the fight in Congress and in the Joint Committee for a remedy that would prevent the rebel states from being *over*represented. (This, we remember, was made necessary by the removal of the "three-fifths of a man" credit for slaves in the original apportionment provisions.) It would have been obviously unfair to permit any state, for the purpose of deciding how many representatives in Congress it should have, to count a portion of its people who were denied the right to vote for such representatives.

So at a time when the nation could not force the states to grant the right to vote to all—because the Fifteenth Amendment had not yet come into being—it could at least be sure that the states did not have voices in Congress for people who did not participate in electing those voices. Thus was born the second numbered clause of the Fourteenth Amendment, hammered out at the same time as the first, the triple-rights clause. Representatives were to be apportioned among the states "according to their numbers," the clause decreed, but when the right to vote was denied to some of the inhabitants "the basis of representation therein *shall* be reduced in the [same] proportion."

The question of the practical application of this constitutional direction had not assumed importance at first. The right to vote had been granted equally throughout the South by the very reconstruction acts that were necessary to get the Fourteenth ratified. Soon afterward, it had been granted equally throughout the country by the Fifteenth Amendment. Although it did not seem that it would ever be necessary to apply the fair representation clause of the Fourteenth Amendment, the machinery to make it work had been created and was ready to be put into operation when needed.

The first census of the population of the United States was taken to determine how many representatives in Congress should be allotted to each state. A provision of the original constitution stated that the census was to be taken every ten years thereafter for that purpose. When the 1870 census was taken, the pollsters attempted to count the number of eligible voters whose rights had been limited, but the results were inconclusive. Congress, nevertheless, in the next apportionment law directed that in the future the number of representatives should be reduced when states were found to have limited the rights of some of their citizens to vote.

When the time came for the decennial redistribution of House seats which was to be based on the 1900 census, the widespread violations of the Fifteenth Amendment had reached scandalous proportions. State after state had succumbed to the epidemic of the 1890s that was begun by the Mississippi plan of making "legal," by state law, the destruction of democracy which had previously been accomplished by force, violence and fraud. The means used were literacy tests, poll taxes, restrictions of other kinds and "grandfather clauses"—all for the purpose of violating the Fifteenth Amendment without openly defying it. The so-called grandfather clauses made it possible to discriminate simply by allowing the automatic registration of those whose grandfathers could vote before 1865—a crude trick guaranteed to bar from the ballot from one fourth to three fifths of the people of every southern state.

One congressman, who is remembered now only because he was a noted grandfather, spoke up in 1901 in joining a handful of his colleagues in making a proper response to the grandfather-clause laws. He was a young representative from Boston whose own people of Irish ancestry were only beginning to shake of the shackles of religious and nativist prejudice. John F. Fitzgerald, known as "Honey Fitz," grandfather of three United States senators, one of whom became president and another attorney general, aided in a fight initiated by Edgar Crumpacker, an heir to Indiana's Radical Republican traditions.

Crumpacker had attacked a report of the House Committee on the Census, which had been ordered to reapportion the number of representatives allotted each state to conform with the 1900 population count. The Indianan insisted that the committee had defaulted its duty because it had ignored restrictions on voting of the type that required a reduction of representation under the Fourteenth Amendment's second paragraph.

Another who joined Crumpacker and Fitzgerald in this fight was a congressman from North Carolina who had been born a slave. George White was to be the last American of African ancestry to sit in the House from the supposedly reconstructed South, and the last from any region until 1929.

As a debater in Congress, White used the skill he had gained after serving six years in the North Carolina state legislature and eight as a state prosecuting attorney. He spoke with eloquence as well as skill, as when he introduced a bill providing for direct national action to restore law and order by putting an end to lynching: "I tremble with horror for the future of our nation when I think what must be the inevitable result if mob violence is not stamped out of existence and law once more permitted to reign supreme."

When the Indiana representative made his move to give life and meaning to the fair representation clause of the Fourteenth Amendment, White joined the embattled minority seeking to enforce the United States Constitution. He showed statistically, state by state, how the number of voters per representative in the South had been affected by the grandfather clauses and other disfranchising laws. In his own North Carolina district—not yet reached by the treacherous tide—more votes had been recorded in the last election than were recorded in each of three states that had been allotted six or seven congressmen each. To this picture of racist exclusion, rewarded in effect by one man-six votes, White responded: "I do not believe that anybody should be permitted to thrive by his own dishonesty and rascality. These frauds in the South, while terribly unjust to the colored man, will certainly react upon the white people."

The effort of the three leaders to persuade the House to do its constitutional duty failed. But not before President John F. Kennedy's grandfather, Honey Fitz, had made his colleagues squirm by recalling two key battles of the then recent Spanish-American War, in one of which the sagging lines of the white "Rough Riders," would have been broken if not rescued by their fellow countrymen of African descent: "We are all proud of the record of the black regiments in the Spanish-American War, and if the white soldier boys whose lives were saved on San Juan Hill and at El Caney . . . were here to speak, I think that they would protest with mighty vigor against the disfranchisement of a race that produced such brave and noble souls."

As the end of George White's last term in Congress approached, he delivered a farewell address. He summarized the achievements of his people under the most adverse circumstances. In the face of lynching, burning at the stake, the humiliation of Jim Crow cars and disfranchisement, he said, "we are forging our way ahead, slowly perhaps, but surely." And as he closed he declared prophetically:

"This, Mr. Chairman, is perhaps the Negroes' temporary farewell to the American Congress; but let me say, Phoenix-like he will rise up some day and come again. These parting words are in behalf of an outraged, heart-broken, bruised and bleeding, but God fearing people . . . full of potential force.

"The only apology that I have to make for the earnestness with which I have spoken is that I am pleading for the life, the liberty, the future happiness, and manhood suffrage of one-eighth of the entire population of the United States."

Part III
RISE:

Revolution and Return to the Constitution

Chapter 22

Grandson
of the Revolution

One August morning in 1906, a hundred Americans of African ancestry assembled in a Virginia field. For three days they had been meeting to discuss their mutual concerns, their past efforts and their future plans. After full debate they had adopted as a program an "address and resolutions" drawn by their leader. To dramatize and to proclaim it they had agreed to move at dawn to a rocky cliff overlooking Harpers Ferry, West Virginia. The place of their meeting had been chosen partly in memory of John Brown, who had launched a fight for freedom for all Americans at that very spot half a century before.

Now they were bent on a peaceful revolution, instead of an armed revolt and guerrilla warfare against a nation strangled by a slaveowners' constitution. Their aim was to restore the freeman's constitution built around Big Fourteen which had been whittled down for forty years until it had become little more than a splinter.

As the first rays of the sun emerged from behind the eastern mountains, reflected in the dewdrops on the leaves and in the grass around them, they sang the chorus of a freedom song. Then one of their number stepped forward to read their revolutionary resolves, the first overt act in their conspiracy to restore the American Constitution to life.

They did not speak only for—or to—black Americans, although there was none present who was "white" by the peculiar definitions adopted and still applied by the former slave states and others infected by segregation. They did include among their grievances such outrages as that "Fifty and more representatives of stolen votes still sit in the nation's capital"—a judgment that echoed the arguments, three years before, of Edgar Crumpacker, John F. "Honey Fitz" Fitzgerald and George H. White; they condemned "the new American creed that says: fear to let the black man even try to rise lest they become the equals of the white." They demanded for their people the right to vote, the right to work and the end of discrimination and segregation.

But they asked for more than what concerned their own people. "Step by step the defenders of the rights of American citizens have retreated," they said. "The battle we wage is not for ourselves alone, but for all true Americans: We want the laws enforced against rich as well as poor; against Capitalist as well as Laborer; against white as well as black. . . . We want justice even for criminals and outlaws. We want the Constitution of the country enforced. . . . We want our children educated. . . . We want the national government to step in and wipe out illiteracy in the South. Either the United States will destroy ignorance or ignorance will destroy the United States."

The group that proclaimed these views was called the Niagara Movement, taking its name from the fact that it first met at Niagara Falls the year before the Harpers Ferry assembly. The man most instrumental in calling it together, and who wrote the address and resolutions read aloud from the rocky cliff over Harpers Ferry, was Dr. W. E. B. Du Bois, a grandson of the American Revolution.

William Edward Burghardt Du Bois was born in 1868, the very year in which the Fourteenth Amendment had been ratified. His place of birth was Great Barrington, Massachusetts, and after having attended the local schools and a southern black university he became the first descendant of a slave to gain the high academic honor of Doctor of Philosophy at Harvard University. As a graduate student at the University of Berlin at the age of twenty-five, he quietly made a resolve which he entrusted to his diary: "be the truth what it may, I will seek it on the pure assumption that it is worth seeking."

Dr. Du Bois returned to the United States in 1894, dedicated to the life of the scholar and a career of writer and teacher. As a member of the faculty at Atlanta University, he began to publish works on history and sociology. But he could not be indifferent to the world outside. The segregated Jim Crow cars of Atlanta he would not tolerate, and fifty years before the Montgomery bus boycott of our time he chose to walk rather than to ride in a seat in a separate section. That violation of equal protection of the law did not sear his soul as much as the due process and equal protection violation that occurred every time an American citizen was seized by a mob or gang, often with the connivance or aid of the police, and taken out and summarily slain in the especially American crime of lynching.

While he continued to accept and serve the biblical mandate that "ye shall know the truth,—and the truth shall make ye free," he found it insufficient. The suffering that he sustained as he contemplated the wrongs that stemmed from the nation's failure to enforce the Fourteenth and its sister amendments prevented him from remaining confined to his academic tower. One of the truths that he had learned in his studies was that only by uniting in a common cause could a people better their lot when oppressed.

One American black who had made a success as speaker and writer—Booker T. Washington—attracted the attention and support of philanthropists by advocating the view that an accommodation to the nonenforcement of the Constitution was a necessary evil. Du Bois had written an essay expressing admiration for this man as an educator but at the same time opposing his basic political philosophy. "We have no right to sit silently by," wrote Du Bois, "while the inevitable seeds are sown for a harvest of disaster to our children, black and white."

A number of his essays, including his criticism of Booker T. Washington, were published in 1903 in a book that has become a classic, *The Souls of Black Folk*. The publication of the book stirred up a great deal of controversy, as well as interest in the writer; he learned from the response that there were many who agreed with him. As a result, he issued a call to begin a movement that would be "for organized determination and aggressive action," and in response a number of his contemporaries gathered for a first session at Niagara Falls. The place was chosen in respect for the memory of the Underground Railroad to freedom, and from it the group took its name.

The Niagara Movement continued to exist for several years after the Harpers Ferry meeting, but it never gained the strength or attracted the attention that would have been needed. Something on a larger scale was required for the tremendous task of restoring the Constitution to working order for the benefit of all Americans.

Meanwhile, the evils against which the Niagara Movement had been formed to fight continued. The Supreme Court approved the Kentucky law that destroyed Berea College as a single, all-American institution. In the case of the white banker Albert Twining, the court reaffirmed the restrictive interpretation begun with the slaughterhouse and Cruikshank mob cases. The court conceded that criticism of its earlier decisions had "never entirely ceased," and even added, concerning the handiwork of its predecessors of 1873: "Undoubtedly, it [the court's decision on the butchers' battle] gave much less effect to the Fourteenth Amendment than some of the public men active in framing it intended, and disappointed many others."

The heart of the original Bill of Rights, the First Amendment in more than name, decreed that "Congress shall make no law . . . abridging the freedom of speech, or of the press." Threatened before the twentieth century only in time of war, when impatience with dissent outweighs dedication to the ideals for which we are supposed to be fighting, the First Amendment's guarantee of press freedom did not come before the Supreme Court for consideration until 1907. The court that had gotten used to turning its back on the black man, and that turned its back repeatedly on the rights of the accused white criminal, now turned its back on the white publisher.

Colorado's Senator Thomas M. Patterson was publisher of two Denver newspapers that had crusaded for reform in the handling of public utility franchises. Such reform had been accomplished by winning a charter form of government for Denver, which provided for a popular vote to extend the monopolies granted gas companies and street railways. The state political "boss" of the day was intimately connected with the Colorado Fuel and Iron Company and was president as well of the Denver City Tramway Company. The law was struck down by the state supreme court.

Patterson's *Times* editorial the next day declared that the court's decision was responsive to the will of "the utility corporations of Denver and the political machine they control." For this he was accused of contempt of court; his defense was based both on the state constitution's pledge of freedom of speech and on the idea that the Fourteenth Amendment—as Bingham had repeatedly stated—brought the First Amendment's protection to bear on the state governments.

In a ruling written by Oliver Wendell Holmes, the Yankee who only later became a dissenter in such matters, the Supreme Court refused to interfere. While unwilling expressly to reject the application of Big Fourteen in such a case, the Holmes majority upheld the conviction. Not many years later, the court was to state that "neither the Fourteenth Amendment nor any other provision of the Constitution of the United States imposes on the states any restrictions about 'freedom of speech.' "

Harlan, outraged, dissented once more and reminded the majority of the importance of the national citizenship created by the very first words of the Fourteenth: ". . . if the rights of free speech and of a free press are, in their essence, attributes of national citizenship, as I think they are, then neither Congress nor any State since the adoption of the Fourteenth Amendment can by legislative enactments or by judicial action, impair or abridge them." He went on to insist also that such rights are part of every man's liberty, not to be taken away without due process of law, and hence twice protected by Big Fourteen.

In the summer of the same year during which the Supreme Court rejected banker Twining's appeal, a series of outrages occurred that eventually led to the larger organization that grew out of the Niagara Movement. This was to become known as the National Association for the Advancement of Colored People, that from then till now was to carry on the struggle that became the central force in the rebirth of the Fourteenth Amendment.

It began after the North was invaded by what had been, until then, a typically southern violation of the right not to be deprived of life without due process of law. The mob action known as "lynching," supposed to bring quick revenge that would discourage acts of sexual violence but actually designed to terrorize all blacks and eliminate those who asserted their rights as Americans, broke out with fury in Springfield, Illinois, where fifty years before Abraham Lincoln had practiced law. Self-defense by one of the intended victims infuriated a mob, whose action turned into attacks on all of the blacks it could find, a rampage that did not abate when the white woman involved denied that she had been attacked. Many persons were wounded and killed, houses burned and stores smashed. The crowd that carried out this lawlessness and disorder was said to include some of the "best people" in Springfield.

Throughout the nation there were many who were shocked—and a few who were stirred into action. One of these was William E. Walling, a white Kentuckian who was also an American Socialist follower of Eugene V. Debs. He and his wife, Anna Strunsky, a Russian revolutionary emigré, went to Springfield to investigate the riots. In a published report, Walling described the savage terror that had been followed by a social and economic boycott designed to drive from town the few blacks who had not fled in fright. He concluded: "Either the spirit of the abolitionists, of Lincoln and Lovejoy must be revived and we must come to treat the Negro on a plane of absolute political and social equality, or Vardaman and Tillman will soon have transferred the race war to the North." Vardaman and Tillman were white southern members of Congress whose unbelievably barbaric anti-Negro speeches and propaganda were looked down upon by the "enlightened" people of the North. Aiming his final shaft at them, Walling closed: "Yet who realizes the seriousness of the situation, and what large and powerful body of citizens is ready to come to their aid?"

A response came from another socialist, a descendant of an abolitionist who had dedicated herself to neighborhood welfare work to aid the oppressed. Mary White Ovington immediately saw how preferable it was to organize to combat injustice rather than merely aid its victims. She proposed that they form a biracial organization aimed at solving the racial problem—really the white problem—that was America's plague. An early volunteer in the cause was Oswald Garrison Villard, grandson of William Lloyd Garrison and very much a crusading editor in his own right.

In an early call to one of the first organizing sessions of the new, militant association, Villard wrote: "If Mr. Lincoln could revisit this country in the flesh, he would be disheartened and discouraged. . . . He would learn that the Supreme Court of the United States, supposedly a bulwark of American liberties, had refused every opportunity to pass squarely upon this disfranchisement of millions. . . . He would learn that the Supreme Court, in the Berea College case, has laid down the principle that an individual state may 'make it a crime for white and colored persons to frequent the same market place at the same time, or appear in an assemblage of citizens convened to consider questions of a public or political nature. . . ."

The signers of the call and the early supporters of the new association form an honor roll of great, some forgotten, Americans of that period. They included Jane Addams, William Dean Howells, Rev. John Haynes Holmes, Henry Parkhurst (who had once rid New York of Tammany Hall for a period), Lincoln Steffens and Rabbi Stephen S. Wise. To mention only some in this way is almost unfair to the balance of the honor roll.

Of course, among the signers, and playing a leading role in the first organizational meetings of the new NAACP, was W. E. B. Du Bois. And when the functioning organization took shape, he was the leading Negro among the full-time workers, having left his academic haven at Atlanta University to become director of research and publicity. The grandson of the American Revolution was enlisted in the third American revolution.

Chapter 23

Sumner's Secretary
Carries On

It was a pleasant afternoon in October, 1867, in Cambridge. Du Bois had not yet been born, and the Fourteenth Amendment was awaiting ratification by the states. A tall, slender, blue-eyed youth of twenty, who had been born in the then fashionable Boston suburb of Roxbury, was sitting indolently in his room, looking unhappily at his pile of law school assignments. He had been a better than average college student, but there had not been much about his life until then that would have made it possible to predict that Moorfield Storey would ever have been more than a successful lawyer and an agreeable "man of the world."

Perhaps it was his performance as college class orator that began the chain of events that brought the visitor to him that day who carried news that was to influence much of the rest of Storey's life. He had reflected, long and hard, in one term paper, on the subject "Whether to abstain from publishing a truth, from fear that the world might not be ready to receive it." Using as his principal example the case of the abolitionists, so prominent during his youth, his conclusion was that the truth could never produce lasting harm and would always be the cause of lasting good. This outlook led to a class day oration that concluded with words which, when published in the Boston papers, attracted the attention of a very distinguished person to the young Harvard alumnus who had said, "We can engage in no more noble warfare than the defense of truth, wherever we may find her opposed or oppressed."

Young Storey's visitor that October afternoon was an emissary from the chairman of the United States Senate Committee on Foreign Relations, the man who, as a son of the Revolution, had fought for Sarah Roberts' right to equality before the law. Now, twenty years later, Charles Sumner had risen to the most distinguished post in the United States Senate. He had the right to designate as Clerk to the Senatorial Committee one who would act as his private secretary. He wanted for the post a young and able Harvard law student.

For Moorfield, this afforded an opportunity to be in the midst of great men, among events that he knew to loom large in our history. It provided at the same time an opportunity (since in those days "reading" in the office of a lawyer was equivalent to class work) to complete preparation for the bar without the drudgery of school work. He fairly jumped at the chance, and had moved to Washington within the month.

While the distinguished autobiographer of those days, Henry Adams, has recorded that "Senator Sumner had as private secretary a young man named Moorfield Storey, who became a dangerous example of frivolity," the young Bostonian did not really surrender entirely to the temptations of Washington social life. It was a time when the President of the United States, who had repudiated the ideals and the idealists who had helped elect his ticket when he had run as candidate for vice-president under Lincoln, came very close to being impeached. Young Storey, in the thick of these things, saw and learned much.

Later in life he was to write a biography of Charles Sumner which would do justice to the nobility and idealism of the man under whose influence he fell. Meanwhile, as he wrote his father, although having come to Washington as an opponent of the impeachment of President Johnson, the daily accumulation of firsthand evidence from the South convinced him of the need to act. "He had filled the offices with unrepentant rebels, and by their assistance and all the power which the vast patronage and influence of the Executive gave him was working to defeat reconstruction, to prevent the success of the loyal element in the election, to prevent the adoption of universal suffrage and the extension of true principles of justice in the South." The effect of all this, he told his father, was to encourage a renewed spirit of rebellion and "a state of things where no loyal man's life was safe, and no loyal man's murderer could be punished." Despite his feelings, and unlike the great men around him, Storey remained cool and objective enough to predict the failure of the impeachment, having had much opportunity to observe the influences, corrupt and otherwise, that were working against its success.

Such major episodes in the life of a young man come inevitably to an end, and Moorfield Storey returned to Boston to resume the life for which he had been preparing when the invitation to serve as Sumner's secretary arrived. For many years his career progressed not too differently from how it might have had the connection with Sumner not entered his life. He became successful and prosperous in his law practice, so much so that by the 1890s he had been elected a member of the Board of Overseers of Harvard College; a token of his position in the community. In 1895 there came the supreme recognition of his professional standing, election to the national presidency of the young American Bar Association.

Meanwhile, his principal attention to outside activities had been a concern with antimachine politics. There was neither occasion nor motivation for support of the issues of freedom and peace that had marked Senator Sumner's career. One of Storey's early allies in "reform" was young Henry Cabot Lodge, but when out of personal ambition he betrayed that cause Storey broke off personal relations with him. Fifteen years later they were to be on opposing sides in a great American crisis of conscience over armed aggression by our armed forces against Asians struggling for freedom. This in turn was what brought Moorfield Storey to resume, as a private citizen, active agitation for the enforcement of the promises contained in the constitutional amendments that were wrought during Sumner's public life.

It was in the aftermath of the 1898 war with Spain that, as we have seen, the cases came to the Supreme Court that evoked from Mr. Dooley the observation that, though the Constitution may not follow the flag, the Supreme Court of his day surely followed the "illiction returns." That aftermath involved a decision by the McKinley administration—which had been elected on a platform pledging "no jingo nonsense"—to continue, after victory over the Spaniards, the war that the latter had been conducting against the native independence movement in the Philippines.

In his opposition to America's war on Asian guerrillas who preferred death to submission to American conquest, Storey made frequent use of a statement of a surviving senatorial colleague of Sumner, General and later Interior Secretary Carl Schurz, who was himself active in the antiwar agitation: "Mr. Schurz has given a far higher and truer meaning to the words, 'Our country, right or wrong;' if right to be kept right, if wrong, to be set right."

During the course of his energetic work in the movement that called itself the Anti-Imperialist League, Storey saw clearly the identity of the moral issue presented by the use of our troops to repress the rights of brown Asians, and the failure of the federal government to do anything to defend the rights of black Americans. There were echoes of Charles Sumner's rhetoric in the Third Party platform that Storey helped to write in 1900: "Resolved, That in declaring that the principles of the Declaration of Independence apply to all men, this Congress means to include the Negro race in America as well as the Filipinos."

The Anti-Imperialist Movement faded away but Moorfield Storey's life was never the same afterwards. From a successful lawyer occasionally interested as a "good citizen" in righteous causes, he became transformed into a persistent activist. In October of 1907, when the Niagara Movement was still struggling for recognition as the advance guard of the fight to return to American constitutionalism, Dr. Du Bois wrote to Storey to congratulate him on a forceful and effective Anti-Imperialist pamphlet he had written. . Storey promptly wrote in response to say how familiar he was with the writings of Du Bois—and how much interest he took in the work of the Movement.

Three years later, when the NAACP absorbed the Niagara group and took on organizational form, with Du Bois as full-time staff director of publicity and research, the president elected by acclamation was Moorfield Storey. He was to continue in that post until his death twenty years later at the age of eighty-four. Hardly had he assumed office when his own profession presented a problem that portrayed well the degraded state of American morality. It became known, in 1911, that three Negro lawyers had become members of the American Bar Association—simply by filling out application blanks and sending them in. Although one of them was an assistant attorney general, the reaction of the membership, reflecting the nation's racial animosity, was such that the ABA Executive Committee "rescinded" the memberships—expelled the three.

This action by a body of members of the bar pledged by oath to support a constitution guaranteeing "equal protection of the laws" aroused the wrath of many. One who denounced the action as illegal was the Attorney General of the United States, George W. Wickersham, from whom we shall hear again. Storey, as past president of the bar association, took the lead in a protest campaign. The battle was won, but the war—for the next couple of decades at least—was lost. The three expelled members were reinstated, but the nature of the questionnaires changed so that what was until 1936 the only national association of lawyers retained the color line.

The time soon came for Storey to use his professional skills in the first of the NAACP court victories that were to constitute the artillery barrages in the third American revolution. The comparison to artillery may be justified by the role of these major court cases: they demolish enemy strong points, or score breakthroughs, but unless the people's movement is alive and strong enough to move forward to occupy contested ground the successful artillery hit gains no territory.

We have seen how the "grandfather clauses" served as a blatant barrier to the right to vote, beginning in the 1890s. This was the nickname of a device so transparent that only those deliberately closing their eyes could fail to see through it: rigid literacy tests and like barriers were set up, and then exceptions provided for those who were entitled to vote in 1866, or whose sons or descendants were. Since the grandfathers of illiterate whites could vote in '66—and the ancestors of blacks of course could not—the exclusion problem was solved.

After twenty years of successful disfranchisement by grandfather clauses, Storey and the bar association persuaded the Department of Justice to challenge one in Oklahoma. Ironically, this was a state that had only been admitted to the union in 1908 and had not, of course, been a member of the Confederacy. Nevertheless, among its immigrants and settlers racism predominated so much that the Mississippi-Louisiana plan of exclusion was put into effect.

Storey, in behalf of the NAACP, appeared as "friend of the court" in the attack on disfranchisement, when the Oklahoma case reached the Supreme Court. Yielding to the unavoidable logic of his position, the court struck the law down. "How can there be room for any serious dispute," asked the chief justice, "concerning the repugnancy of the standard based upon January 1, 1866?" Of course the court ruled that there was none. Such clauses having been in effect for more than twenty years, however, the governors, sheriffs, judges and county registrars of voting in all of the affected states were well entrenched; by the discriminatory use of literacy tests, they were now able to keep from registration the few blacks who had the courage to attempt to take advantage of the breakthrough.

The victory of the constitutional revolution was not to happen overnight, nor was the path to victory to be an easy one. The next great case that was taken on by Moorfield Storey would illustrate that the feeble flicker of life found in the Fourteenth Amendment would be insufficient by itself to rekindle the torch of freedom. The needed change of direction of our constitutional history would require more than a victory in a court case or group of cases. For a period, the path of the law was to be one step forward and two steps back—but this was still an improvement over the history of the first forty years, during which every step was backward in the retreat from the Constitution.

Storey's second great victory was to be in the field of forced ghetto restriction, resisting the attempt by law to limit people in the selection of the place where they might live or work. The attempt to create ghettos by law did not begin in the South, nor was it directed against blacks. San Francisco pioneered the concept in an effort to herd its Chinese-Americans into one area; so gross was the nature of the law that a lower federal court struck it down.

The intolerable conditions of life in the rural areas where most American blacks had lived in the last century brought efforts to escape in which the first destination was the nearest southern or border city. The rising tide of racism against blacks prompted new attempts at the creation of legally made ghettos in the places to which these "internal refugees" would migrate. The city of Louisville drew up a local law for the supposed purpose of preventing "conflict and ill-feeling"; the heart of the measure was a simple prohibition against the purchase of property by blacks in city blocks where a majority of the owners were white, and vice versa. The balancing of restrictions—each race forbidden to buy in the other's "territory"—was planned for the purpose of getting around the San Francisco precedent, aimed at Chinese only.

A test case was planned and taken to the Supreme Court of Kentucky. There the state judges turned down the would-be seller, Buchanan, who was contesting the constitutionality of the Louisville law. Plausibly enough, the Kentucky court reasoned that the local law was valid since the United States Supreme Court had upheld separation of the races by forceful state action in the Berea College case. Storey then took charge of the final appeal to the Supreme Court of the United States.

The man who stood before the court in 1917 to tell the justices that the Fourteenth Amendment forbade a state or city from creating a "ghetto"—perhaps the first time the name of the Jewish restricted areas of feudal Europe was applied to areas in democratic America—was impressive. Seventy years of age, he still stood tall with a commanding presence, with the clear blue eyes and classic features of a patrician Bostonian. He had a courtly dignity and spoke with a grace that would have marked him as unusual in any group.

When he talked, the court was obliged to listen, and with the sound of guns overseas and the probability that American boys were soon to die in the name of "democracy" it listened attentively. "No one outside of a court room," said Storey (implying that in court-rooms men are fooled more easily than outside?), "would imagine for an instant that the predominant purpose of this ordinance was not to prevent the Negro citizens of Louisville, however industrious, thrifty, and well-educated they might be, from approaching that condition vaguely described as 'social equality.'"

The court was unanimous in sustaining Storey's position. While the emphasis of the justices was more on the "property" rights involved than on the violation of equal protection of the laws, it was a significant victory. It was more important for what it prevented than for what it gained. What was prevented was the full-scale introduction of a South African style of total apartheid, with America rigidly and permanently divided into two castes with no hope for change. In a purely practical sense, much of American life had reached this point, but Storey's work in the grandfather-clause case and in the Louisville segregation case left twin beacon lights of a promise, even if remote, of the possibility of change.

While the Buchanan case prevented much, it gained little as a practical matter. The prevalence of white racism had reached the point where landowners in city and suburb achieved by private agreement what they had failed to accomplish by municipal decree. The nature of the agreement, the so-called "restrictive covenant," was such that no subsequent owner could breach the bond, no heir could repudiate his parents' evil promise. Once a real estate dealer had placed a covenant in a deed, the area was treated as "white only," and courts would forbid deviations. When the legality of such arrangements came to the Supreme Court in 1926, they were sustained. Twenty-two years later the court took another look and Storey's victory was retrieved.

Chapter 24

The Ultimate Guardians
of Our Freedom

A wise and witty Harvard Law School professor once wrote, "Nine men in Washington cannot hold a nation to ideals which it is determined to betray. Whether justice is done to the particular defendant is important, but in the long run less important than whether a nation does justice to itself."

Those words were written as Americans began to understand how far their officials—and the people themselves—had departed during and after World War I from the rules of fairness and freedom provided by our Bill of Rights. It was just a quarter century later, on the eve of another period of forced uniformity, that a fine and flinty faced old judge—one never named to the Supreme Court, though thought by many to be more deserving than some who were—told a throng of thousands celebrating "I Am An American Day" in New York's Central Park: "I often wonder whether we do not rest our hopes too much upon constitutions, upon laws and upon courts. These are false hopes; believe me these are false hopes. Liberty lies in the hearts of men and women; when it dies there, no constitution, no law, no court can even do much to help it."

Our story of the birth, near death and return to life of the Fourteenth Amendment is told primarily through the episodes in its history that reached the Supreme Court. Whether a rule is applied to bring about the result it is supposed to achieve depends very much on what it is thought to mean. What the Supreme Court has said is intended—or not intended—by "due process of law" or by "equal protection of the laws" is a guide for action. Much more important than what may happen to the parties of a case is the effect of the court's ruling in governing lawmakers, public officials and especially the lower courts that do so much of the business of umpiring, of applying the rules of the game that affect the daily lives of most people.

Yet, as Professor Thomas Reed Powell wrote, a nation can betray itself, regardless of what nine judges may do or say; and as Learned Hand told his flag-waving audience, courts and laws cannot revive the spirit of liberty when it has died. Judge Hand may have over-stated his case to make his point: it is true that the court's retreats from the Constitution have often been a reflection of the lag in the people's will to obey the rules to which they give lip service; but it is also true, as the chapters that follow will show, that the court can stimulate a revival of a flagging spirit. And in the period with which we are now concerned, the presidency of Woodrow Wilson, the fruit of the court's betrayal of the guarantees of fairness was to be found in popular insensitivity to the meaning of liberty.

The peaceable revolution that was led by men like Du Bois and Storey—that had been given organizational form with the help of women like Mary White Ovington and Anna Strunsky—was aimed at restoring respect for and obedience to the second American con-stitution. It was an essential part of that "second constitution"—the abolition of slavery, the promise of equality and justice throughout the nation, the protection of the right to vote—that the Congress should enforce its guarantees by "appropriate legislation." The Supreme Court's denial of effect to most of that legislation left a void, a vacuum of enforcement machinery.

The efforts and especially the actions in court by the NAACP made a tiny beginning in the filling of that gap. Where the federal government had been forced to abandon its responsibilities, this group of private citizens was carrying on. But in conducting the fight to enforce the Fourteenth and its sister amendments as they were written and intended, the private group was not only handicapped by the line of Supreme Court decisions that began with the exoner-ation and the freeing of the Cruikshank mob of 1873, after the door was opened by the distortions in the ruling on the butchers' battle. They were also up against the appalling effect of four decades of accumulated public acceptance of injustice as a way of life. It was a part of their cause, as Moorfield Storey once said, "to make race prejudice as unfashionable as it is now fashionable."

There was another area where another group of private citizens was attempting to combat the tendency to deny the rights of Ameri-cans. Foremost among the "privileges and immunities" in the Bill of Rights that were intended to be safeguarded against the interference of states, cities and private mobs (such as the mobs that attacked abolitionist meetings and destroyed their printing presses) were free speech and the right of peaceable assembly. Just as the repression of black Americans was due to the desire to make them labor on terms dictated by landowners, there was, for the sake of seeing to it that they would labor under conditions imposed by mine, mill and rail-road operators, restriction and interference with these rights of all Americans. Such restriction and interference was made possible by precisely the same downgrading of human rights protection as had defeated, for the time being, the great purposes of Thaddeus Stevens and Charles Sumner.

Abraham Lincoln once said: "it has so happened, in all ages of the world, that some have labored, & others have without labor enjoyed a large proportion of the fruits. This is wrong and should not continue. To secure to each laborer the whole product of his labor or as nearly as possible, is a worthy object of any good government."

The governments that followed after Lincoln's—in the nation and in the states—had not acted in accordance with Lincoln's idea that a "worthy object" was the securing to laborers "as nearly as possible" the whole product of their work. As we have seen, when some states did move in that direction, the court had distorted the due process clause to interfere with and check their efforts. Working men united in organizations whose purpose was aimed at the worthy object that government had failed to secure, and then were often repelled by the government itself. Sometimes they were halted in their efforts by the state government, sometimes by the nation.

The Hayes administration, which withdrew the few token forces of federal troops from the former slave states in 1877, despite and in the face of continuing violations of federal law, did not hesitate to use troops against strikers throughout the nation in that very same year. The eight-hour day movement was set back in 1886 by the furor and frenzy unleashed by the Haymarket explosion and the placing of the blame on the activist labor leaders who were hanged after trial by a prejudiced jury. The several states began, with federal aid and approval, to build their National Guard organizations as instruments of repression: trained, armed and led with the single purpose of defending the owners and controllers of great wealth from those who sought by self-organization to improve their miserable living conditions.

In 1894, while Albion Tourgee's Lost Cause—the fight against the Jim Crow Louisiana Law—was on its way to the court, the justices approved the issuance of a federal court order against Eugene V. Debs, leader of a great railway strike, and he was jailed for violating the court decree. In the face of protests from Governor Altgeld of Illinois—the same who had freed the last Haymarket prisoners—who protested the violation of his state's rights, the rail employers obtained the aid of United States Army forces to repress the workers who were trying to better their conditions.

In the years that followed, the principal and practically the only organization of working men that survived and grew was the newly founded American Federation of Labor. But the unions that were part of the A.F.L. did not reach or try to assist the great mass of American industrial, farm and forest, or mine workers, the men whose efforts were contributing to the amassing of greater and greater fortunes for their employers and the banks that financed them. These A.F.L. unions, contrary to the traditions of the earlier federations or national labor organizations, and against their own early teachings, began to exclude black Americans from their membership. By the turn of the century black workers were excluded from most of the skilled trades or "crafts" to which the A.F.L. unions were confined; and the workers of all ancestries who did the hard labor of the lumberjack, the miner, the unskilled in many industries were at the mercy of their employers, earning hardly enough to survive and in wretched conditions.

There arrived on this dismal scene in 1905 a new organization, one that saw that the spirit of Lincoln had been stifled and that new methods and new ideas were needed to win just and humane treatment for the great assembly of unorganized and undefended American workers. Its founders and leaders, having lived through the years in which the full force and power of the government was used to aid the owners of capital, the employing class, in securing the labor of the working class on its own terms, shared a common belief in the need for a drastic change. They saw a society in which the result of the control of the government by and in the interest of the greed of the owners was that two percent of the population owned sixty percent of the wealth, in which half, or almost half, of the people of the United States lived at a level very close to starvation.

They were convinced that there was no real hope for the improvement of these conditions except by the introduction of a fraternal cooperative commonwealth, which would come about by removal of the owning class entirely, and management of the factories and the mines by and in the interests of all the people. Until the day could come when all workers, united in one big union, could successfully displace the owners and remove the government from their control, they were pledged and ready, in the words of their leader, William D. Haywood, to go "down into the gutter to get at the mass of the workers and bring them up to a decent plane of living."

Their movement was to inspire, and their members and sympathizers were to write, many ballads that told of their struggles, and fighting songs that they would join in singing in their meeting halls, in the streets and often in jails. One of them, "Solidarity Forever," gave voice to their dream of the benefits to come from the creative, collective action to come from their united efforts:

> In our hands is placed a power greater than their hoarded gold,
> Greater than the might of armies, magnified a thousand fold,
> We can bring to birth a new world from the ashes of the old:
> For the Union makes us strong.

Their founding convention in 1905 took the name Industrial Workers of the World. Often referred to by their initials, I.W.W., they also acquired the nickname of "wobblies," by which they might call each other, or "rebel," or "fellow worker." Their language was frank and simple; their aims unconcealed; their methods as direct and sometimes as violent as the brutal conditions that they had organized to fight against. Not only were the housing and health conditions, the diet and clothing, of the workers they championed dreadful; an official government report conceded that justice was denied to the mass of workers "in the creation, adjudication, and administration of the law."

It must be remembered that during the period in which the I.W.W. flourished it was only the people who were the guardians of the principles of liberty, justice and equality in the United States, for the Supreme Court had turned its back and most officials of government ignored them. At a time when free speech itself was not considered to be protected against the states and cities by the Fourteenth Amendment, the wobblies fought for free speech in the streets. At a time when the court refused to apply the Fourteenth Amendment to secure equal protection of the law to all Americans, and the seeds of the crisis in our cities of the present day were planted by the exclusion of blacks from most labor unions, the ranks of the I.W.W. were open to all. "There are two organizations in this country that have shown that they do care," wrote Mary White Ovington about living up to the United States Constitution: "The first is the National Association for the Advancement of Colored People, the second is the Industrial Workers of the World."

Never in the long history of our country, until recent years, have there been such persistent, militant and courageous struggles in the streets for the principles of free speech as those conducted by the I.W.W. from 1908 to 1916. It was only natural—once it had become clear that they raised the question "Who will control the machines and mines and for whose benefit?"—that those threatened by that question would seek to silence their voices. When an organizing campaign to persuade workers to unite in the organization took place, or when a strike to use the power of the united workers to improve their conditions was on, only one side would be told in the newspapers or in the pulpits of the churches. The advertisers and the big contributors to churches would see to that. The streets were the only place where the wobblies could tell the truth, as they saw it, about their aims and the grievances they sought to remedy.

The employing class was always in a position, especially in those days, to influence and practically to control the politicians who voted in the city councils, or gave orders to the police. That control was used, or was attempted to be used, to keep the I.W.W. speakers off the streets. Either a local law or ordinance was passed that forbade public street speaking, or without even the benefit of a "law" the police would be ordered to arrest and haul away the speakers before they could get very far in their talk.

Now free speech was not an academic or theoretical question for the wobblies. The freedom of the streets was essential for the two ever present aspects of every campaign: to reach the workers who were to be induced to join in a fight to better their conditions; to reach and win the sympathy of the "public" or at least to neutralize it, at a time and in circumstances when the employing class would always seek to incite and control mob activity directed against strikers and leaders of labor. That essential freedom could not have been won in the courts. Although the First Amendment forbade the making of any law abridging the freedom of speech or the right of the people peaceably to assemble—and that freedom, that right, was a privilege or immunity intended to be secured against the interference of states and cities by Big Fourteen—there were few courts that would, in those days, have enforced the Constitution. Some other way had to be found, and it was.

More than twenty and possibly as many as thirty of these "free speech" fights were conducted by the I.W.W. in the western cities and states where its work had been centered. There were many variations in detail, but the basic pattern was the same. When a point was reached where the police and/or a city ordinance was used to stifle the right to speak, and the leaders of a local movement would be hauled down off their soapboxes, a call for help would go out. Rank and file members from many miles away would begin to converge on the city of struggle. A group would get ready at an appointed time and place. One would climb up and start, "Fellow workers and friends . . ." He would be hauled down and dragged away, just as he knew he would. But then another would mount the box and begin again. And another and another and another.

The jails would be filled and the courts obstructed. The spirit of the speakers and the reinforcements never would sag. The jails and the annexes, firehouses and stables—whatever facilities the perplexed city authorities could press into service—would ring with the sound of the rebel songs, the ballads of struggle that the wobblies sang when they were together. In a matter of weeks or months, the authorities would tire, and settle: two or four street corners were allotted for the exercise of the rights that the American Revolution was fought to win and the American Constitution written to preserve. For a few years, at least, the ardor and willingness of the I.W.W. members to suffer enabled liberty to live.

A people who still understood the meaning and value of the freedom they had won would have acclaimed such efforts and appreciated such victories as their own. But by 1913, the Golden Jubilee year of Lincoln's Proclamation of Emancipation, there seemed to be little commitment to liberty and justice for all in the hearts and minds of the American people. How far we had strayed was shown in the very first months of the administration of Woodrow Wilson, who expressed ideas under the slogan "The New Freedom" that offered hope to many. "The masters of the government of the United States are the combined capitalists and manufacturers of the United States," said Wilson in the campaign that won the presidency for him, promising to restore the control of the government to the people.

America was promises, one poet wrote, neglecting to add how many of the promises have been broken ones. Woodrow Wilson's promises included "absolute fair dealing" to all Americans and "justice done the colored people . . . not mere grudging justice but justice executed with liberality and cordial good feeling." Within a month after he took the oath to support, protect and defend the Constitution, Wilson's Cabinet agreed unanimously to inflict the humiliating practice of segregation in the federal civil service. The national government pledged in the Fourteenth Amendment to protect its people against injustice inflicted by state and local governments had not only broken its word, but was even adding injury on its own.

Du Bois wrote that he had "thought it impossible that so high-minded and scholarly a man could repudiate" his "plain straightforward words." But more ominous than the broken promises of one man were the indifference and callousness of the many. Thirty years before, as one acute observer said, segregation of its own clerks by the federal authority would have caused a tornado of protest. "Now it passes almost unnoticed," wrote Paul Haworth. Moorfield Storey published an Open Letter "To the People of the United States," asking, without much response, that they speak out for justice. Segregation in government was allowed to spread, extending even to the gallery of the Senate of the United States.

A nation so indifferent to the spirit of liberty could not have been expected to respond with appreciative warmth to the struggles and sacrifices of members of the I.W.W. for the principle of free speech. It was left, rather, with a sullen recollection of the idea of "violence" as associated with the wobblies, although it was most often the local forces of repression that accounted for the conflict. As the I.W.W. continued its efforts for economic justice for the workingmen it reached, the Great World War of 1914–18 engulfed Europe and increasingly affected America. By the time Congress (which, as we have said, did not represent the American people) declared war supposedly to make the world safe for democracy, those who were in control of the government and the press—very much the same "capitalists and manufacturers" denounced by candidate Wilson—were ready through President Wilson to repress and practically extermi- nate the Industrial Workers of the World. Not only was it intolerable to those who stood to profit from the war that the mass of miners and loggers whose labor was essential to such profit should be led to fight for fair wages and decent conditions; it was totally unacceptable that men should go unmolested who told the truth about the war, who described it as a "war for conquest and exploitation," and one of whose poets sang:

> Mourn not the dead that in the cool earth lie
> Dust unto dust. . . .
> But rather mourn the apathetic throng—
> the cowed and the mean—
> who see the world's great anguish and its wrong
> And dare not speak!

The story of the ruthless repression of the I.W.W., in all its detail, involves the First and Fifth and Sixth and Eighth Amendments, not the Fourteenth, and so is for the most part beyond the scope of this work. But before the major act of persecution—once more, as in 1886, a conspiracy trial in Chicago, but this time with the United States Attorney instead of the state's attorney controlling the court— there was, among many local lawless acts, an episode so shocking that an attempt was made to allay the protests that followed by using for its original purposes one of the civil rights laws passed to enforce Big Fourteen, a law that had lain unused for many years and that was to go back to the dustbin again for many years to come.

A sheriff is a local offical sworn to uphold law and order. Harry C. Wheeler, Sheriff of Bisbee, Arizona, was one of many in our history who have betrayed their oath. In the summer of 1917, at the very time when the Supreme Court was pondering its decision in Moorfield Storey's Kentucky residential segregation case, Sheriff Wheeler led a mob on a mission of lawless violence. Backed by the leading businessmen of his country, Wheeler and a gang of ruffians, including many of those businessmen, sworn in as deputies for the occasion and "under cover of darkness, calmly, premeditatedly, de- liberately swooped down at dawn upon the homes of unsuspecting, unoffending miners who committed no violence, nay more who had threatened no violence but who had every lawful reason to feel se- cure as citizens under the guarantees vouchsafed by the Constitution of the United States of America." Those were the words of the gov- ernor of Arizona himself, chief executive of the state where the at- rocity thus described had occurred.

The forcible, violent, illegal mass kidnapping had been organized in response to an I.W.W.-led strike of copper miners that had been launched that summer in the Bisbee area. There had been no violence by the strikers. A Presidential Mediation Commission investigated the facts and found that the strikers were neither "pro-German" nor "seditious" as the sheriff and the town's businessmen had claimed, that what had been involved was "nothing more than the normal results of the increased cost of living and the speeding up processes to which the mine management had been tempted by the abnormally high market price of copper."

The report of the Mediation Commission came too late to help the families that had been the victims of the deportations described by the governor. The strike was broken and the few allowed to return to their homes were obliged to work on the "copper barons'" terms. Though the president was himself to use federal troops again and again to the same end as the lawless mob of Bisbee, the reaction of the governor and the report of the Mediation Commission made it necessary to attempt to prosecute the sheriff and the leaders of his mob of gentlemen of property and standing.

The case of *United States against Wheeler* was brought to court under one of the long-dormant civil rights acts of the 1870 Congress. No more fundamental civil right can be imagined than the right of U. S. citizens and lawful residents to reside undisturbed in their homes and chosen places of abode. But taking the same narrow view that was used in the slaughterhouse case and in freeing the Cruikshank mob, the Supreme Court freed the Wheeler mob. Violators of the civil rights of white miners could take shelter in the protected area devised for violators of the civil rights of black cotton farmers. Forty years of denial of the authority of the United States to act to guarantee the rights secured by the Fourteenth Amendment had taken their toll. The power expressly granted to the Congress was still denied. But in a series of cases that were before the courts just before and after the Wheeler case, federal judges were finally forced to face their obligation to see to it that state criminal courts did not convict people without due process of law. Another turning point would be reached.

Chapter 25

Leo Frank,
Joe Hill
and Frank Moore

Leo Frank and Joe Hill were to die within a few months of each other. The gulf between their lives and personalities was as wide as the distance between Georgia, where a mob was allowed to kill one of them, and Utah, where a judge's death sentence was carried out. No fair-minded court of justice would have found either guilty of the crime that was the pretext for taking their lives. Neither Frank nor Hill had ever heard of Frank Moore, an Arkansas sharecropper. But when Moore won his fight for life in a case that began the return of vitality to the words "due process of law" in Big Fourteen, it could be said that they had not died in vain.

Born in Texas and brought up in Brooklyn, Leo Frank would have despised Joe Hill and scorned Frank Moore. He was born in comfortable circumstances and college trained when engineering degrees were rare. He was invited to Atlanta to become the very efficient manager of a pencil factory financed by a syndicate dominated by his wealthy Uncle Moses.

Joel Haaglund took the name of Joe Hill when he left his Swedish ship on the West Coast around the turn of the century. Working sometimes as a seaman or on the docks, sometimes as a casual laborer, he saw how necessary it was that working men should organize to better their conditions. He became a member and then an organizer of the Industrial Workers of the World and something more. With a gift for writing rousing songs based on the music of then popular hymns and melodies, Joe Hill became the leading rebel bard in a movement that often won support by the spirit and singing of its rank and file.

Leo Frank would not have been remembered for anything that he had achieved in his lifetime. His modest success in running his capitalist uncle's factory and his prestige as a leader in Atlanta's Jewish community were all he asked from life. He would have been shocked at the words of one of the masterpieces for which Joe Hill is still remembered, the completely irreverent "The Preacher and the

Slave," with its derisive rejection of the "pie in the sky when you die"—which was all that most leaders of organized religion had to offer to the oppressed in those days.

As the time of their deaths drew near in 1915, the thoughts of these two different and distant men dwelt on a similar theme. Leo Frank asked, "Is the technical finesse of the law to forever preclude a hearing of the facts, and human rights to be trampled beneath judicial feet?" At almost the same time Joe Hill wrote, after having first vainly attempted to insist that money being spent for his fight for freedom would have been better used in organizing to build the one big union: "The cause I stand for, that of a fair and honest trial, is worth more than any human life,—much more than mine."

In a land that prides itself on being free, "a fair and honest trial" for one accused of crime is really rock bottom, the very least that every member of society has a right to expect. In one form of words or another it was pledged by every state constitution. It had become quite evident by 1866 that some states did not always keep that pledge. Since it had been settled that we were a nation as well as a union of states, there was every reason for the protection of national citizens by the nation to which they owed allegiance.

For this the words "due process of law" were made a part of Big Fourteen. Whatever else those words might be argued to cover and to mean, they surely mean that no man was to be deprived of life or liberty or property without a fair and honest trial. When the Bill of Rights was written, specific guarantees were provided that were intended to protect that right in federal cases. Not only were the words "due process of law" used; there was also the right not to have to face trial unless indicted by a grand jury, the right not to have to testify against oneself, the right to counsel, and so on. But the reason for all of these special safeguards, the right that they were all intended to protect, was the right to an impartial decision by an unprejudiced tribunal on the question, "Is this defendant guilty beyond a reasonable doubt?"

When Leo Frank's case came to the Supreme Court of the United States the majority was fresh from four decades of voting down the separate guarantees of a fair trial listed in the Bill of Rights in every state case that had come before it. Over and over it had been decided that the specifics—the right to grand jury indictment, the right not to testify against oneself—were not among the "privileges and immunities" of national citizens or a part of "due process of law." Each of these could be dispensed with by a state in a criminal case regardless of Big Fourteen or the men who had written it—who, as the court conceded, would have been surprised and disappointed. In Leo Frank's case no specific safeguard was at stake. To be tested was whether the high court would look at what had happened in a state criminal proceeding that was really no trial at all.

A little girl, a fourteen-year-old worker, had been found murdered in the pencil factory. She had come there to collect her wages on a day on which the plant was closed. Frank, who had been catching up on paper work and had been alone in his office when he gave her the pay envelope, became an object of cruel suspicion that was supported by no definite fact. The double burden he carried of being Jewish and a Northerner was enough to make him fair game. A police department that was pressed by public opinion to find a murderer committed itself to the theory that he was guilty and proceeded to find or to manufacture scraps of evidence on which to convict him. Much of the city's poor and middle class white working population was carried away by a spirit of hate and revenge.

It is a strong statement to say that "there was no trial at all" when all the forms were followed and the legal ritual obeyed. There was a judge presiding who tried to be fair, a jury sworn, able counsel active for Frank, a court clerk and attendants. The whole affair looked and sounded like a trial, except for the last few moments. What happened then illuminated the scene as much as a flash of lightning makes a true picture visible on a dark and stormy night.

"Before I charge the jury," said the judge as the trial drew to a close, "I want to see counsel in my chambers." The defense attorneys followed the judge and the prosecution staff into a small office adjoining the courtroom. There the judge showed the lawyers letters from three Atlanta newspaper editors warning him to take precautions, should the jury find Frank not guilty.

"Gentlemen," said the judge, "I think if the jury acquitted him, the defendant would be lynched." The prosecutor silently agreed. Frank's chief attorney asked, "What solution do you suggest?"

"I have two," said the judge. "I shall alert the commander of the National Guard. And I ask that neither Mr. Frank, nor any of his attorneys be present in the court room when the jury returns its verdict. I fear for all your lives." The judge knew, as did all in the room, that a defendant has an absolute right to be present during every moment of his trial.

"I don't think Frank will waive that right," said one of his lawyers.

"Don't tell him he is waiving it," said the judge.

"He wants vindication," answered the lawyer.

"And I want to preserve law and order." The defense attorneys reluctantly agreed.

The rest of the story is told in the dissenting opinion written on Frank's final appeal by Justice Oliver Wendell Holmes and a new member of the court, Charles Evans Hughes: "The hostility of the crowd was sufficient to lead the judge to confer in the presence of the jury with the chief of police of Atlanta and the Colonel of the Fifth Georgia Regiment, stationed in the city, both of whom were known to the jury. . . . When the verdict was rendered, and before more than one of the jurymen had been polled, there was such a roar of applause that the polling could not go on until order was restored. The noise outside was such that it was difficult for the judge to hear the answers of the jurors, although he was only ten feet from them. With these specifications of fact, the petitioner alleges that the trial was dominated by a hostile mob and was nothing but an empty form."

An empty form—no trial at all—was this "due process of law"? The Supreme Court majority refused to interfere. Frank's plea had been presented to, and turned down by, the Georgia appeals court, and the majority of the nation's highest court refused to go behind that court's ruling to see what the facts were, to find out what had really happened in Atlanta. Was the noise outside so loud that the judge could not hear the answers of the jurors? Did the jury see the judge conferring in open court with the commander of the Georgia National Guard? Is it "due process" or any process of law at all for a trial to be concluded under conditions that prompted the sober estimate that if the jury did not find the defendant guilty a mob would lynch him?

Dissenting from the majority's ruling, speaking up in their own way for Big Fourteen as Justice Harlan had done from his lone post on the bench for so long, Holmes and Hughes declared: "Mob law does not become due process of law by securing the assent of a terrorized jury." Where the trial judge himself, "the expert on the spot," had feared for Frank and his lawyers in case of an acquittal, it was the duty of the nation's highest court "to declare lynch law as little valid when practised by a regularly drawn jury as when administered by one elected by a mob intent on death."

It was to turn out, after all, that Leo Frank was to die a victim of a mob. The governor of Georgia, privately satisfied of Frank's innocence, commuted his sentence of death to life imprisonment on the publicly stated ground that doubt of guilt had been expressed by the trial judge and others. Two months later, the state was the scene of one more act of brutal lawlessness of the kind that had been used repeatedly to terrorize its black population. Two dozen cold-blooded murderers "broke" into the state penitentiary—somehow not being stopped by the armed guards so carefully placed there to keep prisoners from breaking out—and seized and dragged out Leo Frank. They drove unmolested almost two hundred miles across the countryside in a convoy of eight automobiles. When they came to the murdered girl's home town they barbarically tortured Frank to death.

Frank's tragic and brutal death was but one of thousands of lynchings that have stained our history. More serious in its significance was the court decision that had turned down his appeal. It seemed so definitely to mean that the logic of the cruel decisions of past decades would be pushed to the limit—that national citizenship would not be protected by an examination by a national court of whether or not a state's process was fair. An example of the effect of such a ruling on precedent-minded attorneys was found in Joe Hill's case, where, after the Utah courts had turned him down, it was not felt worthwhile even to try an appeal to the Supreme Court.

"You are right in excluding all hope of action by the United States Supreme Court," wrote Frank P. Walsh, an able attorney who had been serving as a member of the United States Commission on Industrial Relations. "Through the interpretation of the various sections of the Constitution by that Court, the right to appeal to it has become a mere paper one." Having known Hill's reputation and work, Walsh added: "What you have written me about Hill's case, of course, strikes a very deep chord of sympathy in my heart, and I would do anything in my power to assist him."

Hill's popularity and success as an I.W.W. balladeer had not interfered with his dedicated work as organizer and agitator. While his songs were sung wherever the dispossessed and the disinherited gathered, on picket lines, at demonstrations, in hobo "jungles," in jails, Hill was never idle. He would go from town to town and state to state, while his comrades won new followers with such songs as "What We Want," written to answer the taunting question often hurled at them:

> We want all the workers in the world to organize
> In a great big union grand
> And when we all united stand
> The world for workers we'll demand
> If the working class could only see and realize
> What mighty power labor has
> Then the exploiting master class
> It would soon fade away.

In the same issue of the movement's newspaper, *Industrial Worker,* appeared another Joe Hill song with a chorus expressing his—and the I.W.W.'s—vision of the future:

> Then we'll sing one song of the Worker's Commonwealth
> Full of beauty, full of love and health.

But within a short time the periodicals that published his songs were circulating pleas for his freedom; a special edition of the I.W.W. *Songbook* was sold to raise funds for his defense. Joe Hill, a newcomer to Salt Lake City, where he had come on organizing business, was charged with the murder of J. B. Morrison, a retired policeman. The man had been shot in his home by armed intruders who made it evident that their motive was not robbery but revenge. Their grudge against Morrison must have antedated Hill's arrival in Salt Lake. The rebel bard's arrest was made possible by a coincidental shooting wound he had suffered in an affair involving a woman and a jealous lover or husband.

Once Joe Hill was seized and charged with Morrison's murder his doom was sealed, even though there was no really positive identification. A storm of newspaper articles attacked the I.W.W. and denounced Hill's membership. Likewise in the period before and during the trial, to whip up a pervasive hostility against him, Joe Hill was vilified for his so-called "criminal record," which consisted of arrests sustained in the normal course of efforts to organize and aid the underdog.

The police were not outdone by the press in behaving just as Atlanta had towards Leo Frank. They managed to produce and induce witnesses to testify against the man detested by the "copper bosses," the chief taxpayers of the area. The attorneys representing Hill were ineffectual, shrinking from their cross-examination of destructive, hostile witnesses, so much so that Joe Hill tried to discharge them. This was blocked by the trial judge, and so Hill was both the victim of an enveloping hostile atmosphere that prevented fair consideration of his guilt or innocence and deprived of the right to counsel of his own choice.

Each case, Frank's and Hill's, resulted in a rising tide of criticism and protest that was not stilled entirely even when the defendant was killed. The legacy of protest and of disappointment at the failure of the defense campaigns undoubtedly contributed to the change in setting that Frank Moore and his fellow freedom fighters found a few years later. But more important than the public's revulsion at the lynching of Leo Frank and their anger at the judicial murder of Joe Hill was the resistance shown throughout the nation by the victims of violence, lawlessness, hostility and prejudice. The 1919 resistance movement of the nation's black Americans, their efforts to organize in their own defense and their willingness to die fighting when attacked, brought about a profound change in outlook. Moorfield Storey returned to court in order to win the recognition of the Supreme Court that Big Fourteen's pledge of "due process of law" imposed on it a duty to supervise and review the action of state courts in cases involving the rights of the nation's citizens.

Frank Moore was but one of a number of Arkansas black farmers who were inspired by the leadership of another man named Hill—Robert Hill, who had been taken from his cabin by the draft law passed to force men into the army in World War I. He had returned to his native Phillips County with a determination to win the "democracy" for his people that Americans had died for overseas in the war declared by a Congress that contained no black men.

The lynching of Leo Frank which so shocked the nation was neither unprecedented nor surprising to people who had seen such murderous outrages average as many as one hundred a year. They knew or sensed that the purpose of the murderers was, in many cases, the same as that of the men of the Cruikshank mob and the hooded night riders of half a century before: to make an example of blacks who would dare to speak up for their rights or to resist being cheated. The object of the state officials who closed their eyes during such crimes or allowed them to go unpunished afterwards was to serve the needs of wealthy landowners—to have a compliant labor supply that would serve on their terms. The black farmers were obliged to work under a system superficially fair yet almost always based on cheating—"sharecropping."

To work for a share of the crop that one labored to produce might have been endurable if the farm workers had prospered when the crop was good and had had an opportunity to improve their conditions. That rarely happened. To find at the end of a harvest and a year's toil that one was in debt, and that one could be jailed for leaving the plantation while in debt, was hardly better than slavery. Not only were the shares dictated by the owners, but the latter did not even live up to their end of the bargain, and they robbed their workers by double bookkeeping.

Robert Hill and Frank Moore and the Arkansas farmers who responded to their call to "Organize!" formed themselves into a local group that they called the Progressive Farmers and Household Union of America. Some of them had been instructed in the use of guns by the very government that, for fifty years, had neglected their right to due process of law before their life, liberty or property was to be taken away. They were willing to risk their lives for the sake of a civil right which the nation should have protected, or should have forced the state of Arkansas to protect: the right to assemble peaceably, which the First Amendment was written to guarantee and the Fourteenth to secure against action or inaction by state governments.

The war, the need for black labor off the plantations, the preaching of government leaders about "democracy" to win support for the war—all had brought about a change in conditions. Events like the lynching of Leo Frank had helped the campaign of the National Association for the Advancement of Colored People against the institution of lynching. Working men's organizations in the nations that were allied with the United States protested such denials of justice as the execution of Joe Hill and the near execution of a California labor leader named Tom Mooney, who languished in prison for a crime he did not commit and was saved from execution by stormy protests in Europe. And during 1919, in one location after another, when attacks were made on black communities, their inhabitants fought back, heeding what poet Claude McKay had written in July:

If we must die, let it not be like hogs
Hunted and penned in an inglorious spot
While round about us bark the mad and hungry dogs
Making their mock at our accursed lot. . . .
Like men we'll face the murderous, cowardly pack,
Pressed to the wall, dying, but—fighting back!

The white planters, merchants and bankers of Phillips County were not ready to sit back and permit the farm laborers, on whose oppression the whole structure of their wealth and social position rested, to unite. With control of the local press and the means of reporting events to the rest of the nation, they began to spread false reports that the blacks were organizing to massacre the whites, to seize their property and to overthrow the local government. Behind the shield of this barrage of lies, they planned to kill and terrorize blacks on a large enough scale to discourage the dissatisfaction of those complaining of the share they had received from the cotton crop.

The attack that followed the press reports opened with a volley of bullets fired by a sheriff and others into a church at the tiny hamlet of Hoop Spur, where over a hundred croppers were meeting to discuss retaining an attorney to press their claims. It did not go as planned. Instead of disbanding and fleeing for the woods, the men inside the church shot back. One of the attackers fell. Soon afterwards, inflamed by false reports about this very incident, armed bands of whites throughout the county roamed about, slaughtering at least one hundred blacks.

The Phillips County massacre succeeded in its immediate object of defeating efforts at self-organization by the local farm workers and sharecroppers. But the next move on the part of the landowners—their effort to teach a stern warning lesson to the brave members of the Progressive Farmers and Household Union and all who might seek to follow their example—was to run aground on the shoals of a slow to emerge Fourteenth Amendment. Neither state nor nation, of course, would fulfill its obligation to furnish equal protection of the laws to the victims of the massacre. The state's efforts to hang and imprison the known members and leaders of the union were to be blocked, after several years of struggle, by the Fourteenth Amendment.

In what was almost a reenactment of some of the features of Leo Frank's trial in Georgia, Frank Moore and eleven other front-rank leaders were convicted of murder and sentenced to die. At the time of the trial, it was evident that none would have survived the lynch mob if the jury had acquitted any of them. Jurors, too, were in danger: they could not have gone on living in Phillips County if they had voted for an acquittal. False testimony there was, this time the result of beatings and torture rather than bribes.

Moorfield Storey was called in to present the case in the Supreme Court of the United States. He took it on with the help of Scipio Jones, a local black attorney from Arkansas, and U. S. Bratton, the white lawyer whom the sharecroppers had been about to retain at the time that their church was fired upon by the advance guard of the lawless and disorderly white mob. Worried as he was about the effect of the precedent in the Frank case, Storey became increasingly hopeful about the outcome in the case that was to become known as *Moore against Dempsey*. While he developed a legal argument that created a basis for a technical distinction in the cases—that Georgia's highest court had examined for itself whether or not Frank's process was "due" but that Arkansas had not done so for Moore—his optimism must have been based on several factors: the change in conditions since the Frank case ten years before, the fact that the Constitution and a people's freedom were on trial, the belief that the United States, victor and participant in a postwar European settlement, could no longer be insensible to world opinion, and above all his choice of Bratton, an emancipated white Southerner, to help in the oral presentation. That courageous man, whose son had almost been lynched by the mob, made it his goal in speaking "to get a mental picture in the minds of the Court as to the exact conditions in Arkansas. I told the Court that conditions had grown up there that were worse than before the Civil War."

Victory was as significant as it was sweet. Holmes and Hughes were in the majority of seven now, rather than being a minority of two. If "the whole proceeding is a mask"—that is, if the trial is simply a form or ceremony the outcome of which has been fixed in advance—the court held that there is no due process of law. For the first time, and for the benefit of all Americans, it was decided that citizens' rights under the United States Constitution could not be trampled on at state court trials, that life and liberty (not merely property, as had been the case until then) were shielded by the pledge of due process of law, and that the duty and the right to redeem that pledge lay with the federal judicial system acting under the Fourteenth Amendment.

Chapter 26

Liberty by
Another Label

Joseph Gilbert was one of many Americans who were sent to prison for expressing their opinions about our intervention in World War I. One fact made his case unusual, one that stood out in the rising tide of repression. When Minnesota prosecuted Joe Gilbert and he fought his case to the Supreme Court—and lost—it at least gave one great justice the opportunity to reopen a debate that had seemed closed for half a century. That was when the slaughter-house decision frustrated the framers' intent to give national protection to the basic privileges and immunities of citizens of the United States.

There is no right—for that is what a "privilege or immunity" really is—more important to American democracy than the right of free speech. Free speech, needless to say, is only important and valuable when it is used. When there is an issue that is really worth arguing about, those on the side related to governmental power are tempted to cut off the debate. That is precisely what happened during the last great national controversy that preceded World War I, the argument about slavery. It was because so many states ignored their own constitutions and repressed the abolitionists, or permitted them to be driven out by mobbism, that Stevens and Bingham wanted a sweeping national guarantee of all privileges and immunities and won its inclusion in the Fourteenth Amendment.

Just as during the abolitionist era, imprisonment and mob violence were suffered by those who openly disagreed with the reasons that President Wilson had given for leading the country into war. There were quite a few, especially since the president had been re-elected in 1916 on a platform claiming that "he kept us out of war," but the government was not content during the war to accept merely the support of the majority that silently swallowed its claims. The administration whose leader admitted after it was all over that "This war was a commercial and industrial war" and that "the seed of war in the modern world is commercial and industrial rivalry" could not tolerate the expression of such ideas while the war was on.

Driven by an almost panic-stricken fear of adverse opinion and debate, Wilson's government sought to impose unanimity of thought and opinion on the nation. For repression, it used the Army and the Department of Justice as its principal agencies. Grievous injury was done to rights supposedly protected from the nation's action, rights with which we are not directly concerned in the story of the Fourteenth Amendment. For inciting its majority to support and play a role in that repression, there was a mobilization of every conceivable agency of public opinion. Cartoonists, songwriters, advertisers billboards, magazines and country newspapers were all conscripted, in effect. They combined to build up a sense of near hysteria on the part of the solid majority that supported the war.

All this was achieved by an official Committee for Public Information, whose own sympathetic historians have written: "Though only too well aware of how hysteria begins and grows, the Committee was forced to deal constantly with the material of panic, fear and intolerance." Although supporting the war to the hilt, and a member of a banking house that had not a little to do with our entry, J. P. Morgan's partner Thomas W. Lamont wrote: "There is altogether too great a tendency to call people names just because they happen to talk intelligently on certain topics. . . . I have heard people called pro-Germans just because they expressed the hope that the war would not last forever." In fact, those who expressed ideas that called into question the assumptions on which we entered the war were denounced as "pro-German"; those with German-sounding names, regardless of what their opinions might be, were harassed with such hoodlumism as the painting of their doors with yellow paint, and worse. Great artists like Fritz Kreisler and Frieda Hempel were driven off the concert stage. The German language was banned from school curricula in some states.

Senators and congressmen who had voted against the declaration of war were subjected to a flood of abuse. One United States district court judge expressed a wish that he could order them before a firing squad. Federal repression of dissent was disguised by its inclusion, without any justification, in a law called the "Espionage Act"; several states followed suit with their own local gag laws. Under these one man was jailed for saying to a patriotic knitting bee, "No soldier ever sees those socks." A woman agitator for the Socialist Party was sent to jail for ten years for saying "I am for the people; the government is for the profiteers."

In Minnesota, one victim was imprisoned for complaining about the food at a military training camp. A farmer, when visited by a Red Cross fund collector, said—and was arrested and sent to jail for so saying—that the government which had gotten us into an unnecessary war could get us out, and that meanwhile the Red Cross should be supported out of tax money.

Joseph Gilbert was the first of these targets of repression to insist on fighting a state law's constitutionality all the way to the Supreme Court. As an organizer for the now almost forgotten Nonpartisan League, he was used to standing up for his rights. The League had been formed by and for the small working farmers of the north-western states, who had seen both political parties connive at their exploitation by the railroads, the grain-elevator operators and the banks and commodity brokers. They united for a socialist kind of agrarian reform as they saw the price of wheat rise, with other costs, while their income stayed the same. Their object was state sponsor-ship of cooperative farming and state ownership or rigid control of the banks and facilities that siphoned off their income.

"We are going over to Europe to make the world safe for democ-racy," said Gilbert at a meeting of his followers, "but I tell you we had better make America safe for democracy first. . . . We were stampeded into this war by newspaper rot to pull England's chest-nuts out of the fire for her. I tell you, if they conscripted wealth like they have conscripted men, this war would not last over forty eight hours."

When the Supreme Court majority approved Gilbert's conviction it claimed for its justification that the war "had been declared by the power constituted by the Constitution to declare it, and in the manner provided for by the Constitution." Justice Oliver Wendell Holmes, who had written the court's opinions in cases that had been recently decided sustaining federal repression of dissent, concurred in the approval of the conviction. But one dissenter spoke up to de-nounce the invasion of liberty that the Minnesota law accomplished. Using words that the Joint Committee on Reconstruction would have approved, Mr. Justice Brandeis declared that the Minnesota law "affects rights, privileges and immunities of one who is a citizen of the United States; and it deprives him of an important part of his liberty. These are rights which are guaranteed protection by the Fed-eral Constitution, and they are invaded by the statute in question."

Louis D. Brandeis had been named to the United States Supreme Court only a few years before. He was descended from a family that had come here as refugees from the European revolutionary struggles of 1848. His uncle, Louis Debbitz, had continued here his fight for freedom by becoming an ardent supporter of the abolition-ist movement. The Brandeis family had first settled in Kentucky, but Boston attracted Louis after he had attended Harvard Law School and he settled there to practice law.

There were enough reminders about of the Boston of Charles Sumner and William Lloyd Garrison to attract him and to instruct him in the city's great traditions. His life was to be influenced by one of those which he tried to help revive, a tradition best expressed by

William Ellery Channing in defense of freedom of speech for abolitionists a decade before the Brandeis family landed in America:
"Freedom of opinion, of speech, and of the press is our most valuable privilege, the very soul of Republican institutions, the safeguard
of all other rights . . . if rulers succeed in silencing every voice but
that which approves them, if nothing reaches the people but what
would lend support to men in power—farewell to liberty."

After a brilliantly successful legal career, the latter part of which
was devoted to voluntary public service, the man who became an
outstanding twentieth-century advocate of Channing's views was
named to the Supreme Court. The nomination was confirmed after a
hard fight. The opposition included not only men repelled by the
work that Brandeis had done for social justice and economic reform
but also many who opposed the first Jew to be named to the court
and were influenced consciously or subconsciously by the poison of
anti-Semitism.

Some of those who opposed the confirmation of Mr. Justice
Brandeis—including Moorfield Storey—were later to find some satisfaction with his work on the court. And while Justice Holmes is better remembered as a spokesman for freedom, Brandeis deserves to
be honored as a successor to Justice Harlan, the really great dissenter, whose views clashed with Holmes' more than once. If
Holmes in his later years on the court seemed to speak out more
often as a spokesman for the liberty of the individual and human
rights, a good deal of the credit should go to Brandeis. There is every
reason to believe that Brandeis contributed to the rebirth of freedom
not only by his own work on the court but also by his influence on
Holmes.

Soon after making his lone effort in Joseph Gilbert's case, Justice
Brandeis was to be convinced that the rest of the members of the
bench could not be persuaded to accept his interpretation of the
"privileges or immunities" clause as a basis for protecting free
speech from curtailment by state laws. The other justices, less than
two years after Gilbert's appeal was turned down, made their stubbornness evident by including a hostile phrase, one totally unnecessary to the decision, in another case. There the Prudential Insurance
Company was trying to test a Missouri law that required such firms
to explain the reasons for the discharge of an employee who had
been with them at least ninety days.

Naturally Holmes and Brandeis agreed that such a law was within
a state's power, as tending to eliminate arbitrary dismissals and the
use of boycotts and blacklists. But not on the ground given by their
fellow justice, which seemed to chill all hopes for the enforcement of
free speech protection. Rejecting an argument that the "privileges or
immunities" clause was supposed to give a company the right of si-

lence about its reasons for firing workers, the justice assigned to write the opinion said: ". . . neither the Fourteenth Amendment, nor any other provision of the Constitution of the United States imposes upon the States any restrictions about 'freedom of speech' or the 'liberty of silence'. . . ."

However, in his dissent in Gilbert's case, Louis Brandeis had laid the foundation for a future fight for liberty under another label. In pointed reference to the tradition that had developed for striking down laws regulating business, he concluded his opinion in favor of Gilbert's freedom by saying, "I cannot believe that the liberty guaranteed under the Fourteenth Amendment includes only liberty to acquire and enjoy property." His words were recalled with perhaps increasing pangs of conscience as the court was to be confronted again and again with the results of the hatred and intolerance that had been whipped up during and immediately after the war of 1917–18. As Brandeis' ideas influenced Holmes, and the two with the aid of able attorneys who had appeared before them persuaded their fellows to join them, a new door was opened. As Brandeis' closing words in Gilbert's case foresaw, the "due process" clause was to be used for protecting the civil rights and liberties that should have been guarded as the privileges and immunities mentioned in Big Fourteen.

One fine opportunity arrived when a Nebraska law was brought to the court on a challenge by Robert T. Meyer who had been convicted of the awful crime of teaching German to a schoolboy. The law that made this a crime was one of a dozen or so, across the country, that reflected the narrow intolerance produced by war propaganda. It was now five years since the war was over, and there was an increasing consensus of shame and regret at the extreme intolerance that Americans and their lawmakers had displayed. Not yet ready for an avowal of the freedom under the Fourteenth that Brandeis spoke for, the court nevertheless could not resist the repentant mood of a nation that sensed it had gone too far. Meyer was freed, but for the wrong reason.

It was still a period when, as we have already seen, the court was regularly striking down state laws that offered modest protection against business and banker cupidity for workers, farmers and consumers. "Liberty of contract" had been the phrase invented to justify the court's use of the due process clause to assume the power to take such action. Due process had been turned topsy-turvy when it was converted into an instrument for the defense of greed and exploitation; now it was turned around again in a curious way.

Mr. Meyer, the "criminal" who had dared to teach the German language to a child whose parents wanted him to learn it, was employed in a private school. For him this was a business and his continued acquisition of property depended on it. In such a case, the court said, Meyer's right to teach and the parents' right to engage him to instruct their children were forms of liberty. Since that was so, the formula used for protecting profits in business, banking and railroad cases was applied: the law "is arbitrary and without reasonable relation to any end within the competence of the state." (Justice Holmes, intent on his own effort to defend a state's power to control big business, chose to vote against the extension of liberty under the unexpected label.)

Two years later the members of a Catholic parochial school society, the Sisters of the Holy Name, were to learn—possibly to their surprise—that they were entitled to the protection of "the profitable features of their business." Catholic parents had been faced with the penalties of an Oregon criminal law commanding them to send their youngsters to public schools. The 1922 law, directed against private and parochial schools, was the result of the resurgence of the Ku Klux Klan. The name of the guerrilla fighters against freedom who terrorized the South and nullified the structure of rights and the voting laws of half a century before was adopted by a new mob of bigots that began at the time of the lynching of Leo Frank. The organization, anti-Jew, anti-Catholic, antiblack and antiradical, had mushroomed throughout the land in the favorable conditions of hatred, fear and intolerance spawned by wartime repression and propaganda. The elimination of parochial schools as a step toward the elimination of Catholics was an object of its political action.

The court, as in the Meyer case, was determined that this type of tyranny on a local scale should be struck down. It was brought closer, but not close enough quite yet, to recognizing that Big Fourteen had been framed to guard against precisely that kind of tyranny. Even though it was not ready to see and to admit that whatever Congress was forbidden to do by the Bill of Rights it was bound to forbid to the states, nevertheless it had to act.

The First Amendment protects the freedom of religion and religious choice, but the court decision did not protect the right to an education in a Catholic school as a matter of the right of conscience. Since it is results that count, and the Sisters of the Holy Name were victorious in their lawsuit, one should not carp, and they did not at the time. But it hardly sounds like a blow for freedom to have the Ku Klux Klan law struck down and thrown out because it would "greatly diminish the value of their property." It was arbitrary and unreasonable, said the court, for the dedicated nuns to be deprived of "the free choice of patrons."

This could not go on, this corruption of language and thought that was employed in deciding hard cases. The court must have known that its central problem was not some vague, mercenary "liberty" to make a living, say at teaching German. Nor was it the profit to be made in selling a Catholic education that had been at stake. The Bill of Rights, in the First Amendment, forbade congressional laws respecting an establishment of religion, or "abridging the freedom of speech or of the press or the right of the people peaceably to assemble."

There was no genuine doubt that these rights were the "privileges or immunities" mentioned in the Fourteenth Amendment and thereby entitled to Supreme Court protection against the states and cities. But the "privileges" and "immunities" had been erased from the amendment by the tortured reasoning used in the slaughterhouse case and by half a century of bad law built into constitutional practice based on that reasoning, Hurtado had hanged and Cruikshank's mob had gone free because of it, and the error was too enormous to correct all at once. Now the other label that Justice Brandeis had proposed in Gilbert's case was to prove acceptable to the court majority.

Benjamin Gitlow was a man whose long-winded and doctrinaire espousal of revolutionary ideas was more likely to put a crowd to sleep, as one historian has suggested, than to incite it to storm the barricades. Nevertheless he was prosecuted by the State of New York for criminal anarchy—a remarkable piece of illiteracy as well as injustice, since anarchy as a philosophy had no more to do with Gitlow's ideas of proletarian dictatorship than atheism had to do with Catholicism. What was significant about his case was that it became just one more of those in which appeals were pressed by sturdy defenders of freedom, carrying on in the courts the fight that the I.W.W. had carried on in the streets for the freedom of speech, which so few Americans had been taught to appreciate or guard. Many of the activities of these lawyer-freedom fighters were coordinated by an organization that was first known as the American Committee Against Militarism, then as the Civil Liberties Bureau and finally as the American Civil Liberties Union.

The defenders of the rights of radicals, who were thereby defending the rights of all Americans, were to lose in case after case that was appealed against the federal repression of the war years. In the major cases involving the First Amendment, free speech received one setback after another, with the court unanimous and Mr. Justice Holmes as its spokesman. Then under the able persuasion of eloquent advocates of freedom such as Walter Heilprin Pollak, and possibly influenced by Justice Brandeis as well, Holmes began to repent and to relent. Both Holmes and Brandeis began to dissent and in their dissents express with eloquence the value and importance of the freedom of speech. Their language bore the marks of the words used almost a century before by Rev. William Ellery Channing, defender of free speech for abolitionists in Boston.

They achieved a major partial victory in Gitlow's case. The court had finally recognized the necessity of acknowledging the power it had been given by Big Fourteen to interfere when high state courts failed, as they had during the abolitionist era, to honor the pledge of the free speech guarantees of their own local bills of rights. While Gitlow's conviction was sustained by the majority, on the basis of the supposed danger of his words, a new turning point was announced. The entire court agreed, less than two years after saying the opposite in the insurance brokers' case, that "we may and do assume that freedom of speech and of the press—which are protected by the First Amendment from abridgment by Congress—are among the funda- mental personal rights and 'liberties' protected by the Due Process Clause of the Fourteenth Amendment from impairment by the states."

There may seem small occasion to rejoice at a victory in principle that is a defeat for the prisoner directly involved. Gitlow and his followers and defenders would have been right in resenting the re- sult. But his defeat, in its own way, was as great a victory for the resurgence of Big Fourteen as Moorfield Storey's successful fight for Frank Moore. (Gitlow did not have to serve long in prison: the gov- ernor of New York was Alfred E. Smith. "Al" Smith was a man of the people who was not afraid to exercise his power of pardon when he agreed with the dissenting minority in a free speech case. He re- leased Gitlow and several others with ringing words in defense of freedom, which many presidents and governors have not since had the courage to recall or act upon.)

The first beneficiaries of Ben Gitlow's victory in defeat were an I.W.W. organizer named Fiske and, a few years later, a camp direc- tor, 19-year-old Yetta Stromberg. Fiske's vindication came too late, for the I.W.W. had been smashed to fragments by the wartime per- secutions. It was some promise for the future, however, that a state could not prosecute one for belonging to an organization whose con- stitution declared that there was a struggle between the employing class and the working class which "must go on until the workers of the World organize as a class, take possession of the earth, and the machinery of production and abolish the wage system." Yetta be- longed to a league of young communists and taught the children at her camp to salute a red flag, saying: "I pledge allegiance to the workers' red flag and to the cause for which it stands, one aim throughout our lives, freedom for the working class." To be con- victed for this, said the court through the chief justice, endangered "The maintenance of the opportunity for free political discussion to the end that government may be responsive to the will of the people." The First Amendment, at least, was protected by the Fourteenth.

Chapter 27

Lawlessness in
Law Enforcement

The decade that was coming to an end had been dominated by increasing concern with crime and lawlessness. Public morals seemed to have deteriorated. National and state laws forbidding, because of its supposedly harmful effect on mind and body, the sale and manufacture of a substance for human consumption (except on drug prescription) were widely ignored. The police and the courts were under fire for having failed effectively to deal with a rising rate of crime, violence in the streets and contempt for law. The President of the United States said in his inaugural address: "Justice must not fail because the agencies of enforcement are either delinquent or inefficiently organized. To consider these evils, to find their remedy, is the most sore necessity of our times."

It was March 4, 1929, the president was Herbert Hoover and the "Lawless Decade" of the 1920s was troubling many. To "find the remedy" for the evil of mounting crime, President Hoover appointed a commission of distinguished Americans. At their head he placed one whose devotion to law, order and the protection of private property could not be doubted. George W. Wickersham had won fame and respect at the conservative bar as a corporation law expert and as counsel for municipal railroads and for bankers like August Belmont. Always active as a Republican, he was selected in 1909 by President Taft to be his attorney general. During that administration he became chief spokesman in its defense against the increasing attacks from progressive Republicans.

Mr. Wickersham and the distinguished citizens and experts associated with him in his investigation labored long and hard. They produced fourteen separate reports, totaling three and a half million words, dealing with all aspects of the problem. They concluded that it was necessary to prepare and submit a complete and separate report on the subject of "Lawlessness in Law Enforcement." They found evidence everywhere of what they called a most "sinister" belief that the end justifies the employment of illegal means to bring offenders to justice. They concluded the opening paragraphs of their study with this warning: "Respect for law, which is the fundamental prerequisite of law observance, hardly can be expected of people in general if the officers charged with enforcement of the law do not set the example of obedience to its precepts."

A significant clue to the Wickersham Commission's sweeping charge that fundamental legal principles were constantly disregarded by many law enforcement officers was to be found in one signature to the report. Dean Roscoe Pound of Harvard Law School, just eleven years and one month earlier, had been one of a voluntary committee of distinguished lawyers who had joined in signing a fact-finding study addressed "To the American People" and titled *Report upon the Illegal Practices of the United States Department of Justice.* That report had been initiated by the American Civil Liberties Union, in one of its earliest major efforts, in response to the series of repressive incitements to postwar hysteria engineered by the United States Department of Justice.

Eminent authority had approved the remarkable 1920 condemnation of the office of the Department of Justice, signed by the same Dean Pound who was chosen in 1930 to aid former Attorney General Wickersham in investigating the breakdown of law and order. The Republican leader and former Supreme Court Justice (to be named Chief Justice by President Hoover in 1930) Charles Evans Hughes had studied the report with care. "We cannot afford to ignore," he said, "the indications that perhaps to an extent unparalleled in our history, the essentials of liberty are being disregarded." The report, he insisted, came from "responsible citizens" and disclosed "violations of personal rights which savor of the worst practises of tyranny."

The report opened with a broad charge by the signers, all of whom were, as they described themselves, "lawyers, whose sworn duty it is to uphold the Constitution and Laws of the United States": they had seen the "continued violation of that Constitution and breaking of those laws by the Department of Justice of the United States Government." How and in what way had this been done? "Under the guise of a campaign for the suppression of radical activities, the office of the Attorney General, acting by its local agents throughout the country, and giving express instructions from Washington, has committed continual illegal acts."

Neither the full story of that shameful episode in our history—commonly known and referred to by the name of the man who authorized it as "the Palmer raids"—nor a complete explanation of how it had happened to occur would belong in this story of Big Fourteen and its sister amendments. But some mention of it must be made here because of the significance of the federal example in inciting the growth and spread of "lawless enforcement of the law" among state agencies, particularly local police. Federal instigation of violations of the rights of American citizenship which the Fourteenth Amendment had been designed to protect against state and local violation helped to produce the conditions denounced and exposed in the Wickersham reports—which in turn contributed almost as much as the black freedom movement to the rebirth and revival of Big Fourteen.

Wickersham's comment about the problem of "ends" and "means" in connection with prevention and punishment of genuinely criminal activity was hardly relevant in 1920, when the end was as illegal as the means. The object itself of the federal campaign, "suppression of radical activities," was as unjustified in a land that had been born in a radical revolution as the means were illegal. The rejection of the basically American radical tradition that began with the revolution of 1776 and found its finest hours in the radical Congress that produced the Fourteenth Amendment can be accounted for in several ways.

One possibility, as John Jay Chapman (grandson of an abolitionist comrade of Garrison) wrote in 1911, was that "the timidity of our public life and private conversation" and the "morbid sensitiveness of the American to new political ideas" are among the "intellectual and moral heritages of slavery [which] are with us still." Another source of the widespread prejudice against radicalism is explained by the episode of "law and order in Chicago" that followed the 1886 Haymarket explosion. When the press and the rest of the leaders of public opinion created a frenzied false belief that made possible the conviction of eight radicals whose guilt had not been proven, a precedent was set that created a pattern repeated in 1920.

Added to these patterns of prejudice and sources of appeal to unreasoning hate and fear was the special combination of events bearing upon World War I. It was not a war for the defense of the United States, but that was not realized or understood at the time except by a minority of dissenting socialists and other radicals, including the members of the I.W.W. Denounced and persecuted as "pro-German" for agitating for such views as President Wilson himself expressed *after* the war, the radicals cheered to see the coming of peace speeded by revolution in Russia and Germany. The people who owned the press, supported the churches and endowed the universities feared the very idea of socialism. They helped to see to it that the prejudices played upon during the war continued after it was over. The ultimate response was what has been called the Great Red Scare of 1919, followed by the Palmer raids.

The attorney general put his case vividly: "The blaze of revolution was sweeping over every American institution of law and order . . .

eating its way into the homes of the American workman, its sharp tongues of revolutionary heat licking at the altars of churches, leaping into the belfry of the school bell, crawling into the sacred corners of American homes, seeking to replace marriage vows with libertine laws, burning up the foundations of society." This was meant to be taken seriously and it was, especially by the bright young man that A. Mitchell Palmer found in the Justice Department and selected to head its Alien Radical Division. His name was J. Edgar Hoover and he was just twenty-four years old, with a long and promising career before him.

Young Mr. Hoover, later to head the Federal Bureau of Investigation for almost five decades, won his chief's notice and his own spurs by a report that he had been commissioned to make on "Negro radicalism," in the aftermath of the successful episode of black self-defense that led to Moorfield Storey's victory in winning freedom for Frank Moore. Hoover found Negro "radicals" to be guilty of a constantly increasing "insubordination," and declared that there was "a well-concerted movement among a certain class of Negro leaders of thought and action to constitute themselves a determined and persistent source of a radical opposition to the Government"; evidence of this was shown, he said, in editorials and poems to be found in major Negro newspapers. What was especially dangerous on the part of Negro leaders, according to Mr. Hoover, was their "ill-governed reaction towards race rioting," their "threat of retaliatory measures in connection with lynching," their "demand for social equality," behind all of which was what he called an "increasingly emphasized feeling of a race consciousness . . . openly, defiantly assertive of its own equality and even superiority." The most able and "dangerous" of such publications was one edited by A. Philip Randolph.

Now Mr. Hoover was to lead on a broader battlefield. A great drive was planned against all alien radicals, and the first step naturally was the gathering of information. Agents were instructed to collect what they could from private individuals and companies, from local and state police and other authorities, and from veterans of the American Protective League, an unofficial association of amateur spy-chasers that had been brought into being during the war. The next major step, as described in the "Report to the American People," was to help create the menace from whose elimination the Bureau was to win glory: "Agents of the Department of Justice have been introduced into radical organizations for the purpose of informing upon their members or inciting them to activities; these agents have even been instructed from Washington to arrange meetings upon certain dates for the express purpose of facilitating wholesale raids and arrests. In support of these illegal acts the Department of Justice has also constituted itself a propaganda bureau, and sent to newspapers and magazines quantities of material designed to excite public opinion against radicals, all at the expense of the government and outside the scope of the Attorney General's duties."

After Mr. Hoover's agents had acted as spies and coordinators, the stage was set for the Big Red Raid. The plan was for groups of agents to make simultaneous surprise attacks on meetings their paid helpers had arranged, all on the fateful night of January 2, 1920. The Palmer-Hoover Bureau of Investigation did not yet have a name that was a household word, and not many agents, so in thirty-three of the largest cities it was necessary to use state and local police and their facilities. The instruction in law enforcement methods and respect for the United States Constitution received by the local police that night has been carefully documented. The general outline of what took place was fairly well put together by one disapproving Wilson aide, Assistant Secretary of Labor Louis F. Post: "Meetings wide open to the general public were roughly broken up. All persons present—citizens and aliens alike, without discrimination—were arbitrarily taken into custody and searched as if they had been burglars caught in the criminal act. Without warrants of arrest men were carried off to police stations and other temporary prisons, subjected there to secret police-office inquisitions commonly known as the 'third degree,' their statements written categorically into mimeographed question blanks, and they were required to swear to them regardless of their accuracy."

Albert de Silver, a young, fairly conservative Wall Street lawyer who had been acting as head of the Civil Liberties Bureau—the organization that was about to reorganize into the American Civil Liberties Union—was on the spot soon after one of the New York raids. He found the offices of a foreign-language newspaper in great confusion, the floors entirely covered with torn books and papers. Books had been destroyed by being ripped down the back, pieces of broken typewriter were mixed up in the wreckage, desks and tables were upset, the contents removed and torn, the drawers lying about the room, in many cases with their panels smashed.

Silver's eyewitness account was part of the "Report to the American People" that had been prepared as a result of the joint effort of the American Civil Liberties Union and the National Popular Government League. Civil Liberties attorneys, then a pitiful handful, did their best, across the land, in an effort to vindicate the human and constitutional rights of the victims. A federal judge in Boston condemned the "lawless disregard of the rights and feelings" of the victims. The mayor of Detroit condemned as "intolerable in a civilized city" the conditions in which Hoover and his cooperating local police held the victims.

The report, signed by Dean Pound, Professor Felix Frankfurter and ten other distinguished jurists, condemned Attorney General Palmer and his Special Assistant J. Edgar Hoover for violating four basic constitutional rights. In violation of the Fourth Amendment, they had arrested and detained people without warrants and disregarded their right "to be secure in their persons, houses and effects, against unreasonable searches and seizures." The Fifth Amendment was deliberately disregarded by the forced interrogation of those arrested. The Sixth was flouted by denying them the right of counsel. Cruel and inhuman punishment and denial of the right to bail, all in violation of the Eighth Amendment, were denounced.

The Palmer raids and J. Edgar Hoover's method of conducting them cannot be said to have been the sole or the earliest involvement of local and state police in multiple violations of the rights of Americans under their constitution. The path had been cleared by Supreme Court decisions in the cases of the New Orleans butchers, the bootlegger, the burglar, the banker and the murderer. But the widespread belief in the philosophy that the ends justify the means, the example set by the national guardians of the shrine of liberty and justice, had a powerful and pervasive effect.

One of those horrified by the developing picture that he saw was Supreme Court Justice Brandeis, who pronounced a warning that was as wise and profound as that of any old testament prophet in a case in which wiretapping was used by federal authorities with the blessing of a narrow majority of the Supreme Court in a prohibition-of-liquor case: "Our Government is the potent, the omnipresent teacher. For good or ill, it teaches the whole people by its example. Crime is contagious. If the Government becomes a lawbreaker, it breeds contempt for law; it invites every man to become a law unto itself; it invites anarchy. To declare that in the administration of the criminal law the end justifies the means—to declare that the Government may commit crimes in order to secure the conviction of a private criminal—would bring terrible retribution."

Chapter 28

The Court Begins
to Curb Lawlessness

For those who made it their business to give some thought to such things, there was a curious consequence to Gitlow's case, which we described as protecting liberty under another label. The result of the case was all to the good, insofar as the future of freedom of speech went. First Amendment rights were covered by the Fourteenth, and as time went on this proved to be the case with freedom of assembly and freedom of religion as well. There was no logic or law that could justify carrying in the first phrase of a broad prohibition and leaving out the balance.

But by the same token it would have been hard to explain why the label "due process of law," which was used to get around the slaughterhouse case and bring freedom of speech in the back door, should not apply to the rest of the Bill of Rights. Why should all but one of the rights which the first founding fathers had said "no just government should refuse" be ignored, while the highest court in the land merely backstopped the first of them?

It is true, but it was not a complete answer, that the Supreme Court was by no means the only guardian of the rights with which we are concerned. The word "backstop" described matters accurately: there were, after all, high state courts and state constitutions. Most of them covered most of the ground of the Bill of Rights. They were supposed to protect citizens against police lawlessness and any other kind of infringement by any official. But just as in a ball game some of the wild pitches and foul balls will get past the catcher and have to be checked by a backstop, foul play by police or prosecutors will sometimes be permitted by high state courts. We have seen that, in the framing of the Fourteenth Amendment, close to the hearts of the men who wrote it was the idea that from that time on all national citizens were to get national protection. States were expected to respect and protect the privileges and immunities of national citizens, but just in case they didn't that was what Congress and the Supreme Court were there for.

This promised protection of 1868 was almost surely supposed to come from the first of the triple rivets, "privileges or immunities." "Due process" was intended for something quite different, as illustrated by Storey's victory in Frank Moore's case—a genuine trial ("process"), not simply going through the motions under the fear of a mob. The third rivet, equal protection, was ninety percent removed from Big Fourteen in Plessy's case, and it was still some time before it was to be restored so as to eliminate the nonsense of "separate but equal." In Gitlow's case the idea of free speech—even though turned down in that decision—was recognized as being entitled to protection, but under the wrong and mystifying label of "due process." That covered one—but only one—of the valuable privileges and immunities specified in the First Amendment. The rest of the First Amendment rights, assembly, freedom of religion, etc., were to be some time in receiving clear recognition. The other provisions in the Bill of Rights were to take an agonizingly long period, one marked in some parts of its course by a "three steps forward, two steps backward" kind of development.

The movement—the peaceable revolution whose aim was a return to the Constitution as amended by Big Fourteen—gained new impetus in 1930 with the Wickersham Commission's reports on "Lawlessness in Law Enforcement." The scholars and experts (including Dean Roscoe Pound, who had joined a decade earlier in writing the report on law violations by the Department of Justice) exposed and denounced nationwide disregard for law by police, prosecutors and judges. When President Hoover's commission demanded that "officers charged with enforcement of the law . . . set the example of obedience to its precepts," a major new force was added to the fight against the subversion of the people's privileges and immunities.

To the struggle of the blacks who fought back and won the rebirth of "due process" in sharecropper leader Moore's case, to the agony of the rebels and dissenters and the efforts of their defenders—as shown in the I.W.W.'s "free speech" fights and the American Civil Liberties Union's campaign in Gitlow's case—to the weight in the scales of these "radical" struggles for constitutional law and order there was added a consensus of American constitutional lawyers and scholars who appealed to an untapped source of conscience and responsibility.

Their pitiless probe into lawlessness in law enforcement began with the warning that was quoted in introducing the indications of a probable connection between the lawlessness of the Department of Justice in Palmer's raids and the later spreading lawlessness of state and local police poisoned by young J. Edgar Hoover and his agents with the pernicious idea that the end justifies the means. "It is a fundamental principle of our law," continued the Wickersham report, "constantly reaffirmed by courts and almost as constantly disregarded by many law enforcement officers, that everyone is presumed to be innocent of crime until convicted." This was stressed for reasons obvious to those who know and love and honor our Constitution: the police lawlessness about to be outlined and condemned came from a reversal of the presumption of innocence by inquisitors: the police had come to treat the objects of their suspicion (or the victims of their need to show results) as guilty unless they could prove their innocence.

After summarizing the basic and historic rights of those accused of crime, the report suggests agreement with the prevailing notion that "these rights have been very generally disregarded by the police"; the principal charge in this connection made by former Attorney General Wickersham, Dean Pound and their colleagues was that "confessions of guilt frequently are unlawfully extorted by the police from prisoners by means of cruel treatment, colloquially known as the third degree."

Echoing in part the condemnation of the Federal Bureau of Investigation that the "report" to the American people of 1920 had voiced, the Wickersham commissioners said: "The practice of the third degree involves the violation of such fundamental rights as those of (1) personal liberty; (2) bail; (3) protection from personal assault and battery; (4) the presumption of innocence until conviction of guilt by due process of law; and (5) the right to employ counsel who shall have access to him at reasonable hours. Holding prisoners *incommunicado* in order to persuade or extort confession is all too frequently resorted to by the police."

Quoting the report of their own staff experts with approval, the commissioners agreed that "The third degree brutalizes the police, hardens the prisoner against society, and lowers the esteem in which the administration of justice is held by the public." Summarizing some of the other aspects of the law enforcers' lawlessness under the heading of "unfairness in prosecutions," the commissioners accepted the staff's condemnation of the practices listed under the general description of "abuses relating to the time and place of trial, denial of counsel, or other safeguards granted by the law to the accused during trial, and the various forms of misconduct by prosecutors and judges in the court room."

When the conservative and prestigious jurists of the commission described what they had found as "shocking in its character and extent, violative of American traditions and institutions, and not to be tolerated," that was as far as they could go. They had no power to do anything to check the evils they had found and reported. The mere condemnation of the Wickersham Commission was of no importance to the many petty local tyrants—police chiefs, detective bureau heads, mayors and sheriffs—who knew about and permitted or participated in such outrages.

Some of the victims who could afford skilled and courageous attorneys were able to appeal to the higher courts of the states where such practices had flourished, and sometimes they won their own cases. But that had always been true, and in the past it had not served to check or discourage the lawlessness that had spread so far and wide. Sometimes those who could afford to appeal would find their state's bill of rights to be unenforceable "antiques"; local judges would simply find the charges unproved, or take the word of the local police.

Such denial of justice might have been the concern of the United States government, except that by its refusal to interfere in the case of Sheriff Wheeler's deportation of the I.W.W. strikers from Bisbee, Arizona, the Supreme Court had reaffirmed its denial of vitality to federal civil rights laws that still remained on the books. Too many senators and representatives in Congress came from states where voting rights were denied and would have objected strenuously to efforts at enforcement that might shatter or shake the structures of tyranny which brought them into public life and gained them seniority in Congress, with its special ability to strangle appropriations for law enforcement. Public opinion could not affect the majorities in Congress who tolerated minority rule, for America was suffering from a crisis that overshadowed its law enforcement crisis.

When President Herbert Hoover's administration began in 1929, the stock market was rising, profits seemed to get greater every year, there seemed no limit to the profits to come from stock speculation and investment, and the president announced: "We in America today are nearer to the final triumph over poverty than ever before in the history of our land." Soon afterwards the nation was plagued by a business crisis following a stock market crash that brought an end to inflation and with it business failures, farm foreclosures and widespread unemployment. White and black workers suffered together, although the blacks, lacking resources and savings, suffered far more.

Caught up together as victims of the economic catastrophe were nine young black men and boys who, together with a number of whites, were traveling across the Alabama countryside looking for work. The poor and unemployed could only travel in those days by stealing rides on freight trains. One such train pulled into the little town of Scottsboro, Alabama, in March 1931, and the young whites who had been aboard picked a fight with the young blacks and began a chain of events that opened the door for the long and painful struggle that was to vindicate old John Marshall Harlan, win the national protection that Thad Stevens and John Bingham had thought they had delivered, and provide the backstop that would check the evils, the shocking practices "violative of American traditions," that had been denounced by the Wickersham Commission.

The place where, one by one, the privileges and immunities of American citizens were to be restored to them and protected against erosion and violation by cities, counties and states was a new marble palace that had been built for the Supreme Court, carrying carved on its front portico the words "Equal Justice Under Law." The cornerstone for the new Supreme Court Building had been laid October 13, 1932. Precisely two days before, Walter Heilprin Pollak—who had stood before the court to win in Gitlow's case the pledge that the court would guard, under Big Fourteen, the First Amendment's "free speech" privilege/immunity—had risen to argue the case for the black youngsters who had come to be known throughout the country as "the Scottsboro Boys." The Sixth Amendment to the United States Constitution had long provided that a defendant in a criminal case, under "American traditions and institutions," was entitled to representation by counsel in a major criminal case. The nature of the case of the Scottsboro boys, the character of the struggle that had been waged for them, and the able advocacy of Walter Pollak were to establish that, in a capital case at least, the Fourteenth Amendment required that the Sixth Amendment be enforced against the states.

Much more was involved in the Scottsboro cases than the issue of right of counsel on which the Supreme Court first decided that a new trial had to be granted. At first, all that seemed to be the trouble was the fact that young black men had stood their ground and fought back when attacked by young white men (equally tragic victims of unemployment) on a train where all were trespassers. It turned out that two of the whites on the train—in boys' clothes—were women, living wretched lives like so many of their sisters, who had occasionally to earn their bread by selling their bodies. When the local authorities learned of this, it seemed a classic case to take the usual revenge on blacks who threatened the structure of a post-reconstruction society that was based on the essential cornerstone that the meanest, most coarse and deprived white was "superior" to the finest and most genteel of blacks.

To enforce that rule of social "etiquette" a racial myth had been invented that had helped to cause thousands of mob killings during the half century that followed the freeing of the murderous members of the Cruikshank gang. The myth centered about a fancied need to maintain a racial "purity" for whites that was supposedly threatened by a (wholly fictitious) appetite that blacks were supposed to have for relations with white women. Unless blacks acted as if they believed in their own inferiority, so ran the fantasy, they might be tempted to assault white women or lure them into intermarriage or sexual relations. Every breach of the code that forbade this, and indeed every action or gesture that might lead to such a breach, had to be quickly and ruthlessly punished by nothing less than death. Until about 1920, most governors and senators, especially in the South, condoned—and some even incited—the utterly lawless infliction of death by lynching, often accompanied by the most cold-blooded, barbaric and brutal torture.

When this savagery spilled over the racial line and cost the life of Leo Frank—and when Frank Moore and his fellow fighting sharecroppers, like other blacks in town and country who had heard talk of a war for "democracy," began to fight back—the conditions were created for something very much like success for an antilynching campaign that had been mounted by the NAACP in 1916. The Association had been founded by men and women stirred to action by repeated acts of lawless disorder by northern whites. From its very beginning, Moorfield Storey's organization had investigated and protested individual outrages. Its investigation into one revolting episode in Coatesville, Pennsylvania, summed up its findings by attributing the evil to "an upper class materialized, a middle class vulgarized, a lower class brutalized." (In connection with that very Coatesville crime, John Jay Chapman, who had rented a vacant store in town for a prayer meeting of commemoration and protest—attended by three people—described his "glimpse into the unconscious soul of this country. I saw a seldom revealed picture of the American heart and of the America nature. I seemed to be looking into the heart of a criminal—a cold thing, an awful thing.")

Over the years the antilynching campaign of the NAACP mounted. Southern-born President Wilson, having led the nation into a war that he preached was against tyranny and oppression, was even induced (after repeated efforts) to call upon local officials to oppose lynching actively—since, as the president knew and said, it could not exist "where the community does not countenance it." Moorfield Storey spoke out at bar association meetings, lashing out at lawyers, educators and clergymen who had so long been silent. Some courageous governors and mayors actually stood up and defied mob rule. Congressman L. C. Dyer of Missouri introduced the first federal antilynching bill. Since crimes like murder and mob assault were traditionally punishable by state law, some doubted the "constitutionality" of a national antilynching law in the face of the hostile decisions of the Supreme Court of the 1870s and 1880s; others soon saw that such a law was nothing less than an attempt under the fifth paragraph of Big Fourteen to enforce by "appropriate legislation" the right granted in the first, that one's life could not be taken away save by "due process of law."

The Dyer Anti-Lynching Bill actually passed the House of Representatives by 1922; although killed in the Senate then and thereafter by filibuster—the rule that unlimited debate could not be cut off except by two-thirds vote—its near enactment created a force that was almost as effective in helping to stamp out the traditional form of open mob lynching as an actual law would have been. Fearful of arousing new national pressures for full federal antilynching action, local authorities turned more and more often to the all-white courts, where all-white juries passed upon questions of life and death as well as less important cases that might come before them. Though inherently unjust in their makeup, and rarely likely to dispense evenhanded justice in matters of racial controversy, the local courts offered at least a slim chance of a fair trial to a defendant who was adequately represented by counsel. It was always possible that jurors might be selected who had both conscience and courage.

The innocent Scottsboro defendants were saved from outright mob lynching and their fate entrusted to the courts on the insistence of an Alabama governor who called out the National Guard promptly on the first word of danger. That had come when the two white women who had been aboard the train in men's clothes had somehow been persuaded, or moved on their own to save face, to charge them with rape, that trigger word for racial hostility that had cost the lives of thousands of innocent Americans. As it happened, a local doctor who examined them was later to reveal privately to the first judge assigned to the case that there was no physical evidence to support the accusation, but his information did not become known until thirty years afterwards.

The trials that were staged to satisfy the townspeople and hill folk held back by bayonets were not much more than a mere formality, not a real contest at all. It was not so much the all-white juries that kept these first trials from being tests of guilt or innocence, or the howling mob outside, as had happened in Frank Moore's case. No kind of defense was put up, nothing but the most perfunctory legal representation, the casual presence of a local lawyer and an observer from Tennessee, called in by one of the families of the young men. Neither "defense counsel" did anything—or had the opportunity to do anything in the way of investigation or preparation for defense. Within two weeks after the fight on the freight train, the Scottsboro victims were convicted, and all but one thirteen-year-old boy sentenced to death.

That might have been the end of them and the case had it not been for the intervention of a radical workers' legal aid organization known as the International Labor Defense. The NAACP had remained silent at first, having no local branch nearby to keep it informed, and its national secretary having been misled by false reports in southern newspapers that the young men were well represented by able counsel. The International Labor Defense (I.L.D.) had been brought into being by the American Communist Party, which had itself come into being when the socialists in the United States divided over the issues of World War I and the Russian revolution that helped to end that war. These communists considered themselves the heirs to the native American radical tradition of the I.W.W. and the socialism of Eugene V. Debs, and Debs himself had been a member of the first national board of the I.L.D. Numbered among them were men and women of great sincerity and idealism who were willing to sacrifice themselves courageously for the cause they believed to be just.

What had sparked the I.L.D. into immediate action on the Scottsboro case was the report of a local observer in communication with its New York headquarters who said that there were all the signs of a new Sacco-Vanzetti case. It was in the long effort to save the lives of two Italian immigrants, themselves pacifists and radicals, that the I.L.D. workers, although playing only a minor role there, had learned much that was to stand them in good stead in their effort to win justice in the Scottsboro case. That earlier struggle had failed— only four years before the Scottsboro arrests—but it had begun eleven years before and had come very close to success because it had aroused the energy and enthusiasm of many Americans of conscience as well as the attention and concern of people and governments the world over.

The Sacco-Vanzetti tragedy had no direct effect on the history of the Fourteenth Amendment, although it has a double connection with our story—and, like Joe Hill, Sacco and Vanzetti would not have died if their treatment by state court judges had been tested by the standards that the amendment was meant to impose. Charged with the crime of murder during a payroll robbery and convicted by a jury inflamed with the feelings so well expressed by the trial judge—who blurted out afterwards, "Did you see what I did to those anarchist bastards?"—the men who died in the electric chair in Boston in 1927 were really, as Anatole France told the world, "convicted for a crime of opinion."

They had been arrested in the aftermath of the Palmer-Hoover raids, and one of them had become enmeshed in the consequence of a visit to New York to inquire after a comrade, illegally detained by Bureau of Investigation men, who committed suicide. Agents of the Bureau, according to their sworn statements later, who knew all along that Sacco and Vanzetti "had nothing to do with the South Braintree murder" nevertheless aided in their prosecution in the belief that the result would aid their own Red Hunt. Lawlessness by lawmen was a factor that the Supreme Court could not ignore when in the Scottsboro case it came to grips with the question, "Can the Fourteenth Amendment permit such lawlessness as the conviction of victims of a state court that did not provide representation by counsel?"

The other indirect link between Sacco-Vanzetti and Scottsboro was the repeated attention focused on the forms and the processes of American justice. It was not because America was disliked or considered to be a despotic land that an extraordinary outcry arose the world over at the prospect of the execution of the two whites or the nine blacks. It was especially because for so long we had had the reputation of the land of opportunity, the cradle of revolution, the land of the "free," that the unjust treatment of two humble Italian immigrants so stirred opinion among friendly nations. When a distinguished Massachusetts newspaper, *The Springfield Republican,* could write "a dog ought not to be shot on the weight of the evidence brought out in the Dedham trial of Sacco and Vanzetti," it was no wonder that the nations that we now think of as the "free world" expressed their revulsion. An international public opinion alerted in 1927 by the electrocution of two poor men in Massachusetts was about to express itself again at the even more ghastly miscarriage of justice that brought with it from Alabama the picture of the oppression of a tenth of a nation within a nation.

The combination of pressures on the conscience of the court brought about the beginning of a second stage in the revival of the Fourteenth Amendment as a shield against any state action that violated the federal Bill of Rights. The sixty-year period of evasion of the purposes of John Bingham and Thaddeus Stevens was not quite over; but the court went far enough that one of the two dissenters bemoaned it as "an extension of federal authority in a field hitherto occupied exclusively by the several states."

Of course it was just that. The court looked into what had happened in a state court trial and said in contradiction to the solemn lie of a state's highest court that there had been no adequate representation by counsel. But by what authority had the highest federal court done this? In the Bill of Rights, the Sixth Amendment pledges the individual's right to have counsel in a criminal case. The framers of the Fourteenth had designed it to secure to Americans in every state the protection of the Bill of Rights. The court yielded an inch, of the yards of protection, by using "liberty" once more under another label. Instead of conceding that, as a privilege and immunity of Americans, the Sixth Amendment's right of counsel was made mandatory by Big Fourteen, the court said only that it was not "due process" in that capital case for a trial to be conducted without counsel for the defense. Its decision was to prove to be a partial and misleading concession, and yet it was a great reversal of what had been a growing trend. A journey of a thousand miles can begin with a few steps.

Chapter 29

Chipping Away
at Inequality:
the "Fatal Injustice"

The ordeal of the Scottsboro boys continued. They were to return to the nation's highest court after a new round of "guilty" verdicts, but before they did a most revealing interruption occurred. The first of the new trials took place in the courtroom of an Alabaman whose conscience would not let him be a party to a judicial lynching.

James E. Horton was the first of a number of native southern judges who were to risk and then suffer community hostility and the loss of their hard-won posts in the course of doing their duty to their profession and their country. He presided at one of the trials, saw and studied the witnesses and weighed the evidence and then received the inevitable verdict from the all-white jury. As is customary before passing sentence, he heard and considered the defense lawyers' application (called a "motion") to throw out the verdict as having been arrived at against the weight of the evidence.

"Deliberate injustice is more fatal to the one who imposes it than to the one on whom it is imposed," Judge Horton said in what could have been intended as an appeal to his fellow white Southerners to consider the injury that they had been doing themselves for two thirds of a century. The case of the prosecution, he ruled, "bears on its face indications of improbability, is contradicted by other evidence, and in addition thereto the evidence greatly preponderates in favor of the defendant. It, therefore, becomes the duty of the Court under the law to grant the motion made by the defendant in this case."

The gallant judge was saying, in legal language, that there was more than a reasonable doubt of the guilt of the boys, that they were in all probability innocent. But the judge's decision, instead of closing the cases, became only a forgotten interlude. The state attorney general brought pressure on Alabama's chief justice to reassign the cases to another judge who would be less concerned about justice. The next election was to see the defeat of Judge Horton; meanwhile, juries were to rubber-stamp the dread verdicts again.

The second round of Scottsboro appeals to the Supreme Court was based on the central fact that was the consequence, and at the same time the cause, of the caste society's continued stability, ever since its foundations were assured by the Supreme Court's decision in Plessy's case forty years before: no blacks were permitted to serve on juries in Alabama. Yet no law was on the books permitting or requiring this exclusion—that would have been unconstitutional under a Supreme Court decision dating back to fifteen years before Plessy, one of the few in some sixty-five years which obeyed the equal protection of the laws clause of Big Fourteen. There was in fact a federal law—section four of Sumner's Civil Rights Act of 1875—that made it a federal crime to omit citizens from juries because of their race or skin color.

The fate of this federal law—a law central to the administration of justice and hence at the heart of law and order—was not unlike that of Big Fourteen's pledge to guarantee the equality of all men before the law. It had been nullified and become a dead letter. Although it had always been the law of the land that no qualified citizen should be excluded from jury service because of "race, color, or previous condition of servitude," no one in Alabama or in many other states could remember, in the 1930s, ever having seen a black man on a jury. Yet no United States attorney general had sought to punish anyone for this long-lived and widespread violation of the law (or has since 1935 even though some have called for "new laws" on the subject).

Few people ever get to serve on juries and still fewer ever have to face them. That does not mean that the exclusion of a race from jury service is or was a small matter. The states whose democracy was destroyed by disfranchisement had for decades seen only white judges elected or appointed, and only white sheriffs, jury officials and prosecuting attorneys. The lily-white jury system encouraged lawless aggression by the race that was permitted to serve against the race that was excluded, since the aggressor was assured of immunity from punishment. Mob violence and brutality on the part of law enforcement officials toward members of the excluded minority were likewise promoted. All of this injustice served to support continued repression.

The opportunity to rise—self-improvement in what has been called the "American way"—was curtailed by the absence of justice in civil courts, where men should have been able to sue for remedies for private wrongdoing. Cheating and exploitation by the race whose members served on juries were encouraged and became rampant. The white jury system was not the sole and perhaps not the most important link in a chain of circumstances which produced inequality and injustice which were as "fatal," to use Judge Horton's word, to the oppressor as they were to the oppressed. They could not be eliminated overnight, nor could the dreadful consequences of so many decades of injustice, but the time had come to make a beginning and that beginning was provided by the worldwide struggle to save the Scottsboro defendants.

The Supreme Court was and is powerless to direct federal prosecutors to punish criminals such as the many hundreds of jury commissioners who had deliberately excluded a part of the population from exercising their civic right and duty. But it did have the power to see to it that no man could be convicted of a crime by a jury from which a part of the population had been excluded. The court had resoundingly declared in 1880 that it was essential, in order to make certain that "the law in the states should be the same for the black as for the white," that "their neighbors, fellows, associates, persons having the same legal status" should not be arbitrarily excluded from jury service. But it had not done much about the discrepancy between legality and reality until 1935, when domestic and foreign street demonstrations denounced the Scottsboro trials as examples of American racism and cried "shame!"

In delivering the court's opinion in the second round of Scottsboro appeals, Chief Justice Hughes avowed that the court was making no new law: there was, he said, "no controversy as to the principle involved." Of course there was not: even the Alabama courts conceded the principle; what they denied was the *fact* of exclusion. Nine Washington justices far removed from the hurly-burly of courtroom drama had not been used to going into "facts" in constitutional cases, except in perverted due process cases in which utilities claimed "confiscation" by rate-fixing: only when questions of profit were involved would they go into facts—such as the value of the investment on which the claimed rate of return had to be based. But now the pressures of civilization and decency had caught up with the court and the nation. Overseas, Europe's strongest nation had fallen into the hands of men who claimed that *they* were the master race; the Nazis were preparing for a worldwide militaristic role through barbaric repression at home. The American court could no longer turn its back: "That the question is one of fact," said the chief justice, "does not relieve us of the duty to determine whether in truth a federal right has been denied."

The change was really a change in attitude, not in "law," and it permeated the court more and more as the years rolled by and as justices hardened in older ways retired and died. Instead of the chilly aloofness that marked even the opinions of Mr. Justice Holmes before the Frank case and before the arrival of Louis D. Brandeis on the court, there was a new mood. The decisions began to show an increasing concern for the real truth and for the actual consequences in cases that presented the question of "equal protection of the laws," as well as the other commandments of the Fourteenth Amendment. The Scottsboro cases and the agitation that surrounded them had led to the breaking up of a congealed indifference to a condition in our land which could best be described as "barbaric." Barbaric in the sense that a people could not call itself civilized because it perpetrated or tolerated the treatment of human beings in the way that black Americans had been treated in the early twentieth century.

The Scottsboro boys themselves were not exonerated in the Alabama courts, but they were not executed and all were ultimately freed. A new round of trials began, and with only token compliance with the jury requirements that the Supreme Court had declared it would enforce. Jury "panels"—the lists from which the jurors were chosen—included a couple of blacks, but the selection at the trials resulted in all-white juries, as before. The habits and prejudices of a social order are not eradicated overnight or by a ruling that one of its bastions is unsound. Convictions began again, but before they went very far a compromise was worked out. Four of the defendants were to be freed immediately, others gradually over the years. Unfortunately the Fourteenth Amendment does not require that the innocent be freed, only that no one shall be convicted without due process of law and equal protection under the laws.

The bastions of inequality were numerous and sturdy; some had been erected with the aid of earlier court decisions. The breach in one wall of injustice brought about by the second Scottsboro decision should neither be magnified nor belittled. It was a beginning, though, and an important one, at scraping away an integral feature of a thoroughly un-American court system that was an essential feature of an unjust society. Yet it was only a beginning and there remained many barriers to be assaulted before America could effectively combat the malignant results of the Supreme Court's tolerance of the idea which Thad Stevens and his fellow framers of Big Fourteen had thought they had made intolerable. That pernicious idea, that there was a difference between black and white which justified difference in treatment or segregation by state law or private custom, was at the root of too many American institutions and in the mentality of too many of our people.

Having returned to the Constitution—at least in the jury cases—the Supreme Court continued to do its duty in that area. Case after case was to be brought up in the years to come from states that had violated the rights of those brought to trial. Subterfuges, tricks and ingenious excuses were all rejected. A native Alabaman, who as a United States senator had fought against special privilege and for the common man, was appointed to the court by Franklin D. Roosevelt in

1937. Hugo L. Black, like James Horton, respected law and justice enough to see the sinful and illegal quality of the two-caste society from which he had risen.

Justice Black became the spokesman for the court in one of its insistent repetitions of the law on the subject. "Equal protection to all is the basic principle upon which justice under law rests," he wrote in granting a new trial to Hugh Pierre, a black man from Louisiana whose attorneys had shown that from 1896 to 1936 no Negro had served on a jury in his parish. A single sliver of equal protection had been won. The court's determination to stand fast in the jury cases did not mean that full and equal justice had been achieved in American courts. There were too many states that had never seen a black judge, sheriff, prosecuting attorney or court clerk. It did not even mean that the jury system had been reformed: hundreds of cases failed to achieve review by the Supreme Court for lack of attorneys or ignorance of the plight of many. Yet a standard had been laid down that men of integrity, with respect for law, could follow; the day of reckoning for the many other illegal preferences and privileges permitted by judges and lawmakers in violation of the Fourteenth Amendment had been brought closer.

The National Association for the Advancement of Colored People (which had played an important, if secondary, role in the Scottsboro cases) was already prepared to move on the many difficult and varied fronts on which the fight to make the Constitution supreme again had to be waged. Its tradition of limited volunteer counsel no longer curtailed its efforts nor was it going to be primarily on the defensive in the 1930s and thereafter. A wealthy young white man named Charles Garland grew up to believe that no one has a right to enjoy wealth unless he has earned it. He placed his personal fortune in a public service fund whose grant made it possible for the NAACP to plan a full-time legal staff. That gift, while it lasted, was a monetary arsenal that financed the heavy litigation costs which continue to this day—costs which really discharge the obligations of the federal government to enforce its own constitution.

The staff that came into being to wage the fight was aided in its efforts by the increasing militancy of the black people who were released, to a great extent by the success of the NAACP's campaign for a federal antilynching law and the struggle to free the Scottsboro defendants, from the fear that had held many back for so long. Blacks and whites responded together to the eloquent denunciations by our leaders of the Nazis and the master race theory which were both creeping across Europe. Naturally our own homemade master race theory seemed less plausible in the face of developments abroad. The new mood in the land included a change in the ranks of organized labor, where the radical leadership of the new CIO unions insisted on equality in job opportunities.

In this setting was begun the multiple campaign to establish the illegality of the restrictions on the right to vote, on the right to choose housing and above all on educational opportunity—as well as the many humiliating and irritating denials that were the trappings of a segregated system. Persistence as well as ingenuity and skill were needed for the fight. And even some victories that followed defeats were to be nullified by the refusal of a large and stubborn mass of people to respect or obey the law when it ran counter to their own prejudices. The "fatal injustice" of inequality continued to plague those who inflicted it as well as those who suffered from it. The legal right of all Americans to equal treatment was gradually reestablished, step by painful step, but the actual conditions of life—in voting, in housing, in educational opportunity—were to remain affected by the weight of the accumulated injustice of the past.

The restoration of the right of all Americans to vote was a constant objective of the NAACP. Its victory in the fight that Moorfield Storey had led against the grandfather clauses was only a beginning in the restoration of democracy to the states that were really white dictatorships. Devices created to preserve this tyranny were as many layered as an onion and each layer had to be peeled off to regain the government by the consent of the governed that Jefferson and Madison had led a revolution to win. The next layer to be removed was the white primary.

Like the fascist dictatorships that appeared in the Old World a few decades ago, the New World states that denied the vote to part of their people had become one-party regimes. They were ruled by white cliques, and outside of their circle there was no hope that any poor white or poor black could influence the process by which nominations, which were the equivalent of election, were made. Governing and law enforcement posts, as well as Washington representatives, were selected by an in-group of planters, bankers and merchants.

When this method of control was threatened by the introduction of the direct primary method of voting for nominees of the single party, which occurred at the same time that blacks began to become disillusioned with the party of Abraham Lincoln (which barely had token existence in the one-party states), the white South took prompt action to exclude black voters from the Democratic party's primaries. One of the first blacks to have the courage to volunteer to challenge the legality of voter exclusion was Dr. A. L. Nixon of El Paso, Texas, and the National Association for the Advancement of Colored People took his case to court.

Voting in primaries to select nominees was not yet clearly seen to be a right protected by the Fifteenth Amendment. So, when Dr. Nixon's case came before the Supreme Court, the Texas law excluding blacks from Democratic party primaries was struck down under the equal protection command of Big Fourteen. The Texas law's defenders had argued that under earlier cases the states had been allowed to "classify" people and businesses, and that if the classification was "rational," and people within a class were treated alike, it had been allowed to stand. For example, not all landlords were required to have fire escapes: owners of three-story buildings might be obliged to, and two-story buildings exempted. "States may do a good deal of classifying that it is difficult to believe is rational," said Justice Holmes for the court, "but there are limits, and it is too clear for extended argument that color cannot be made the basis of a statutory classification affecting the right" to vote. This pronouncement was in 1927, and, if the court and the American people had had the intellectual honesty to pursue the logic of that simple statement, the classification by race permitted by the court in Plessy's case in railroad cars—and by then extended unbelievably—would have clearly been seen to be unconstitutional.

Neither intellectual honesty nor logic could easily or quickly be brought to effective force in a nation that had been so thoroughly infected with racial hostility. Justice Holmes himself sensed this as he remarked on the bench but off the record at the very moment of decision in Dr. Nixon's case: "I know that our good brethren, the Negroes of Texas, will now rejoice that they possess at the primary the rights which heretofore they have enjoyed at the general election." He knew that a whole arsenal of methods had been used effectively to abridge the right to vote at general elections and he was ironically forecasting that they would be used in primaries as well.

So predisposed was the court and the nation to acquiesce in the denial of democracy by the states whose white power structures chose to do so that the nominal victory in the white primary case was permitted to be erased. The simple device of repealing the state law that excluded part of its people from voting in primaries and allowing the exclusion to be perpetrated by the "private" party convention was held by the court in a 1935 case—the same year as the second Scottsboro case—not to be a violation of the Constitution's commandment that no state should deny the equal protection of the laws to any person. Incredible as it may seem now, the argument that was accepted then was that it was not the "state" that had done the wrong but a group of "private" citizens. That this private group was in effect deciding who would be the nominee and hence the successful candidate as well the court ignored, using a tortured process of reasoning that did not survive for long.

In less than a decade the court wiped out this particular stain on its, and the nation's, honor. It was the decade during which black Americans—freed to a large extent in the South from the rape-mythology-fostered lynch law that had been eroded by the mighty Scottsboro struggle—moved forward on new fronts north and south to win allies in their freedom fight. It was also the decade that saw black and white Americans drafted to fight and die supposedly to combat the threat to the "free world" by the "master race" of Nazi Germany. Continuing their fight with the persistence of men who knew that they were morally and legally right, NAACP lawyers persuaded the court to confess its own error—as it had frankly failed to do in the Scottsboro cases—and end all legal sanction for the white primary.

This 1944 victory was far from the end of the struggle for equality at the ballot box, or for equality of right and treatment in so many other respects. The incubus of past injustices weighed heavily on a society in which the beneficiaries of illegal privilege suffered from the spiritual corrosion that made the infliction of inequality a "fatal injustice" to them as well as to their victims. Other barriers to the democratic right of free access to the ballot box remained, and years of struggle and chipping away—so often at the seemingly disheartening rate of two steps forward, three steps back—were to follow.

The effort to win the freedom to live in a place of one's own free choice and the battle for equal educational opportunity were to tell much the same story. Each of these continuing efforts to win back from the court and the conscience of the country the rights that the Constitution had been amended to give to all Americans required repeated assaults. The housing and education wrongs, and the campaigns to overcome and make amends for them are most often described as separate narratives. They are really part of a single tale, though, for restricted housing and inadequate education interact and their consequences continue as a vicious circle of oppression that threatens us today and tomorrow.

Moorfield Storey had won, in the Louisville residential segregation case of 1917, the ruling that local and state laws which required "apartheid"—racial separation in residential neighborhoods—could not stand up against the freedom mandate of the Fourteenth. The nation and the court slid backward: within a decade, in a 1926 decision, the court had allowed the bankers and brokers of the real estate industry to create an exact equivalent of the unlawful Louisville ordinance. This was the so-called restrictive covenant, whereby blacks could be forced, by court decree, to remain outside residential areas whose owners or developers had agreed that they were to be posted "For White Only."

The covenants (agreements recorded in deeds to property) were more vicious and harmful than any local ordinance could be. A law could always be repealed or modified by the board, council or legislature that passed it: all that was needed was a change in heart and mind, which theoretically could be brought about by public enlightenment. Conscience could not cause covenants to be repealed. There weighed heavily upon the ownership and freedom of action of a possibly enlightened son the dead hand of his racist father or grandfather, a dead hand that no one could lift and whose rigid restriction would win the enforcement order of the courts.

Once more, as in the case of the fight for voting rights (and as in each of the efforts to chip away at the many-layered walls of inequality), defeat did not daunt the National Association for the Advancement of Colored People and its supporters. Though spurned by courts and stoned—or worse—by mobs, they patiently fought on. In one case, decided in 1940, Mr. and Mrs. Carl Hansberry of Chicago asserted their right to buy a house in a more attractive area; the Illinois Supreme Court, like the highest courts in many other states following the United States Supreme Court's 1926 decision, supported the whites who wanted to bar them. On a technical point, the Hansberry family won their case in the highest court in the land. But their new neighbors made their victory so unpleasant for them that the heart of their gifted little daughter, Lorraine, was seared with the memory of the rejection they sustained.

Most of the nation's courts continued to enforce the unfair restrictive agreements for eight more long years. Then Mr. and Mrs. J. D. Shelley brought their appeal to Washington from a Missouri decree that ousted them from their home. Louis Kraemer, one of their neighbors, had sought successfully to enforce an agreement signed by the 1911 owner of the tract on which their homes were located. Now, in the aftermath of World War II, many joined the NAACP in its fight—organizations such as the Elks, the National Lawyers Guild (but not the American Bar Association), the American Jewish Congress, the American Unitarian Association and even the United States Department of Justice.

A unanimous court "made history" merely by admitting what seemed terribly simple and obvious once it had been said, that for a state court to enforce a private agreement which imposed racial discrimination was a denial of equal protection under the law.

Although the death knell for the courtroom enforcement of restrictive covenants had been sounded, the evil that men had perpetrated for so long was to live on after them. Not only had housing patterns been established and popular prejudice been reinforced by the long decades of state-sponsored curtailment of free choice of places to live; but the federal government itself, which had come to participate so widely in housing activity, had also been an open party to the crime. Until 1948, the Federal Housing Administration had actually encouraged homogeneous—meaning all white or all black—neighborhoods and had recommended restrictive covenants as a means of achieving that end. The illegality of this form of inequality had been established, but the undoing of this injustice remained a task that seemed to prove too much for a nation proud of its giant feats of technology.

Chapter 30

It Took
Another Amendment . . . .

Susan Brownell Anthony saw one great flaw in the Fourteenth Amendment—a single word inserted in the second clause that seemed so harshly to contradict the intent of the first. The word was "male." When she and her sister suffragists failed to block the adoption of the amendment—and despite the remaining injustice of the suffrage (second) clause—she nevertheless resolved to fight to enforce the rights (first) clause. As a result she became the first American to defy the law and to risk jail for the sake of Big Fourteen. She then became the first woman to write the text of an amendment to the Constitution, the Nineteenth, ratified in 1920, fourteen years after her death.

The rights clause declared that "all persons born or naturalized" here are "citizens of the United States," decreed that no state could "abridge the privileges or immunities of citizens" and promised to "any person" the equal protection of the laws. But, inconsistently, the suffrage clause (that never-to-be-enforced compromise that was supposed to reduce representation when voting rights were curtailed) spoke only of "male inhabitants" and "male citizens." Were women not people? Susan B. Anthony spent most of her life fighting to answer that question with a resounding affirmative.

The movement for "Women's Liberation" had already gotten some steam up—and not inconsiderable success—when Miss Anthony joined it in 1851. From the time of the eighteenth-century enlightenment in Europe and the first American revolution, the artificial privileges and the historic injustices of the past—between rich and poor, aristocrat and humbly born, white and black, men and women—had come increasingly into question. Isolated voices were heard, and not from women alone, protesting the cluster of iniquities that were the mark of a "man's world."

There assembled at Seneca Falls, New York, in July 1848 a group of women and men, black and white, who brought into being the first of the organized movements that have sought to win the right of women to be recognized as free and full partners in the home and in society. Patterning their manifesto on the Declaration of Independence they declared, "We hold these truths to be self-evident: that all men and women are created equal." The inspiration for many who attended was a groundbreaking by one who could not attend, one who died within a year on her way home from participating in the Italian revolution of 1848. "We would have every arbitrary barrier thrown down," Margaret Fuller had written. "We would have every path laid open to Woman as freely as to Man."

There were not merely legal barriers to overcome. The Seneca Falls Declaration, indicting man's treatment of woman much as the rebellious colonists had accused George III, had summed up their plight and their grievance over the psychological factor in their repression: "He has endeavored, in every way that he could, to destroy her confidence in her own powers, to lessen her self-respect, and to make her willing to lead a dependent and abject life."

Susan B. Anthony responded to the call of the Seneca Falls convention and accepted as her life's work the double mission of persuading men to lower the legal barriers and inspiring women to understand that it was their right and obligation to comprehend the nature of the injustices they suffered and to rebel against them. Just as there had been many whites (including Miss Anthony and her comrades) who saw the injury done to all Americans by the barbarism of racism in the North and by slavery in the South, there were men who perceived the merit of her struggle. The radical transcendentalist preacher Theodore Parker sensed and expressed it very well: "The domestic function of woman does not exhaust her powers. To make one half the human race consume its energies in the function of housekeeper, wife and mother is a monstrous waste of the most precious material God ever made."

Despite the immense contribution which the women of the North had made to the turn of sentiment that produced the Freedom Amendment—and with the knowledge on the part of some that woman's cause was morally just—the men who drew up the Fourteenth inserted the word "male" in its suffrage clause. Susan Anthony was not content to let that be the last word. She had studied and reflected much on the value of the neutral word "person" in the first clause and its promise of equal protection to all, especially its guarantee of the privileges and immunities of all citizens. She was born in the United States and entitled to the full protection of every privilege and immunity that every other American citizen was promised.

She led a spectacular protest and demonstration planned to test the letter of the law against the letter of the Fourteenth Amendment. After having come home to Rochester from a lecture tour, during which she had insisted that the right to vote was a privilege and immunity of all citizens, she organized fifty local women to attempt to register and vote in the 1872 election. With a group of sixteen in all, in her home election district, she presented herself at the registration desk. When the inspectors of election, the guardians of the registration books, hemmed and hawed, she read aloud the sweeping words of the first clause of Big Fourteen: "*All* persons born or naturalized in the United States, and subject to the jurisdiction thereof, are citizens of the United States and of the State wherein they reside. No State shall make or enforce any law which shall abridge the privileges or immunities of citizens of the United States. . . ." The inspectors wilted in Susan's district and permitted her to register; in the other districts the balance of her group was turned down.

On the eve of election day, a Rochester newspaper warned Miss Anthony and her sturdy group of the consequences that they risked. Three years in jail and a $500 fine was the penalty for any person voting without a legal right. Miss Anthony, undaunted, retained counsel, a former judge of the highest court of New York State. He listened to her story and reread the amendment and then said that he thought her argument sound and that he would protect her to the best of his ability.

The "Rochester Sixteen" voted. The federal authorities were frightened. They did not want to create martyrs, nor provide a test case whereby Miss Anthony might win her point. But they certainly did not want the sixteen to grow into hundreds and then thousands at succeeding elections. After three weeks of hesitation, they sent a federal marshal to arrest Miss Anthony on Thanksgiving Day.

She prepared for the trial by going to the jurors before they were even called for courtroom service. Up and down Monroe County she stumped, speaking in every district, explaining the reason for and the justice behind her vote. She did her work so well that the prosecutor asked for a change of venue to neighboring Ontario County, fearing that no jury in her home county would convict her. Not easily discouraged, Susan Anthony covered much of the new county in the three weeks that remained before the trial.

Now she was to encounter male justice, and to find that for her it was no more evenhanded than were many cases of white justice for blacks. The presiding judge, J. Ward Hunt, had been only recently appointed and was the protégé of a political machine that wanted to put the question to rest. He refused to let Miss Anthony testify in her own behalf, and when both sides had rested, in a clearly illegal ruling, he refused to let the case go to the jury. Instead, he "directed" them to find a verdict of guilty, a legal device that caused such a verdict to be entered regardless of what the jurors might say.

Having entered the guilty verdict, the judge was obliged, before passing the sentence that had been planned in advance—a $100 fine, in order to avoid an appeal—to ask under time-honored procedures if the prisoner had anything to say to contest the sentence. Susan had the last word—and she repeatedly defied the court's orders to sit down. After her opening blast—"your ordered verdict of guilty has trampled under foot every vital principle of our government"—she objected to Judge Hunt's refusal to hear a repetition of her attorney's arguments and told him: "I am not arguing the question, but simply stating the reasons why sentence cannot in justice be pronounced against me." The judge interrupted.

Judge Hunt: "The Court cannot allow the prisoner to go on."

Miss Anthony: "But your Honor will not deny me this one and only poor privilege of protest against this high-handed outrage. . . ."

The Judge: "The prisoner must sit down, the Court cannot allow it."

The Prisoner: ". . . As the slaves who got their freedom had to take it over or under or through the unjust forms of the law, precisely so now must women take it to get their right to a voice in this government; and I have taken mine, and mean to take it at every opportunity."

The Judge: "The Court orders the prisoner to sit down. It will not allow another word."

Miss Anthony: ". . . Failing to get this justice, failing even to get a trial by a jury—not of my peers—I ask not leniency at your hands but rather the full rigor of the law."

After hearing the sentence, Susan declared: "I will never pay a dollar of your unjust penalty. And I shall earnestly and persistently continue to urge all women to the practical recognition of the old Revolutionary maxim, 'Resistance to tyranny is obedience to God.' "

She did not pay her fine, but the authorities did not dare to imprison her. Her case and her immediate purpose were frustrated, however, by two rulings by the Supreme Court. It had already cut the heart out of the rights clause of Big Fourteen by its decision in the slaughterhouse case which destroyed the privileges and immunities guarantees that were at the heart of her argument. On the same day the butchers' battle was decided, the court (which had divided five to four in that case) turned its back by an eight-to-one vote on Myra Bradwell.

Mrs. Bradwell had married an Illinois lower court judge and had started to study law with his assistance. She found nothing mysterious or particularly "male" in the subject matter and by 1869 had shown enough mastery to be appointed editor of the *Chicago Legal News,* a bar journal. When she applied for membership in the Illinois bar the following year so that she could practice her profession, the old male judges recoiled in horror: "That God designed the sexes to occupy different spheres of action, and that it belonged to men to make, apply and execute the laws, was regarded as an almost axiomatic truth. . . ." For women "to engage in the hot strifes of the

Bar" would tend to "destroy the deference and delicacy with which it is the pride of our ruder sex to treat her."

Mrs. Bradwell might well have preferred to do without the delicacy and gain her rights. She moved on to the Supreme Court of the United States and there complained that the right to engage in the practice of the law was her privilege as a United States citizen, and that she was denied the equal protection of the laws as well by the decision excluding her. The slaughterhouse majority had not the least difficulty deciding her case, having that very day practically abolished federal protection of the rights of citizens. And the minority in that case—except for Chief Justice Chase, who dissented vigorously—not wishing to tread on the ground that they had just condemned, proclaimed: "The constitution of the family organization, which is founded in the divine ordinance, as well as in the nature of things, indicates the domestic sphere as that which properly belongs to the domain and functions of womanhood. The paramount destiny and mission of woman are to fulfill the noble and benign offices of wife and mother."

Meanwhile Mrs. Virginia Minor, Missouri women's rights leader, had filed suit against a local election official to compel him to let her register and vote. With the aid of her lawyer-husband, she had developed a theory not unlike Miss Anthony's, which had been elaborated in the movement newspaper *The Revolution*. When her case reached the Supreme Court, a last attempt was made to force the issue. The court unanimously turned down the appeal. There was no longer any hope that the Fourteenth Amendment could be relied upon, and Susan Anthony sat down to compose the words that were to become, forty-five years later, the Nineteenth Amendment to the United States Constitution: "The right of citizens of the United States to vote shall not be denied or abridged by the United States or by any State on account of sex."

During the period of the mounting battle for the Anthony amendment—which dealt only with political inequality—the movement that had been launched for much broader purposes at Seneca Falls continued to assault the multiple barriers to legal, social and economic equality. Since many, if not most, of these were embodied in state laws, and since sentiment in some states—particularly the western states, where the contribution and sacrifice of pioneers was a more recent memory—was more easily moved than in others, there were varying degrees of success.

As the years rolled on, from the nineteenth century into the twentieth, the insistence of women, as well as many enlightened men, that there was no rational basis for denying college educations to girls produced a significant response. Women's colleges and coeducational schools multiplied enormously. But there was still stubborn resistance to the removal of the sexual barrier at the graduate and professional line. Medical schools remained closed to women for decades and law schools continued for an even longer period to defend a male monopoly. Some disciplines, such as architecture and engineering, were even worse.

Progress in other areas in which the laws had seemed to treat women as inferior beings—not quite human or adult—was uneven, but it never quite stopped. One by one, the separate states dropped the laws that forbade married women to own or control property. As recently as 1920, when the struggle for the Susan Anthony voting rights amendment succeeded, a dozen states still followed the old practice: a woman, no matter how capable, was at the mercy of a husband who might prove incapable of managing money or property, unless he was so unfit that he could be placed in an institution. Women who worked for a living might not be able to control what was done with their own earnings—only two thirds of the states had changed that rule by 1920. They had barely won, in most states, the right to equal consideration in gaining guardianship of their children in case of conflict.

The gains that were made and the rights that were secured were the product of agitation and political action. In not one instance was the Fourteenth Amendment's promise of equal protection kept by the courts whose judges had sworn to uphold the Constitution. When challenges were made to the continuing inequity, the only response was given in terms of "classification": women as a class could legitimately be treated differently from men as a class. The judges who made such decisions upholding differences in privileges or rights based on an irrelevant difference in sex were all men, needless to say. The equal protection gained by women was entirely the product of their own struggle.

One instructive episode that occurred during a woman's suffrage parade in the capital of the land of the free and the home of the brave was recorded by W. E. B. Du Bois in the NAACP's monthly magazine, *The Crisis*. More than a hundred persons were crushed as mobs of male hoodlums jostled, shoved into and tried to break up the parade; some shouted "Granny, go home, we came to see chicken, not hens"; others jumped on the running boards of cars to snatch at flags carried by demonstrators, or tried to tear off parts of their garments.

"Wasn't it glorious?" wrote Du Bois. "Does it not make you burn with shame to be a mere black man when such mighty deeds are done by Leaders of Civilization. . . . Does it not make you 'want to be white'?" He went on proudly to quote one white woman, who had observed: "I wish to speak a word in favor of the colored people during the suffrage parade. Not one of them was boisterous or rude as with great difficulty we passed along the unprotected avenue. The difference between them and those insolent, bold white men was remarkable. They were quiet and respectable and earnest, and seemed sorry for the indignities which were incessantly heaped upon us."

When the right to vote was won by national constitutional amendment, it was achieved only after a period of rising militancy which has had no precedent in our political history. The leaders and the followers, imbued with the conviction that a great wrong was to be undone and that no means necessary were too "extreme," did not merely ring doorbells, make speeches, draw up petitions and write letters to congressmen. They picketed the White House, persistently and *en masse,* for perhaps the first time in our history. They stormed the parties' National Conventions: in Chicago, for example, in 1916 five thousand marched from the Loop to the Coliseum to overwhelm a Republican Convention's resolutions committee. They filled the streets and blocked traffic in illegal, nonviolent (until they were attacked) demonstrations at which they went limp and refused to cooperate in being arrested: they had to be peeled off and pulled away one by one, and often the ranks of the traffic-blockers were refilled from the reserves of militants faster than the police could remove them.

But, as one woman editor wrote fifty years afterwards, looking at the legal, economic and psychological-social condition of her sex in America, "What Did the Nineteenth Amendment Amend?" Implied in and asserted by the very asking of the question was this double charge—that merely giving the right to vote did not, in itself, eliminate any of the other inequalities that had been permitted to flourish in violation of the literal language of Big Fourteen, and that possessing the right to vote did not prevent what has proved to be a real backsliding in women's role in life and consequently their self-image as equal human beings.

The catalogue of current inequalities and injustices is staggering. Until a lower federal court held otherwise in 1966—and its decision is not yet accepted everywhere—the exclusion of women from juries was held to be compatible with the Fourteenth Amendment. State-supported colleges are permitted to deny to women the same educational opportunities that are given to men. Different treatment in licensing individuals for state-regulated occupations has been permitted. Longer prison sentences for women than for men, for the same offenses, are considered acceptable in many areas.

The mentality of the nine men who sit on the Supreme Court has not visibly changed since 1948, when a two-thirds majority upheld a Michigan law requiring the licensing of bartenders but forbidding women to be licensed unless they were the wives or daughters of male owners. With a hardly suppressed chuckle, Justice Frankfurter referred to "the ale wife, sprightly and ribald, in Shakespeare," and observed that although "women had achieved virtues that men have long claimed as their prerogatives and now indulge in vices that men have long practiced" the states may still draw sharp lines between the sexes. Even the dissenters, who were led by Justice Douglas, omitted mention of the injustice done to the many women totally excluded from the work and rested their objections on the narrower discrimination against female bar owners.

Examples such as these indicate that there is truth in the argument of present-day Women's Liberation leaders who insist that the path to equality lies not so much in fighting for new court rulings that will enforce the Fourteenth Amendment as in a new and categorical amendment that would provide that "Equality of rights under the law shall not be denied or abridged by the United States or by any state on account of sex."

As much as in relations between blacks and whites, the imposition of inequality in relations between the sexes is a "fatal injustice" with rugged roots and it cannot be eliminated merely by changing laws. And just as the struggle of blacks for equal justice has been aided by whites who have sensed the injury to themselves that injustice produces, some men have been lucid and understanding in their approach to the woman's rights battle. A pioneer in this endeavor was one who had been a radical abolitionist, a colonel of a black regiment in the Civil War and a former minister who spent most of his career as a writer. Thomas Wentworth Higginson, as a frequent essayist on women and men, met many of the backward ideas of the men and women of his day and persuasively rebutted them.

The common notion, put more crudely in the 1870s but often repeated now, that woman's role as "intended by nature" is primarily (if not only) that of wife and mother Higginson answered by saying that she is above all a human being and no more constituted for maternity only than men for paternity: "The life which is common to the sexes is the principal life; the life which each sex leads, 'as such,' is a minor and subordinate thing. . . . The mental and moral laws of the universe touch us first and chiefly as human beings. We eat our breakfasts as human beings, not as men or women; and it is the same with nine tenths of our interests and duties in life. In legislating or philosophizing for woman, we must neither forget that she has an organization distinct from that of man, nor must we exaggerate the fact."

Nevertheless, the shallow ideas that Higginson attacked have had a vitality that has kept them flourishing to this day. In recent decades there was revived a concept of women as segregated from the life of action and the life of the mind and belonging rather to a world of consumption and self-adornment. In response to and in rebellion against this concept, which was so forcefully exploited that the percentage of women effectively using their talents decreased in the 1950s and the 1960s, there came into being the modern equivalent of the movement once led by Susan B. Anthony and her brothers and sisters.

The great obstacle has hardly changed since their day and it was well and truly described by John Stuart Mill, their contemporary, the British writer, philosopher and statesman: "All causes, social and natural, combine to make it unlikely that women should be collectively rebellious to the power of men. They are so far in a position different from all other subject classes, that their masters require something more from them than actual service. Men do not want solely the obedience of women, they want their sentiments. All men, except the most brutish, desire to have, in the woman most nearly connected with them, not a forced slave but a willing one, not a slave merely, but a favorite. They have therefore put everything in practice to enslave their minds. The masters of all other slaves rely, for maintaining obedience, on fear; either fear of themselves or religious fears. The masters of women wanted more than simple obedience and they turned the whole force of education to effect their purpose. All women are brought up from the very earliest years in the belief that their ideal of character is the very opposite to that of men; not self-will, and government by self-control, but submission and yielding to the control of others. All the moralities tell them that it is the duty of women, and all the current sentimentalities that it is their nature to live for others; to make complete abnegation of themselves, and to have no life but in their affections." It is all this that above all must be amended.

Chapter 31

Tourgee Triumphant
—On Paper

When the second Scottsboro case was in the Supreme Court, a young Southerner was just beginning to practice law. He had been born and raised in Baltimore, son of a school teacher and a steward, but he was never a sensational student until he reached law school. There he distinguished himself, leading his class despite the handicap of having to work his way through school, at the same time commuting from Baltimore to Washington to attend. Every morning he rose at 5:30 to catch the train to Washington, and he rarely reached home before ten at night. In Maryland's own law school, whites only were permitted.

Why did Thurgood Marshall take on the burden of traveling eighty miles a day to study, leaving the state where he wanted to practice in order to do so? Perhaps because he felt that it was more important that he become a lawyer and join the fight against such injustices than that he tarry on the path to become a test case himself in the fight. Or it may have been simple inertia—of the kind that was so widespread before the fight for the Scottsboro boys began—the personal accommodation that was made whenever a roadblock was encountered that had been around so long that it seemed a natural part of the landscape.

Whatever the reason for his personal choice, young attorney Marshall fairly leaped at the chance that he was offered two years after his own admission to the bar by an even younger Amherst alumnus. Donald Murray entered Marshall's tiny Baltimore office one day in 1935 to say that he sought the counsel of a lawyer who would bring suit to compel the Maryland state law school to admit him. He had been emboldened to make the effort by the notice served by the second Scottsboro ruling to the effect that Big Fourteen's commandment that no state could deny anyone equal protection of the laws was to be obeyed in jury cases. As Thurgood Marshall listened to the young man tell of his willingness to have his life stand still during the long wait for the outcome of a lawsuit, and to face humiliation or physical danger if he won, he sensed the thrill of a great opportunity.

Neither Murray nor Marshall was the first to wish to tackle the task of combating inequality of educational opportunity. They both came upon the scene after a master plan had been drafted by a group of NAACP leaders who had concluded that the time had come to move to complete the constitutional revolution that Du Bois had sparked in 1906 and that Moorfield Storey had initiated with three Supreme Court victories.

Their objective was the promised land of full equality under the law; their Moses was Charles H. Houston, grandson of slaves and dean of the law school that Thurgood Marshall had attended. Their central thrust was the sweeping away of "educational inequities"; on the flanks they had already opened fire, as we have seen, on voting, jury and housing injustices.

Under Houston's guidance, Marshall began Murray's lawsuit, a case that was to become historic as the first successful attack on the barriers to educational equality for American citizens. He asked the Maryland court for a writ, an order compelling the state university to admit Donald Murray to its all-white—and only—law school. The state's attorney general resisted: he invoked the ghosts of the Supreme Court justices who had turned down Albion Tourgee's plea for Homer Plessy. Since blacks could be awarded scholarships to attend out-of-state segregated law schools, they insisted, the standard of "equal but separate accommodations" had been met. Not so, said Maryland's highest court after hearing Marshall. If there is to be separation, the equality must be genuine. An out-of-state tuition grant cannot make up for the cost of living away from home. What was more important was that—as the young man who had traveled three hours a day to study in the District of Columbia had eloquently urged—there could be no equality in forcing a student to learn law in a state in which he did not intend to practice.

This was first blood in a campaign that still continues. Looking back, it might seem to be a minor victory: not even a Supreme Court decision, but simply one case in one state's high court directing the admission of one student. The principle of "separate" in the "equal but separate" formula that had been the bulwark of the cruel monstrosity of segregation was untouched. All that was won was the right to request the court to enforce the equality that had always been required by law—on paper. That was all, but it was a great deal.

It was not merely that it was followed up by instances of voluntary compliance and a developing series of Supreme Court cases that tested equal opportunity at the graduate school level of higher education. There, in one form or another, the inexorable requirements of the demand for equality repeatedly forced a breach in the wall of separateness. Out-of-state was not equal to in-state; a tiny and shabby law school with a miniature library was not equal to a law school that was properly set up; a graduate student could not be required to eat and study separately when the very dialogue and interchange with other students that were necessary for the completeness of his studies were cut off.

Fifteen years after Donald Murray walked into young Thurgood Marshall's tiny office, the tall, easygoing and able Marylander celebrated a Supreme Court victory in the somewhat more adequate office of the NAACP in New York which he had deprecated as "tush-tush" when promoted and transferred there. It was another law school case and it marked a turning point in the battle over which he was now general in chief. Opposing a young Texan's effort to enter the "white" law school, the state argued that the separate black school that it offered was as costly to it, per student, as the white. It also urged that the state-dictated separation was necessary for peaceful concentration on studies.

Marshall answered the last point by calling Don Murray down from Maryland to testify about what had happened when he entered the university there:

Q. Were you ostracized in any way?
A. No, I was not.
Q. Were you segregated in any way?
A. No, I was not.
Q. Were you mistreated in any way?
A. No, I was not.

Marshall then turned to the dire predictions of unrest that had been tossed about after his Murray victory:

Q. Attorney General O'Connor signed a legal paper predicting the worst if you were admitted, did he not?
A. Yes.
Q. Who gave you your diploma when you graduated from the University of Maryland?
A. Governor O'Connor. [The same man who had been attorney general.]
Q. And Charles T. LeViness signed that paper predicting trouble as Assistant Attorney General?
A. Yes.
Q. Who gave you your first job when you left law school?
A. Charles T. LeViness.

In his argument in the Supreme Court for *Sweatt vs. Painter,* Marshall not only showed the deficiencies of the "black" law school that Texas had provided. He also convinced all of the justices (for they were unanimous behind Chief Justice Vinson on the point) that separateness could not ever be equal, not even if more money were spent on the black law school than on the white. The chief justice responded to Marshall's adroit presentation by writing: "The law school to which Texas is willing to admit Sweatt excludes from its student body members of racial groups which number 85% of the population of the State and include most of the lawyers, witnesses, jurors, judges and other officials with whom petitioner will be inevitably dealing when he becomes a member of the Texas Bar. With such a substantial and significant segment of society excluded, we cannot conclude that the education offered him is substantially equal to that which he would receive if admitted to the University of Texas Law School."

Meanwhile there had also been launched, in accordance with the NAACP's original master plan, a number of insistent attacks on the actual inequities and disparities in educational opportunity at the elementary and secondary school levels in states were schools were segregated. The mere word "inequality" is hardly sufficient to describe the immense differences between the kind and the quality of schooling that was given at the time this drive began in the early 1930s. Behind the facade or pretense of "equal but separate" there had developed a division so extremely unfair and unjust that a mere statistical listing could hardly express it adequately.

The nation whose constitution provided that *all persons* born or naturalized in the United States were citizens whose privileges and immunities could not be impaired by any state and who were guaranteed equal protection under the laws had come to an atrocious condition. In nine southern states in the 1930s, the educational expenditure per pupil was $41 for whites and $16 for blacks. The value of the school buildings was $200 per child for those used by the favored race and $50 for the children of the darker. The ratio of books provided was 4:1 per pupil in favor of whites. Before 1930 there was not a single public high school for blacks in one state.

The laws with regard to compulsory education were often drawn so as to leave out black children. Some counties were given local option, the choice to decide if all children should be educated or only some. The motive behind that was made quite clear in some states in which children were excused—this should read "excluded"—from school during the cotton-picking season.

The caliber of the teachers was directly affected by these differences, and to such an extent that mere figures cannot sufficiently describe it. Many schools were places of custody rather than educational institutions, with a high percentage, at one time seventy percent, of teachers in black elementary schools themselves having had less than a sixth grade education. Needless to say, the nation that permitted these conditions to exist, under the hypocritical and false description of "equal but separate," is still paying the price for this enormous crime. All of its people, black and white, will suffer from it for years to come.

The NAACP's "master plan" included lawsuits to end many thousands of inequalities in thousands of school districts in the states of one third of the nation. The original memorandum suggested that the fight for equalization would make "the cost of a dual system so prohibitive as to speed the abolishment of separate schools." The NAACP also hoped to arouse the conscience of the American people by drawing public attention to the criminally huge difference in treatment. Admittedly, the funds and the manpower which the NAACP had available were so limited that they could not hope to do more than a small part of the job.

Marshall and his associates began this assignment shortly after the victory in the Murray case. They were successful, as far as they went. The first objective was the equalization of teachers' salaries, a fight that was carried on painfully and slowly, county by county. Over a period of fifteen years, fifty such lawsuits were successfully handled. Throughout the thousand counties and the many thousands of school districts that had been guilty, the gap did begin to narrow. Millions of dollars were added to the payrolls of teachers in black schools. In many cases, white women teachers were aided as well: the court orders were broad enough to require the raising of their salary levels to match those of the men.

With all the minor advances that had been made, the nature and dimensions of the basic problem remained the same. Two groups of American citizens were being treated differently by state law and state action on a matter that was vital to their ability to survive and to strive for advancement in a modern, increasingly technological society. But the harm that was done affected more than their education, and the infliction of a lower caste label by segregation did not injure the blacks alone. Marshall and his associates never forgot Charles Sumner's words, addressed to the Massachusetts courts almost two decades before Big Fourteen was written. "The whites themselves are injured by the separation"; when taught to regard a portion of the human family "as a separate and degraded class," they "become less fit for the duties of citizenship."

That idea, which had reverberated in the words of Alabama's Judge Horton when he declared in the Scottsboro case that injustice injured him who imposed it, weighed heavily in the mind of another white southern judge in 1951, when Thurgood Marshall appeared before him for a return engagement. J. Waties Waring of Charleston was born in 1880 into a South Carolina family that had owned slaves and had lived in the South for eight generations. He had been educated in Charleston and practiced law there for forty-two years, interrupted only by a tour of duty as federal prosecutor. His appointment as a United States District Judge had placed him in a position in which, as he viewed the stream of southern life reflected in the cases that came to court, the enormity of the injustice that his fellow Americans did to each other was forced on his consciousness.

Perhaps Thurgood Marshall helped. He had come to South Carolina in July of 1947 to ask the federal court to put down the state's rebellion against the Supreme Court ruling forbidding racial discrimination in primary elections. Judge Waring responded by refusing to permit the trick of allowing the primary to be run by the party (instead of the state) to be used as an excuse for exclusion: "It is time for South Carolina to rejoin the Union," he said.

Judge Waring's decision was sustained by higher courts, but the state's lawmakers continued to respond to the lawless incitations of a United States senator who had said, "Regardless of any Supreme Court decisions and any laws that may be passed by Congress, we of the South will maintain our political and social institutions as we believe to be in the best interest of our people." The judge condemned "this deliberate attempt to evade" and warned that "It is time that either the present officials of the Party, or such as may be in the future chosen, realize that the people of the United States expect them to follow the American way of elections." Under his injunction, thirty thousand blacks voted in South Carolina's 1948 primary.

But this example of law and order was not to the taste of one South Carolina congressman, L. Mendel Rivers, who was to survive until the 1970s as a leading defender of military supremacy and the war on Vietnam. Calling for the impeachment of Judge Waring, Rivers warned "Unless he is removed there will be bloodshed." Waring and his wife were ostracized and isolated by the very whites—some of their own old friends included—whom he had been trying to free from the burden of living in a land dominated by racial hostility. Crosses were burned on his lawn and rocks thrown through his window. He wrote privately to Ted Poston, a black New York newspaperman whom he had met, to ask that he be sure to see to it that "unprejudiced investigators" be sent to Charleston if he or his wife were killed.

"Negroes have thanked me for giving them the right to vote and that is sweetly flattering," he said of this crisis in his life that was finally to force him to resign and flee with his wife so that their last years could be lived in peace; "but my colleagues in the law know that I gave them nothing. The right to vote belonged to them as much as to me, and I was just fortunate enough to be a judge, deciding the question according to law."

Judge Waring held out in South Carolina long enough to participate in the case that was to lead to Thurgood Marshall's greatest—and Albion Tourgee's belated—victory. The suit of parents and children against the Clarendon County School Board had begun after a

1949 petition for equal educational facilities was turned down. While the case was pending in court, Marshall had convinced an NAACP lawyers' conference that the time had come to make a direct attack at the vital center that was poisoning American education. That center was the idea that the forced separation of people by race was an indignity that the courts had to be made to understand, or rather to admit. Blacks always knew it; white Americans of conscience had increasingly come to see it, too—and, especially during and after World War II, they fought against the western and eastern exponents of master race theories. A Presidential Commission on Civil Rights had been directed in December 1946 to report on "more adequate and effective means and procedures" to secure those rights, and this broadly representative group of distinguished citizens had reported: "Not even the most mathematically precise equality of segregated institutions can properly be considered equality under the law. No argument or rationalization can alter this basic fact: a law which forbids a group of American citizens to associate with other citizens in the ordinary course of daily living creates inequality by imposing a caste status on the minority group."

It had been just fifty years since Albion Tourgee had put it to the Supreme Court that "legalization of caste" was obnoxious to the spirit of republican institutions" and had won a response only from Kentuckian Harlan, who had said "There is no caste here." Just as Harlan had spoken for freedom and equality—but only in solitary dissent—Judge Waring was to be the lone dissenter in the round of school segregation cases that were to culminate in Tourgee's vindication. He was outvoted by two colleagues in the special three-man panel that was called to hear the South Carolina case, but that was only one branch of a five-pronged attack. The NAACP had begun, or joined in supporting, appeals to the courts in Virginia, Delaware, Kansas and the District of Columbia which were to come before the Supreme Court at the same time. In his dissent, Waring stood alone among the dozen and a half judges who heard the five cases before they reached the Supreme Court.

Judge Waring minced no words. Marshall had fought hard and had prepared his case carefully. He sought not merely to ask the courts to reconsider the shoddy precedents that had gone into the writing of the majority opinion in Plessy's case. He also prepared the groundwork for the claim that expert testimony showed that segregation produced injury to personality and that adequate education could not be secured in a restricted group that was being prepared to live in a multiracial society. It should be apparent, even without such testimony, Waring said, "that segregation in education can never produce equality and that it is an evil that must be eradicated. . . . I am of the opinion that all of the legal guideposts, expert testimony, common sense and reason point unerringly to the conclusion that the system of segregation in education adopted and practiced in the State of South Carolina must go and must go now. Segregation is *per se* (in and of itself) inequality."

The five cases were argued together in the Supreme Court in December 1952 and argued again the following year. The parent suing in the Kansas case was Oliver Brown, and by chance he won fame and immortality. His fight for the right of his little girl to go to a school five blocks away—her "neighborhood" school, even though marked "white" by the school board—happened to receive top billing when the cases were accepted and heard together in the court.

One of the nine justices who heard the case was Robert H. Jackson of New York, who came from a small town near where Albion Tourgee had lived during his last years. While the court was mulling over the cases, Justice Jackson wrote to friends and neighbors upstate about their former fellow townsman, now dead almost fifty years: "The *Plessy* case arose in Louisiana and how Tourgee got into it I have not learned. In any event, I have gone to his old brief filed here, and there is no argument made today that he would not make to the Court. He says, 'Justice is pictured blind and her daughter, the Law, ought at least to be color-blind.' . . . Tourgee's brief was filed April 6, 1896 and now, just fifty-four years after, the question is again being argued whether his position will be adopted and what was a defeat for him in '96 be a post-mortem victory."

The court met on May 17, 1954, to hand down its decision. It was to prove to be, as Justice Jackson had intimated, a postmortem victory for Albion W. Tourgee. No man had ever won so resounding a victory, so long after his death, as the old carpetbagger in the cases grouped under the single title *Brown vs. the Board of Education.* The heart of the ruling was simply that forced segregation was in violation of the United States Constitution, that it deprived those who were its victims of the equal protection of the laws as pledged by the Fourteenth Amendment.

Affecting, as it did, ten million children in fifty thousand schools, the court's ruling was newsworthy, it was important, it was of transcendent significance. But one thing that should never have been said was that it was surprising. Every decision, every step of the way—from the day that Thurgood Marshall had won Donald Murray's rights in 1936 until the equally important NAACP victories for Sweatt and McLaurin in 1950—had pointed in the direction that had led to the ultimate repudiation of the ruling in Plessy's case, in which Justice Harlan had been a minority of one who was right.

"Thurgood Marshall has been immortalized!" said one black leader when he learned of the decision. Of course he had been, and yet there was glory enough for many to share in the return to the Constitution and the restoration of equal protection which the decision signified. There were Judge Waring and Judge Harlan, white Southerners both, with the courage and integrity to speak out and to dare, even knowing they would be alone, to dissent. There were the many other attorneys and organizations that had filed briefs in support of his pleadings to the court. There were the brave parents and children who risked and often endured verbal and physical violence when they volunteered to be the "plaintiffs," the individuals who sued in the court actions. And there was the entire black freedom movement, in and out of the NAACP, which had kept alive the tradition of protest and had insisted that America make good on the promises of its constitution.

It would have been less painful if one had been able to end this chapter on this note and to say—as Justice Harlan had said of the Plessy decision, it was "quite as pernicious as the decision made by this tribunal in the Dred Scott case"—that the Brown ruling undid the evil that had been done in Plessy's case. Far from it. Evil is not undone easily, and on two immense counts there is still a great gap between promise and performance in the aftermath of the Brown decision. Even if overnight all Americans had responded to the court's leadership, there would have been millions of victims of segregated education from the previous era entitled to remedial treatment. But the great task of making up for the past was never rightly started. Nor was the task of preparing for the future accomplished in good faith. Just as the opportunity for reconstruction was missed in 1865, our 1955 leadership fell far short of responding to the opportunity that the court had presented.

Just as no one man can be given credit for the court's return to the Constitution in 1954, so no one man can be taxed with the blame for the failure of the nation to obey the law as laid down by the court. There is guilt enough to go around for the fiasco of so many years of tokenism that followed Thurgood Marshall's historic victory, and the first to bear the burden of blame is the court itself. Instead of beginning its approach to the future with firmness and a determination to make up for the decades of illegality and unjust deprivation that Americans had suffered, it retreated. And by that retreat it not only continued the injustice of the previous period for millions of school years; it also emboldened a new period of resistance that has made the return to law and decency a mirage that continues to recede into a seemingly unattainable future.

The court in the *Brown* case was deciding only the disputes between five groups of parents and pupils, on one hand, and five local educational government-controlled bodies, on the other. But it was aware that thousands of school districts and millions of parents and children would be affected by the ruling that outlawed the very idea of two separate school systems in any one state or district, one black and one white. Having laid down the law, having spoken clearly and with unanimity concerning what the Constitution required, the court flinched. It showed a timidity in enforcing the law against white administrators that contrasted with the courage with which it had declared the rights of black and white children to have an equal educational opportunity.

First, in the aftermath of the Brown decision, the court delayed for a year in sending the cases back to the districts from which they came, taking the entire period to ponder implementation. Then the formula which it adopted in what came to be called the second Brown decision was expressed in the fuzzy phrase "all deliberate speed," one which the court itself said meant that "additional time" could be granted to obey the law, once a "reasonable start" had been made. Thus did the justices show that beneath their black judicial robes they were, after all, white men.

They could have served notice on America that equality was an absolute right of all, that further subversion of the Constitution could not be tolerated, that inconveniences and difficulties were less important than the rights which it had finally admitted existed. When they failed to do so, they made possible the indefinite postponement of the rights of Americans and opened the door to the destruction of the education of an entire school generation—sixteen grades of children in a dozen states.

It was almost exactly like the aftermath of the Civil War. Then the vanquished might have submitted to the reconstruction of society on the just and equal basis advocated by Thaddeus Stevens and John Bingham, chief architects of Big Fourteen, had they not been encouraged to use defiance and guerrilla rebellion by the president himself, Andrew Johnson. Now the governors and local gentry who ran the segregated schools were inspired to practice disobedience and defiance by the court's vacillation, followed by a series of most unfortunate actions and inactions by the President of the United States, Dwight D. Eisenhower.

Through vigorous moral and political leadership, the president could have helped immensely in making up for the court's failure in the second Brown decision to direct immediate enforcement. Instead, he gave verbal aid and comfort to the leaders of the resistance—who did not, at the beginning, represent a clear majority of the local leaders. (For example, one Louisiana senator, Russel Long, said immediately following the 1954 decision, "Although I completely disagree with the decision, my oath of office requires me to accept it as the law.") But the president's shilly-shallying over the issue, culminating in a refusal to deny a widespread rumor that he had expressed disapproval of the decision, aided a rising tide of refusal to obey the law that has made the victory of Albion Tourgee and Thurgood Marshall, and of Charles Sumner and Boston's Sarah Roberts, too, a paper triumph, until now, in many places.

Chapter 32

Mr. Justice Black
Revisits Congressman Bingham

The great American historian Charles A. Beard was invited to attend a small dinner party in Washington in 1934. To his left, at the table, was a tanned, slim and amiable gentleman whose name professor Beard did not catch. They talked casually on many subjects. Beard found his neighbor to be not only deeply interested in history but quite well versed in it. One exchange showed the stranger to have made scholarly searches of his own on the subject of land tenure. Further aroused to curiosity by the man's spirit, judicial temper and eagerness to get to the bottom of things, the professor inquired later of the host about his neighbor and found him to have been Alabama's senator Hugo L. Black.

Made a Supreme Court justice in 1937, the former senator might have been thinking of many things in his own and in his country's past as he ascended the high bench three years later on Lincoln's birthday to deliver the court's unanimous decision in a case that had come from Florida. It was a "criminal" case—four poor blacks had vaguely confessed to a brutal murder—but, as the Alabaman saw the case, the method by which the "confessions" had been secured was the crime that he was anxious to expose and denounce. The jailors and the prosecutors had acted illegally, he believed.

He could have thought of his own early days as an attorney when as county solicitor he had discovered that one town's police headquarters concealed an interrogation room that was practically a torture chamber, a place where many held or beaten would sign confessions whether or not they were guilty of the crime to which they had confessed. When leading local citizens backed his denunciation of the police, a newspaper in Birmingham, the nearest metropolis, belittled what he had done and doubted its value, insisting that what he had exposed were routine "conditions such as are prevalent in every other city." County solicitor Black was undeterred and successfully pressed for grand jury approval of a report that declared that, innocent or guilty, no American ever loses his "right to be treated as a human being by reason of the fact that he is charged with—or any officer suspects that he is guilty of—a crime."

Justice Black undoubtedly recalled the report of President Hoover's Wickersham Commission, sent to the Senate while he was still a member of that body. He and his brother justices were well aware that neither the president nor Congress had taken any steps, afterwards, to aid in the restoration of law and order by regaining the public's respect for law, which the former attorney general's group declared had been lost because of lawlessness in law enforcement. The commission's principal indictment of the police methods that had come to prevail in so many states was directed, as we have seen, at the practice called the third degree—concentrating criminal investigation on one suspect and confining the investigation to the interrogation of that suspect.

Even before Justice Black, or any of his fellow "liberals"—the justices appointed beginning in 1937 by President Roosevelt—had joined the high court, it had followed up its intrusion into the province of state criminal procedure in the Scottsboro cases by overthrowing a Mississippi conviction whose record, Chief Justice Hughes had said, "reads more like pages torn from some medieval account" than a trial held under an enlightened constitutional government. The confessions unanimously rejected by the court in the case of another Brown, who with two other blacks was beaten with a leather strap with buckle at the end, were declared to be the product of a wrong so fundamental, so revolting to the sense of justice, "that it made the whole proceeding a mere pretense of a trial." This phrase, comparable to the one employed in Moorfield Storey's victory for Moore (the rebellious sharecropper of 1919), enabled the court to declare that it was not molesting the precedent laid down in the case of the banker Twining, in which it had been held that the Fifth Amendment's guarantee against an accused's being obliged to be a witness against himself was not made a limitation on the states by Big Fourteen.

The situation in the Florida case which had been entrusted to Justice Black's legal hand was somewhat different. There had not been the lawless physical torture that was admitted to in Mississippi's Brown case by one deputy sheriff who claimed he had whipped the defendants "not too much for a negro; not as much as I would have done if it had been left to me." Isaiah Chambers and his fellow Floridians had not been physically mistreated: instead, they had been subjected to the mental torture of continuous interrogation until they "broke," to use the word employed by one deputy sheriff.

It was not so easy as it had been in the Moore case in Arkansas or the Brown case in Mississippi to declare the trial a "pretense" or a "sham." Yet Justice Black and the court were determined to do what was within their power; Black was not yet ready, though, to recognize that the court's duty as well as its power lay in the language of the Fifth Amendment's commandment that no person could be "compelled in any criminal case to be a witness against himself." Turning to his sense of history, the justice peppered his opinion with such declarations as these: "Tyrannical government had immemorially utilized dictatorial procedure and punishment to make scapegoats of the weak, or of the helpless political, religious, or racial minorities and those who differed, who would not conform, and who resisted tyranny. . . . The testimony of centuries, in governments of varying kinds over populations of different races and beliefs, stood as proof that physical and mental torture and coercion had brought about the tragically unjust sacrifices of some who were the noblest and most useful of their generations. The rack, the thumbscrew, the wheel, solitary confinement, protracted questioning and cross questioning, and other ingenious forms of entrapment of the helpless or unpopular had left their wake of mutilated bodies and shattered minds along the way to the cross, the guillotine, the stake, and the hangman's noose."

Within the framework of this lesson in history, Justice Black led the court to support the "historical truth that the rights and liberties of people accused of crime could not be safely entrusted to secret inquisitorial processes." This in turn made it possible to justify the court's new kind of interference in state criminal procedures: one could not as easily say of the Florida Chambers group that it underwent a sham or the mere pretense of a trial. Instead, having decided that "no such practice as that disclosed by this record shall send any accused to his death," the court decreed that a trial based on evidence extorted by such questioning was a violation of due process of law because it was so abhorrent to any honest sense of justice.

By the sweeping language of his opinion, the justice also settled another score. For three years a cloud had hung over his name because, after his nomination as Supreme Court justice had been confirmed, an enterprising reporter for a newspaper chain hostile to the progressive causes for which he had fought as senator had dug up and disclosed the fact that in the early 1920s Black had been, for a brief period, a member of the newly revived Ku Klux Klan. There had been an uproar that had slowly died away after the new justice-to-be had insisted that his brief period of membership should not speak as loudly as his own earlier record. A sense of uneasiness had been left behind, but the Chambers decision was enough to satisfy all but the hypocritical foes of the new justice, the ones who opposed him because he was a champion of American constitutional freedom.

The doubters need only have read the salient passage in the Chambers decision—an answer as much to Klan as to police lawlessness: "We are not impressed," said Mr. Justice Black in measured tones, "by the argument that law enforcement methods such as those under review are necessary to uphold our laws. The Constitution proscribes such lawless means irrespective of the end."

Not long afterwards, professor Beard wrote a little book, *The Republic,* in which he tried to convey through Platonic dialogue the meaning of the entire structure of our constitutional government. He chose Justice Black's Chambers opinion to illustrate the "tremendous effect in the development of grand justice" that the Supreme Court can have, and said of it: "The whole document ought to be read by all citizens who care for the perpetuity of the Republic." But no single opinion, unfortunately, can speak for all time or by itself safeguard the liberties of a free people any more than a written constitution can. And, just as the ultimate guardians of our freedom are the people themselves, the constant foes of our freedom are those who are tempted, out of human frailty, laziness or arrogance, to trespass on that freedom.

The real issue that the Chambers case decided was left unstated through no fault of Justice Black's. The court consists of nine men who come from different backgrounds and have separate personalities. They may sometimes come to a unanimous agreement as to what is the just result in a particular case, for a sense of decency and justice does not depend on whether a judge is conservative or liberal. Even so, they can have great difficulty in agreeing on the expression of the principle that explains their action.

The Chambers case itself furnished a very good example. The men of so many different characters who made up the 1940 court— ranging from a rabid reactionary who had ascended the bench in 1914 to a recently appointed radical, in the honorable and early American sense of the word—were united in agreeing that the police methods there recorded, though not involving physical abuse or torture, were abhorrent and intolerable. They could not agree on the clear and simple basis for freeing the defendants that is evident in the immunity given to Americans by the original Bill of Rights: "nor shall any person be compelled in any criminal case to be a witness against himself." That would have substantiated old Justice Harlan's repeated insistence that the immunities and privileges of American citizenship itemized in the Bill of Rights were safeguarded from state and local interference by Big Fourteen, as Bingham and Thaddeus Stevens and the men of the Thirty-Ninth Congress had intended when they wrote it.

Because the court was not ready to turn its back on the repeated majorities who had outvoted the Great Dissenter, the return to the Constitution has been a rocky road. Setbacks along that road were still to come. For example, the Sixth Amendment grants in *"all* criminal prosecutions" the right of the accused "to have the Assistance of Counsel for his defense." That privilege or immunity had been won, under another label, in the Scottsboro cases during their first trip to the court ten years before a penniless white farmhand named Smith Betts arrived to ask for his rights as an American.

Betts insisted that he was innocent of the crime of robbery with which he had been charged. He had told the Maryland court that he could not afford an attorney, but that court had failed to appoint one to defend him. After he was convicted, Betts appealed for the aid of the United States Supreme Court. He was turned down by a 6-3 vote, the majority repeating the old formula that "the Fourteenth Amendment does not incorporate, as such, the specific guarantees found in the Sixth Amendment." The majority had decided to limit the Scottsboro ruling to capital crimes, without any warrant in the Constitution for doing so.

Hugo Black spoke out for the dissenters. It was a mockery, he said, to talk of solemn guarantees for a full and fair trial and yet deprive a poor man on trial of the aid of counsel necessary to make those guarantees of any value. He confronted the real issue, and put it flatly into words: "I believe that the Fourteenth Amendment made the Sixth applicable to the states. But this view, although often urged in dissents, has never been accepted by a majority of this Court."

With those words, Black began an effort that never ceased to gather a majority. He delved deeply into the history of the Fourteenth Amendment, into the reasons for its wording and the debates in the Congress that had framed it. He mounted his most vigorous offensive in 1947 to persuade the court that the Bill of Rights had become the shield of the American citizen against state and city governmental action as well as against the federal rulers, and he failed by only one vote.

Never has a Supreme Court opinion been freighted with such a convincing array of historical evidence as that which was offered by Justice Black in the appendix to his 1947 dissent in the case of *Adamson vs. California.* He began at the beginning, the appointment and the mission of the Joint Committee on Reconstruction. He analyzed and summarized the various drafts of the Fourteenth and turned repeatedly to the remarks of its chief draftsman, Congressman John A. Bingham. He followed the exchanges among supporters and foes of the new amendment in the committee, in the House and in the Senate, where adoption was completed before ratification by the states. And he concluded his appendix with the words, "For further exposition of these views see also the vigorous dissenting opinions of Mr. Justice Harlan. . . ."

Hugo LaFayette Black did live to see his dissent in Smith Betts' case upheld in the case of Clarence Gideon, another poor white man who protested his denial of the right of counsel twenty years later.

While Black's historical analysis of the constitutional protection of the rights of Americans intended by Bingham and Stevens has yet to prevail, the court has come to recognize, one member by one, that most of the privileges and immunities contained in the Bill of Rights should be the shield of every American.

On a Monday in June of 1969, just two years after his name had been sent to the Senate as a nominee for the supreme bench, a former Maryland lawyer began to deliver the latest of the court's decisions recognizing still another of the immunities in the Bill of Rights which are guarded against abuse by the states. Early in the administration of President John F. Kennedy, Thurgood Marshall had been plucked from leadership in the NAACP's continuing fight to give meaning to Big Fourteen's promise of equal protection as head of a separate legal arm, the NAACP Legal Defense and Educational Fund, Inc. After a tour of duty as a federal court of appeals judge and then as the Solicitor General of the United States, Marshall had joined the court whose return to the Constitution had been so immensely aided by his advocacy over the years.

Thirty-two years before, when Marshall had won Donald Murray's right to go to the state law school, young Justice Black had joined the court in declining to enforce against the states the prohibition contained in the Fifth Amendment that ". . . nor shall any person be subject for the same offense to be twice put in jeopardy of life or limb." Whatever the reason for his assent to that decision—his comparative newness as a justice or, more probably, the great reputation of Justice Cardozo, who had been led into the error of delivering the decision by his uncritical acceptance of the errors of the past—Black soon repented. In a later dissent of his own he observed: "Fear and abhorrence of governmental power to try people twice for the same conduct is one of the oldest ideas found in Western civilization. Its roots run deep into Greek and Roman times. Even in the Dark Ages, when so many other principles of justice were lost, the idea that one trial and one punishment were enough remained alive through the canon law and the teachings of early Christian writers."

Now Thurgood Marshall assumed his role in the process of putting together the privileges and immunities of state citizens that Bingham and Stevens had fought for, and the destruction of which old Justice Harlan had repeatedly protested for three decades. Marshall looked back at the decade during which the decision in banker Twining's case had been overruled, giving back to state citizens national protection against being compelled to testify against themselves; he reviewed the decision in burglar Maxwell's case, which had been overruled by the logic that trial by jury cannot be destroyed by the states in serious criminal cases; and finally he considered the decision in Smith Betts' case, which had been overruled when Clarence Gideon's case consummated the long fight begun at Scottsboro for the right of counsel for all Americans. After summarizing that progress, Mr. Justice Marshall said of the court's decision for which he wrote the opinion, "We today only recognize the inevitable."

It is one thing, however, to say that the return to the Constitution was "inevitable," and quite another to say that it is definite and final. There is an air of uncertainty in the very use of the wrong label— "due process of law"—for the liberty that would have been more clearly reestablished had its protection been granted under the privileges and immunities guarantee of Big Fourteen. There was also a current of dissent within the court, and by historical irony it came from a justice named John Marshall Harlan, grandson of the great dissenter most of whose views had finally prevailed.

But the real danger to the reestablished constitutional guarantees does not come primarily from the court's doctrinal difficulties or from the persistence of followers of the later Justice Harlan to the notions of justices whose horizons were limited by the false assumptions that were built into the court's judging processes during the years it drifted away from the Constitution. Just as we saw that the ultimate guardians of our freedom are the people themselves, and that no bill of rights can long survive in a nation whose people have lost the spirit of liberty, so the durability of the resurgent rights we have won is endangered by a massive propaganda war against them that has been led by two sorts of foes of the Constitution.

One group of the discontented are those whose grievance with the court and the Constitution stems principally from their longing for a way of life that was built on the twisted reasoning that permitted segregation to be substituted for slavery as a means of gaining the supposed advantages of a caste system. To discredit and undermine the court's rulings requiring equal protection under the laws, they have allied themselves with the other group, the lawless and the lazy among law enforcement officers whose lawlessness has created the kind of disrespect for law among the oppressed and underprivileged that promotes crime in conditions of poverty and privation. Objecting in general to any application of the Bill of Rights to the states, they have directed their greatest fire against the line of decisions that were made practically inevitable by the logic of the Chambers ruling—the decisions that have given genuine meaning to the founding fathers' decree that no man shall be compelled to testify against himself.

To the extent that crime in our society may have increased because of poverty amidst affluence, because of drug addiction flowing from frustration and alienation, and because of disrespect for the law as a result of lawlessness in high office and among low officials, these foes of the Constitution have tortured the facts and turned events to their own use. They have succeeded in conveying an impression that crime has increased because the court has respected and enforced the rights of all Americans. Consequently, there is now a constant danger that a climate has been created in which the toll of time will see the replacement of justices who have aided the return to the Constitution by those who will once more allow it to be undone.

The lawless lethargy which tempts so many police officers to return to the kind of coercive interrogation of prisoners that the court has frustrated is best illustrated by an anecdote. It comes from a discussion that British barristers had during the preparation of a Code of Criminal Procedure for India just a century ago. Why, one of the more civilized jurists wanted to know, did native police wish so fervently to be allowed to torture prisoners? One experienced officer replied: "There is a great deal of laziness in it. It is far pleasanter to sit comfortably in the shade rubbing red pepper into a poor devil's eyes than to go about in the sun hunting up evidence." What was won from the court in the struggle to regain the protection of the Fourteenth Amendment for blacks and the poor, radicals and dissenters, was its safeguard for all Americans against the equivalent of such practices.

Many judges in high state courts have been mobilized by the foes of freedom to join their crusade. But one who was not fooled or tempted by injured dignity to ally himself with the underminers gave them an effective answer: "All our difficulties, it is sometimes alleged, can be traced to a few Supreme Court decisions or to Federal intervention in the affairs of the states or to too much toleration of individual freedom.

"I would venture to suggest that perhaps just the opposite is the case. That our difficulties are not caused by the recent Supreme Court decisions, but by the fact that those decisions and the principles which they embody did not come decades earlier.

"For many years America tolerated social injustices, racial injustice and fundamental defects in the area of criminal law. And on no profession does the responsibility for that injustice rest heavier than upon the legal profession whose members, for the most part, stood by with muted tongues while constitutional amendments were ignored and while citizens were oppressed."

The speaker was the Honorable Kenneth Keating, former Republican United States senator from New York State, later judge of the Court of Appeals of New York and President Nixon's Ambassador to India until recently.

Chapter 33

Too Late?

Have the Supreme Court decisions that Judge Keating suggested should have come "decades earlier" arrived too late? That is the great question that America faces now.

Habits of thought and conduct are not easily changed. Special privileges and supposed advantages are not readily relinquished. Injustice does not, like a chalk mark on a blackboard, leave a superficial stain that can be readily erased. The restoration of rights too long withheld is not enough to solve our difficulties. The weight of past error is a curse threatening the future as well as a plague for the present.

The strength of the Fourteenth and its sister freedom amendments has been displayed again and again in recent years. They have served, at least on paper, to illustrate the breadth of the wisdom of the founding fathers of 1866. The errors and the evils of the first seventy-five years of our history provided a nearly perfect guide to those who had met to inquire into and to correct them. What was and is still lacking could hardly have been supplied by foresight: a tool for remedying the effects of the accumulated departures from the Constitution.

The return to the Constitution was marked not only by a belated attention to the specific evils that Americans were supposed to have been safeguarded against by the Thirteenth, Fourteenth and Fifteenth Amendments. (To have told the detailed story of each might have made too long a story, but the constitutional guarantees include the right of every American to live and own a home where he chooses, the right to earn a living on the same terms as any other American, the right of the poor to appeal convictions for alleged crime on the same terms as those sufficiently well off to purchase the stenographer's minutes of the trial, the right of the young when charged with a crime to have the assurances in procedure that have come to be recognized as the constitutional protection of those over sixteen or eighteen.) But the return to the Constitution also established that the clauses of the three amendments which specified the powers of Congress—"to enforce this article by appropriate legislation"—meant what they said and were not to be hamstrung as they had been in the cases of the blacks murdered by the Cruikshank mob and the whites deported from their homes by Sheriff Wheeler's gang of respectable citizens.

The restoration of the vitality of the clauses giving the powers of Congress came in the aftermath of the school desegregation cases of 1954. When the unanimous court admitted by what it did that Du Bois and the Niagara Movement revolutionaries of 1906 had been right, there was a chain reaction. The initial response was sparked by a tired lady named Rosa Parks who refused to go to the back of a Montgomery, Alabama, bus to stand when there were seats in the "white" section of the bus. There followed the thirteen-month Montgomery bus boycott, whose story is told by the hero who emerged, Dr. Martin Luther King, in *Stride Towards Freedom*.

Afterwards came a movement of direct nonviolent protest that reached epic levels with the freedom ride and sit-in movements of the early 1960s, followed by voter registration drives that were needed to overcome the timidity born of long disuse and the insistent and ingenious resistance that continued. Murder in Mississippi in 1964 and brutal assault in Alabama in 1965 led to new Supreme Court tests: one of an old law that had lain unused and another of a new law that was passed to guarantee voting rights by full federal action. The court erased the stain of the decisions in the Cruikshank case and the civil rights cases (from which Justice Harlan had dissented so well) by clear rulings sustaining the power of Congress to secure the rights declared in the amendments. With an uncanny—if possibly unconscious—recognition that its rulings were coming too late, the newly vigilant court fashioned a remedy for a twentieth-century dilution of democracy.

The word "malapportionment" does not arouse the same sense of injustice that "disfranchisement" does. The drama associated with the deprivation of the rights of particular individuals is lacking: the picture of men and women, whole families and communities, barred from the polls by cheap trickery or frightened away by threats and violence. Yet the result is equally vicious. When the lines of districts created to select federal congressmen or state lawmakers are so drawn that 50,000 voters can choose a representative in one and 250,000 in another, the people of the larger district are really given only one fifth of a vote each.

"In a democratic country nothing is worse than disfranchisement," said one southern federal appeals judge in 1959. "And there is no such thing as being just a little bit disfranchised. A free man's right to vote is a full right to vote or it is no right to vote." Judge John

Minor Wisdom of Louisiana, writing for the federal court of appeals for the circuit including Alabama, was expressing his regret at his powerlessness (as he thought), under prior Supreme Court decisions, to interfere with the mutilation of the city borders of Tuskegee.

What had happened was simple. The city of Tuskegee had a population of five times as many blacks as whites. Until the 1950s the combined effect of intimidation and election board cheating had been to keep the number of white voters greater. As the signs and symbols of inequality had been chipped away, it had been decided that another method had to be found to keep the city within the control of a tiny part of its population. The white primary had been outlawed. Tuskegee was a university town, seat of a long-established black college, and it had become increasingly difficult to use the pretense of a "literacy" test to exclude voters. At the point at which the slow increase in the number of black voters posed a threat that government of all the people would be installed in the city, drastic action was taken.

The traditional city limits were chopped, sliced and mangled beyond all recognition. The new lines were drawn by the state legislature so that all but half a dozen black potential voters were left outside city limits. The boundaries of the municipality zigged and zagged in short and long stretches and at weird angles that had no relation to the countryside. A new twist had been given to the old idea of "running out of town" those who sought to exercise their rights as Americans: the town was pulled and twisted away from and around them.

The stage had been set for a new challenge to a court that had become mindful over barely two decades of its obligations and its opportunities under Big Fourteen and its companion amendments. Charles Gomillion, social science department chairman of Tuskegee Institute, had led a group of local blacks in suing Mayor Phil Lightfoot in federal court to cancel the "gerrymander" (traditional nickname for boundary lines warped to distort voting impact). Judge Wisdom, who had said so well that there was "no such thing as being just a little bit disfranchised," condemned what had been done but felt powerless to interfere.

Only fourteen years before Robert Carter, successor to Thurgood Marshall at NAACP when the latter left to head a separate Defense and Educational Fund, walked up the marble staircase under the inscription "Equal Justice Under Law" to argue the case of *Gomillion vs. Lightfoot,* the Supreme Court had seemed to say that it would not—or could not—act in such cases. In 1946, over the vigorous dissent of Justice Hugo Black, the court had declined to act on the complaint of Illinois voters who showed that their right to vote had ceased to be "a full right to vote" because Illinois had failed, for forty-five years, to redistribute its districts for seats in the national House of Representatives. Although populations in Illinois congressional districts ranged from 112,000 to 914,000—and so the voters in the smaller district had a vote with more than eight times the weight of those in the larger—three of the justices, joined by a fourth for different reasons, but enough to make a majority, said "courts ought not to enter this political thicket," and that "the remedy for unfairness in districting is to secure state legislatures that will apportion properly, or to invoke the ample powers of Congress."

Fine words, without real meaning. The very fact of unfair apportionment had increasingly corroded the democratic process in America during the twentieth century—in addition to and apart from the absence of democracy in states where blacks had been illegally kept from becoming voters. In states, cities and Congress as well, the beneficiaries of imbalance, the wielders of majority power selected by minority constituencies, were not prepared to restore equality in representation at the cost of giving away their own control. With perception and understanding, Justice Black, joined by Justice William O. Douglas and Frank Murphy, tried to break up this condition, saying that "glaringly unequal representation in the Congress in favor of special classes and groups should be invalidated, 'whether accomplished ingeniously or ingenuously.' "

The effect of the court's disinclination, for the time being, to enter what one of the justices had dubbed the "political thicket" was to permit the continued deterioration of democratic government. It is easier for corrupt and vested interests to influence and control lawmakers from malapportioned constituencies, and those who are able to perpetuate their offices, their seniority (so important in decisive steps in the legislative process), without responsibility to the vast majority of voters naturally fail to serve the public interest. In the early sixties the effect of assorted and accumulated distortions and dilutions of democracy was such that one United States senator expressed his "deep conviction that the legislatures of America, local, state, and national, are presently the greatest menace in our country to the successful operation of the democratic process."

A specific and particularly ugly example of the impact of the combined evils of malapportionment and disfranchisement was noted in one former Virginia state senator's study of the illegal resistance of many areas to the school desegregation decisions. That resistance on the part of local school boards was compounded and encouraged by the actions of state legislatures in which the swing votes emanated from the white representatives of the Black Belt counties (areas with heavy black populations but few black voters). Such counties, holding between eight and thirteen percent of the states' populations, had from twenty to thirty percent of the representatives in the state lawmaking bodies during the crucial period of resistance that undermined so sadly the effect of the court's return to the Constitution in the school cases.

In the Tuskegee case the practitioners of minority control had been too ruthless and had gone too far. Political thicket or not, the manipulation of voter representation by the discriminatory drawing of district lines was too scandalous an injury to constitutional rights for the court to allow it to go untouched. Chief Justice Marshall had said in the early days of our republic that "The very essence of civil liberty certainly consists in the right of every individual to claim the protection of the laws, whenever he receives an injury." And no one could say, as the justices who turned down the Illinois appeal had, that the remedy for unfairness lay with state lawmakers: it was they who had inflicted it.

The fight of the Tuskegee blacks for their rights was carried on in the community from which Alabama's lawmakers had sought to exclude them, as well as in the courts. The shops and business institutions of the minority whose control over a majority the lawmakers tried to make permanent were boycotted. It became evident that the blacks would not quietly accept exclusion from the power to make decisions in the little city where they had been born and raised and where they worked for most of their lives. The Supreme Court was obliged to respond to the blatant injustice of what had been done: the state is not "omnipotent" in the drawing of district or city lines, it said; "state power" may not be used as "an instrument for circumventing a federally protected right."

The court's statement marked a breakthrough in recognizing the essential purpose of Thaddeus Stevens and John Bingham and the other draftsmen of Big Fourteen—this time in an area which they might not have actually foreseen ninety-five years before. Once it had been established that racial discrimination could not be hidden behind the camouflage of a "political" issue, it would not be long before it was recognized that other kinds of discrimination were open to questioning and correction. Malapportionment for the purpose, or with the effect, of giving greater voting power to rural voters over city voters, to rich voters over poorer voters, to one ethnic group rather than another, was doomed.

It was quite clear by 1962 that neither state legislatures nor Congress was going to begin to restore the basic principles of fairness in the process of setting up and maintaining district lines. In certain instances the inequities were the result of deliberate actions; in others they were caused by inaction, the failure to remedy unbalanced districts that had developed over the years as people migrated, as villages were born or died, as industries shifted or as farms were abandoned. Whether the cause was intentional or the product of inertia, equal protection of the laws was being denied to the under-represented voters.

A group of angry Tennesseans, mainly if not all white, were the first to take advantage of Professor Gomillion's victory. They were not exactly pioneers, but they were the most recent wave of Americans who persisted in refusing to take no for an answer when they were denied equality. The Illinois grievants of two decades before had been cheated of proper congressional representation and the issue in Tennessee was raised by legislative inaction in failing to redistrict for the state lawmaking body. But the principle at stake was precisely the same.

They won a round in the state court in which they began their fight. But the state's lawyers appealed and the highest Tennessee court rejected the suit. If the state legislature is illegal, asked the high court (in horror), how could it pass laws that would make it possible to elect a legal one? The court had put its finger on a pretty serious point, although it drew the wrong conclusion from it. Strictly speaking, many state and federal laws had been thoroughly illegal because the rules laid down for electing lawmakers by the Fourteenth and Fifteenth Amendments had been ignored. Even Woodrow Wilson's declaration of war on Germany, passed by a Congress in which no black man sat, and for defying which so many had been persecuted and jailed, was thoroughly illegal. The illegitimacy of a system based on constitutional violation cannot be waved away or swept under a rug.

The Tennessee insurgents chose not to draw the conclusion that they could exercise their right of revolution. Instead they chose to mount a nonviolent rebellion by pressing for a court ruling to obtain legality in state government. To start a new suit against the secretary of state, Joseph Carr, they chose as leading plaintiff a Memphis justice of the peace named Charles W. Baker. (It has been suggested that they did this because the first great constitutional ruling was won by a District of Columbia J. P. who sued James Madison.) The historic lineup of *Baker vs. Carr* was on its way to final decision.

The first federal court to which Baker and his attorneys appealed, like the lower federal courts in Charles Gomillion's fight, declared that the Tennesseans had indeed been deprived of their rights by the disproportionate districting but disclaimed power to act. The fight was then carried to the United States Supreme Court. Many combatants joined the fray. Across the nation so many areas resented the corruption and dilution of democracy which had developed that a spotlight shone on the marble palace marked "Equal Justice Under Law" almost as brightly as it had on the eve of the ruling in *Brown vs. the Board of Education.*

To Justice William J. Brennan, Jr., who had been appointed to the court in 1956, fell the privilege of writing the opinion in Baker's case, one of the great constitutional decisions of our time. Son of an Irish immigrant who had worked as a stoker and steam fitter, Mr. Justice Brennan had been an able lawyer, a devoted public servant and a well-regarded judge of the New Jersey Supreme Court before coming to Washington. His vote, together with those of Justice Douglas and Chief Justice Warren, had helped win the ultimate victory of the views which had been expressed in dissent by the elder Justice Harlan in the nineteenth century and by Mr. Justice Black early in his career as a justice representing the best of the South.

In Great Britain, at the time of our first revolution, there existed the appearance of democratic parliamentary government. The abuses that provoked the revolution were the manifestations of a reality that was quite different. An outstanding deficiency was the institution of the "rotten borough", the district without a real constituency, for which MPs were handpicked. As Justice Black, now on the victorious side, had pointed out in dissenting in the first Illinois case of 1946, a malapportioned district was no better than a rotten borough. Now the court was announcing that it was open to business to hear complaints against unequal representation, and it was soon to make it plain that no level of government would be exempt.

When the principle in Baker's case was applied, in 1964, to the drawing of congressional districts, the later Harlan dissented. One ground for his protest was that the majority decision placed "grave doubt on the constitutionality of the House of Representatives" and put "in jeopardy the seats of almost all members of the House." But this is hardly a reason for refusing to enforce the Constitution. On the contrary, it raises the question of whether the implications of such past illegality should not be pressed to the uttermost.

If they were—concerning not only past malapportionment but also disfranchisement—there would be much to undo and to remake. Laws passed by tainted votes and governmental machinery welded together by unrepresentative majorities are of questionable legitimacy. The passing of power and influence to a military establishment nurtured by the cooperative indulgence of House and Senate committee chairmen who never had a right to be congressmen presents a challenge to the future of America. But the only effective answer to that challenge can be given by the ultimate guardians of our liberty—the people themselves. The court can return to the Constitution, as it has in many ways, but it cannot restore it or enforce on a nation that repudiates its founding fathers of 1789 and 1866 the ideals which they handed down to us.

The Supreme Court's decisions in the apportionment cases made the deepest penetration that it has been possible to make under Big Fourteen into the very vitals of the governmental power structure. The privileges and immunities of American citizens have only limited value when their protection is restricted to what can be secured by court decisions. One man may be freed from unjust imprisonment, ten may breach the walls of "restricted" areas, one hundred may be allowed to gain employment in a trade from which they have been illegally excluded, a thousand may be protected in their right to vote—all without seriously affecting the pyramid of privilege based on past violations of the Constitution. But nothing that courts have done or can do will supply restitution for all who have suffered injustice. In the apportionment cases, at least, a full remedy for the present is provided.

The experience of the recent past shows us how undisturbed is the basic control of society and how secure is the wealth that was accumulated in large part by reason of the injustices of the past and with the aid of evasions and violations of the Thirteenth, Fourteenth and Fifteenth Amendments. The third American revolution has been won on paper; it seems remote from accomplishment in deed. The question that every American must ask himself is whether or not the return to the Constitution has taken place too late.

Appendix

CONSTITUTIONAL
AMENDMENTS

The Bill of Rights and the Freedom Amendments†

Articles in Addition to, and Amendment of, the Constitution of the United States of America, Proposed by Congress, and Ratified by the Legislatures of the Several States Pursuant to the Fifth Article of the Original Constitution

ARTICLE I.[1]
Congress shall make no law respecting an establishment of religion, or prohibiting the free exercise thereof; or abridging the freedom of speech, or of the press; or the right of the people peaceably to assemble, and to petition the Government for a redress of grievances.

ARTICLE II.
A well regulated Militia, being necessary to the security of a free State, the right of the people to keep and bear Arms, shall not be infringed.

ARTICLE III.
No Soldier shall, in time of peace be quartered in any house, without the consent of the Owner, nor in time of war, but in a manner to be prescribed by law.

[1]The first ten amendments to the Constitution of the United States were proposed to the legislatures of the several States by the First Congress, on the 25th of September 1789. They were ratified by the following States, and the notifications of ratification by the governors thereof were successively communicated by the President to Congress: New Jersey, November 20, 1789; Maryland, December 19, 1789; North Carolina, December 22, 1789; South Carolina, January 19, 1790; New Hampshire, January 25, 1790; Delaware, January 28, 1790; Pennsylvania, March 10, 1790; New York, March 27, 1790; Rhode Island, June 15, 1790; Vermont, November 3, 1791; and Virginia, December 15, 1791. The legislatures of Connecticut, Georgia, and Massachusetts ratified them on April 19, 1939, March 24, 1939 and March 2, 1939, respectively.

†Source: 73d Congress, 1st Session, Senate Document No. 79 (Washington, 1934).

ARTICLE IV.

The right of the people to be secure in their persons, houses, papers, and effects, against unreasonable searches and seizures, shall not be violated, and no Warrants shall issue, but upon probable cause, supported by Oath or affirmation, and particularly describing the place to be searched, and the persons or things to be seized.

ARTICLE V.

No person shall be held to answer for a capital, or otherwise infamous crime, unless on a presentment or indictment of a Grand Jury, except in cases arising in the land or naval forces, or in the Militia, when in actual service in time of War or public danger; nor shall any person be subject for the same offence to be twice put in jeopardy of life or limb; nor shall be compelled in any criminal case to be a witness against himself, nor be deprived of life, liberty, or property, without due process of law; nor shall private property be taken for public use, without just compensation.

ARTICLE VI.

In all criminal prosecutions, the accused shall enjoy the right to a speedy and public trial, by an impartial jury of the State and district wherein the crime shall have been committed, which district shall have been previously ascertained by law, and to be informed of the nature and cause of the accusation; to be confronted with the witnesses against him; to have compulsory process for obtaining Witnesses in his favor, and to have the Assistance of Counsel for his defence.

ARTICLE VII.

In Suits at common law, where the value in controversy shall exceed twenty dollars, the right of trial by jury shall be preserved, and no fact tried by a jury, shall be otherwise reexamined in any Court of the United States, than according to the rules of the common law.

ARTICLE VIII.

Excessive bail shall not be required, nor excessive fines imposed, nor cruel and unusual punishments inflicted.

ARTICLE IX.

The enumeration in the Constitution, of certain rights, shall not be construed to deny or disparage others retained by the people.

ARTICLE X.

The powers not delegated to the United States by the Constitution, nor prohibited by it to the States, are reserved to the States respectively, or to the people.

:: :: ::

ARTICLE XIII.[2]

Section I. Neither slavery nor involuntary servitude, except as a punishment for crime whereof the party shall have been duly convicted, shall exist within the United States, or any place subject to their jurisdiction.

Section 2. Congress shall have power to enforce this article by appropriate legislation.

ARTICLE XIV.[3]

Section 1. **All persons born or naturalized in the United States, and subject to the jurisdiction thereof, are citizens of the United States and of the State wherein they reside. No State shall make or enforce any law which shall abridge the privileges or immunities of citizens of the United States; nor shall any State deprive any person of life, liberty, or property, without due process of law; nor deny to any person within its jurisdiction the equal protection of the laws.**

Section 2. Representatives shall be apportioned among the several States according to their respective numbers, counting the whole number of persons in each State, excluding Indians not taxed. But when the right to vote at any election for the choice of electors for President and Vice President of the United States, Representatives in Congress, the Executive and Judicial officers of a State, or the members of the Legislature thereof, is denied to any of the male inhabitants of such State, being twenty-one years of age, and citizens of the United States, or in any way abridged, except for participation in rebellion, or other crime, the basis of representation therein shall be reduced in the proportion which the number of such male citizens shall bear to the whole number of male citizens twenty-one years of age in such State.

[2]The Thirteenth Amendment was proposed by resolution of Congress which the President approved on February 1, 1865. It was declared in a proclamation of the Secretary of State, dated December 18, 1865, to have been ratified by 27 States. Subsequent records of the Department of State show that the 13th Amendment was ratified by 6 more of the 36 States. It was rejected by 2 (Delaware and Mississippi).

[3]The Fourteenth Amendment was proposed by resolution of Congress on June 13, 1866. By a concurrent resolution of Congress adopted July 21, 1868, it was declared to have been ratified by "three fourths and more of the several States of the Union", and the Secretary of State was required duly to promulgate the amendment as a part of the Constitution. He accordingly issued a proclamation, dated July 28, 1868, declaring the amendment to have been ratified by 30 States, "being more than three fourths." Records of the Department of State show that the 14th Amendment was subsequently ratified by 3 more of the 37 States. It was rejected by 3 (Delaware, Kentucky, and Maryland).

Section 5. **The Congress shall have the power to enforce, by appropriate legislation, the provisions of this article.**

ARTICLE XV.[4]

Section 1. The right of citizens of the United States to vote shall not be denied or abridged by the United States or by any State on account of race, color, or previous condition of servitude.

Section 2. The Congress shall have power to enforce this article by appropriate legislation.

[4]The Fifteenth Amendment was proposed by resolution of Congress on February 26, 1869. It was declared in a proclamation of the Secretary of State, dated March 30, 1870, to have been ratified by 29 States, which "constitute three fourths." Records of the Department of State show that the 15th Amendment was subsequently ratified by 2 more of the 37 States. It was rejected by 3 (California, Delaware, and Kentucky).

Suggestions for Further Reading

(and a word of acknowledgment)

I have consulted a broad variety of materials in the preparation of this book—scholarly studies, monographs, biographies, reported court opinions, historical works and popular histories, and a large number of the sometimes recondite professional papers that appear in law reviews published by the students and faculty of many American law schools. It is not practicable to pinpoint references to the complete catalogue of these sources, nor would it be possible to make suitable acknowledgment to the people, occasions or works that have been especially helpful.

The idea for this book began when the writer, whose profession is the law and whose avocation of recent years has been "white studies"—with emphasis on books and essays on neglected or mistreated Americans who have figured in our constitutional history, men like Thomas Wentworth Higginson, Ulysses S. Grant, Charles Sumner, W. E. B. Du Bois, Thaddeus Stevens—was asked to review the late Judge Loren Miller's 1966 book, *The Petitioners,* a detailed and able study subtitled "The Story of the Supreme Court of the United States and the Negro." The lack of capacity of the "liberal" commissioning editor to accept as within the bounds of publishable controversy a review essay applying the title "A Century of Dishonor" to the first hundred years of the Fourteenth Amendment—the essay was later published in part in Irving Howe's *Dissent* and in its entirety in the United Secularists' *Progressive World*—entitles that editor to a kind of counteracknowledgment.

Apart from the works of general or special interest listed below, particular appreciation must be expressed for Louis B. Boudin's now almost forgotten *Government by Judiciary,* especially vol. II (New York, 1932), and his *N. Y. U. Law Quarterly Review* essay, "Truth and Fiction About the Fourteenth Amendment" (16 *N.Y.U.L.Q.R.* 19). Four other inaccessible (to the lay reader) law review articles deserve special mention:

Waite, (Judge) E. F., "How Eccentric Was Mr. Justice Harlan?" 37 *Minnesota Law Review* 173 (1953).

Watt, R. F., and Orlikoff, R. M., "The Coming Vindication of Mr. Justice Harlan," 44 *Illinois Law Review* 13 (1949).

Holmes, R. M., "The Fourteenth Amendment and the Bill of Rights," 7 *South Carolina Law Quarterly Review* 596 (1955).

Frank, J. P., and Munro, R. F., "The Original Understanding of 'Equal Protection of the Laws,' " 50 *Columbia Law Review* 131 (1950).

In connection with the Fifth Amendment's privilege against self-incrimination that was incorporated in the Fourteenth, see Dean Griswold's *The Fifth Amendment Today* (Cambridge, 1955). I wish I could reproduce (from the January, 1969, *Ameri-*

can Legion Magazine) Richard Curti's popular essay, "How to Convict Criminals Without Their Testimony."

The Fourteenth Amendment

Ten Broek, Jacobus, *Equality Under Law* (N.Y., 1965). (Originally published as *Anti Slavery Origins of the Fourteenth Amendment.)*

Graham, Howard J., *Everyman's Constitution: Historical Essays on the Fourteenth Amendment* (Madison, 1968).

Harris, Robert J., *The Quest for Equality* (Baton Rouge, 1960).

Corwin, Edward S., *American Constitutional History* (New York, 1964).

James, Joseph B., *The Framing of the Fourteenth Amendment* (Urbana, 1965).

N. Y. U. has published a group of centennial essays, Bernard Schwartz, ed., *The Fourteenth Amendment: A Century in American Law and Life.*

The Bill of Rights

Brant, Irving, *The Bill of Rights: Its Origin and Meaning* (Indianapolis, 1965; paperback, New York, 1967). Best of its kind.

Fraenkel, Osmond K., *The Rights We Have: A Handbook of Civil Liberties* (New York, 1971. A popular treatment. By "Mr. Civil Liberties").

Cahn, Edmond, ed., *The Great Rights* (New York, 1963; N. Y. U.'s Madison Lectures).

Rutland, Robert A., *The Birth of the Bill of Rights 1776–1791* (New York, 1962; paperback).

Douglas, William O., *A Living Bill of Rights* (New York, 1961).

Douglas, William O., *The Right of the People* (New York, 1958; paperback, 1961).

Dorsen, Norman, ed., *The Rights of Americans* (New York, 1970).

Reitman, Alan, ed., *The Price of Liberty* (New York, 1968).

Teachers and lay students alike will find especially stimulating and useful a two-volume set by Sobul, D., *The Bill of Rights: A Handbook* and Sobul, Schwartz and Cohen, *The Bill of Rights: A Source Book* (New York, 1969); and see "A Program for Improving Bill of Rights Teaching in High Schools" (The Report of the Williamstown Workshop), Civil Liberties Educational Foundation, New York, 1962. A most useful lay and school tool is a 32-page *Layman's Guide To Individual Rights Under the United States Constitution*, 92nd. Cong. 2nd Sess., printed for the Senate Judiciary Committee and available from G.P.O. or your congressperson.

The Court and the Constitution

Pfeffer, Leo, *This Honorable Court* (Boston, 1965). Best of its kind.

Bates, E. S., *The Story of the Supreme Court* (Indianapolis, 1936; paperback, 1963).

Mitchell, Broadus, and Mitchell, Louise P., *A Biography of the Constitution* (New York, 1964).

Abraham, Henry J., *Freedom and the Court* (2nd ed., New York, 1972).

Schwartz, Bernard, *The Supreme Court* (New York, 1957).

Konefsky, Samuel J., *The Legacy of Holmes and Brandeis* (New York, 1956).

Frank, John P., *Marble Palace: The Supreme Court in American Life* (New York, 1958).

Sources: Cases and Materials

Outstanding as a collection of documentary materials is Emerson, Haber and Dorsen, eds., *Political and Civil Rights in the United States* (Boston, 1967), containing not only texts of selected Supreme Court decisions but also excerpts from laws and regulations, public documents and legal essays. Less voluminous, but useful, is Pollak, Louis H., ed., *The Constitution and the Supreme Court: A Documentary History* (2 vols.; Cleveland, 1966). A variety of collections of Supreme Court decisions in constitutional cases is in print of which by far the most useful is Konvitz, Milton R., *Bill of Rights Reader* (4th ed., 1968). Another documentary collection often consulted was Blaustein and Zangrando, *Civil Rights and the American Negro* (New York, 1968). Irving Dilliard's collection of Justice Black's opinions, *One Man's Stand for Freedom* (New York, 1963), and Stephen J. Friedman's of Brennan's, *An Affair with Freedom* (New York, 1967), were also useful. (The many valuable publications of the United States Commission on Civil Rights should not be overlooked. See also, American Civil Liberties Union, annual reports.)

For the recent period, mention should be made of the valuable public service of Joseph P. Robison of the Commission on Law and Social Action of the American Jewish Congress, who during the past fourteen years has prepared an annual monograph on the civil rights and civil liberties decisions of the Supreme Court for the term just completed. (One can keep in current touch with the national ACLU's monthly *Civil Liberties* and the periodicals of its local affiliates notably *Civil Liberties in New York;* the NAACP's monthly *The Crisis;* the newsletter of The Southern Poverty Law Center; *Rights,* published bimonthly by the Emergency Civil Liberties Committee and its annual *Bill of Rights Journal.)*

Special Subjects and Subdivisions

Chapters 6–11 (congressional reconstruction and the amendments). By no means exhaustive, the following were useful and stimulating:

Clemenceau, Georges, *American Reconstruction: 1865–1870* (New York, 1928).

Cox, LaWanda, and Cox, John H., *Politics, Principle and Prejudice: 1865–1866* (New York, 1963).

Du Bois, W. E. B., *Black Reconstruction* (New York, 1935; paperback, 1964).

Dunning, William A., *Essays on Civil War & Reconstruction* (New York, 1897; paperback, 1965).

Hyman, Harold M., *The Radical Republicans and Reconstruction: 1861–1870* (Indianapolis, 1967).

Chapters 12–21:

Cummings and McFarland, *Federal Justice* (New York, 1937).

David, Henry, *The History of the Haymarket Affair* (New York, 1936; paperback, 1963). Special mention should be made of Zeisler, Sigmund, "Reminiscences of the Anarchist Case," 21 *Illinois Law Review* 224.

Olsen, Otto H., *Carpetbagger's Crusade: The Life of Albion W. Tourgee* (Baltimore, 1965).

Olsen, Otto H., *The Thin Disguise: Plessy vs. Ferguson, A Documentary Presentation (1864–1896)* (New York, 1967).

For these chapters, as well as Chapters 22–33, much follow-up reading can be done in standard works of black (Negro) history, of which the best is still John Hope Franklin's *From Slavery to Freedom.* Also useful is Aptheker, Herbert, *A Documentary History of the Negro People in the United States,* 2 vols. (New York, 1951; paperback, New York, 1962). The pages of the *Journal of Negro History* (vols. I–LVI, 1915 to date) can be and have been profitably consulted. Another useful work in this area is Sterling, Dorothy, *Tear Down the Walls!* (Garden City, 1968). Ralph Ginzburg, imprisoned by the federal authorities in violation of the First Amendment, should be mentioned for *100 Years of Lynchings* (New York, 1962).

Chapters 22–33:

Kellog, Charles F., *NAACP: A History* (Baltimore, 1967).

Chafee, Jr., Zechariah, *Free Speech in the United States* (Cambridge, 1941).

Waskow, Arthur, *From Race Riot to Sit-In* (New York, 1966; paperback, 1967).

Johnson, Donald, *The Challenge to American Freedoms* (Louisville, 1963).

Joughin, Louis, and Morgan, Edmund, *The Legacy of Sacco & Vanzetti* (New York, 1948; paperback, Chicago, 1964).

Carter, Dan T., *Scottsboro: A Tragedy of the American South* (Baton Rouge, 1969).

Black, Hugo L., *A Constitutional Faith* (New York, 1968).

Lewis, Anthony, *Gideon's Trumpet* (New York, 1964; paperback).

Blaustein and Ferguson, *Desegregation & the Law* (New York, 1962).

Murphy, Paul L., *The Constitution in Crisis Times: 1918-1969* (New York, 1972).

Major Court Decisions Referred to in the Body of This Book

The student, or the stubbornly curious reader, may wish to read some of the court decisions that are woven into the narrative. The official United States Reports (——— US ———) are available in non-law libraries with adequate reference departments; the unofficial sometimes are (——— S. Ct. ———) and since the latter appear in print more quickly in pamphlet "advance sheet" form, some of the most recent decisions in the Foreword to the Beacon Edition are so referred to. For convenience, the following are given by chapter and page, since in many cases the reference to the case in text does not have case name.

Index